GRAMSCI'S HISTORICISM

90 0680511 X

GRAMSCI'S
HISTORICISM
A REALIST INTERPRETATION

ESTEVE MORERA

ROUTLEDGE
LONDON AND NEW YORK

First published 1990
by Routledge
11 New Fetter Lane, London, EC4P 4EE

Simultaneously published in the USA and Canada
by Routledge
a division of Routledge, Chapman and Hall, Inc.
29 West 35th Street, New York, NY 10001

© 1990 Esteve Morera

Typeset by LaserScript Limited, Mitcham, Surrey
Printed and bound in Great Britain by
Biddles Ltd, Guildford and King's Lynn

British Library Cataloguing in Publication Data
Morera, Esteve, 1946–
Gramsci's historicism : a realist
interpretation
1. Italy. Marxism. Gramsci, Antonio –
critical studies
I. Title
335.4'092'4

Library of Congress Cataloging–in–Publication Data
Morera, Esteve, 1946–
Gramsci's historicism : a realist interpretation / Esteve Morera.
p.cm.
Bibliography
Includes index.
1. Gramsci, Antonio, 1891–1937 – Views on history.   2. Marxian
historiography.   [1. Gramsci, Antonio, 1891–1937.   Quaderni del
carcere.]   I. Title.
HX289.7.G73M67 1989
335.43'092'4 – dc19
89–5996
CIP

ISBN 0–415–03540–6

CONTENTS

ACKNOWLEDGEMENTS

Special thanks are due to Frank Cunningham and Danny Goldstick. Without their helpful comments on several drafts of this book, the result would have been far less satisfactory. I would also like to thank Winnie Dobbs and Sholem Peliowski for their help and encouragement, as well as Chris Rojek and Claire Watkins of Routledge for their assistance. Finally, for her unwavering support throughout the production of this book, I owe my deepest appreciation to Alina Márquez to whom it is dedicated.

INTRODUCTION

In an article on the reception of Gramsci in the English-speaking world, Geoff Eley concludes: 'The philosophers have had their say. The historians should now take the stage'.[1] This would be good advice, had Gramsci's philosophy been sufficiently clarified, explained, and evaluated. Although the literature on Gramsci is now quite voluminous, the bulk of interpretations has been devoted to political philosophy, political theory, and political practice. Yet, some of the fundamental philosophical issues that Gramsci broached in the *Prison Notebooks* have only been dealt with in passing. Perhaps this is not a state of affairs altogether to be decried – Gramsci's philosophy may not be as influential or as profound as that of other Marxist thinkers. It is certainly not without many ambiguities and inconsistencies. If it deserves any serious attention, it is because his philosophical assumptions do preclude some interpretations of his thought in general, and support others. An important aspect of Gramsci's philosophy is its relation to the thought of Croce. Historians, intellectual historians at any rate, need a deeper analysis of Gramsci's philosophy if they are to assess his position in the development of Italian culture in the 1920s and 1930s.

A crucial issue in philosophical analysis of Gramsci's *Prison Notebooks* is the elucidation of the concept of historicism, a concept that plays a vital role both in Gramsci's own thinking and in that of his interpreters. Unfortunately, and this is the main reason for disregarding Eley's advice, many commentators have simply assumed that the term 'historicism' has a generally clear and unambiguous meaning, and have proceeded to interpret Gramsci's prison writings on the basis of what they thought that

1

meaning was. Thus, a variety of Gramscian historicisms have emerged. For some, historicism is the theory that only knowledge of history is knowledge – real theoretical, philosophical knowledge – and science is only understood as an aspect, a rather mundane one at that, of historical self-consciousness. Closely related to this view, there is the historicism that truth is relative to its historical conditions. For others, historicism is the theory that only history is real, and that nothing exists outside history. For still others, historicism is the rejection of any form of essentialism. Finally, many have thought that, if historicism means anything, it must be that the economy does not determine politics, or does not determine it fully. In short, 'historicism' has become an empty term into which one could put anything one likes as a powerful armour against everything one dislikes (such as materialism, economism, determinism, essentialism, etc.).

For the above reasons, the unspecified meaning of 'historicism' has also led to attributing to Gramsci's thought political theories of different stripes. Emphasis on the political character of history, on the negation of determinism, etc., leads to theories of political intervention which are different from the ones of those who have defended a Leninist Gramsci. However, whether Leninist or Crocean, scientific or humanist, realist or idealist, Gramsci's thought is now seen as one of the first, and one of the greatest, foes of economism, though there is no agreement on what his anti-economism is. In short, the lack of precise and extended analysis of the concept of historicism in the *Prison Notebooks* has had a chameleon effect: Gramsci's theory has varied with the seasons, to paraphrase the title of Davidson's essay. Of course, most interpretations of the work of past thinkers undergo this process of adaptation to new intellectual fashions. The ambiguities necessarily present in any work, especially if it is a work that breaks new ground, are always open to competing interpretations and appropriations. In Gramsci's case, however, this is far more evident because of the unfinished character of the *Prison Notebooks*. We shall return to this presently.

Colletti has pointed out that there are two vastly different meanings of 'historicism'. There is, first, the historicism of Marx, which concerns 'history or science, that is, *sociology*, or history of a socio-economic formation, of a *species* or phenomenon-type, hence of *repeatable* processes'. Second, there is an idealist historicism 'that today goes by Marx's name', which 'in practice, is reduced to relating a philosophy to the immediate historical milieu that has seen its birth: where the accuracy of historical judgement is identified precisely with the importance of singular and irrepeatable features that characterize that given milieu'.[2]

In general, this idealist historicism finds its roots in Vico, Kant, and Hegel. Two main varieties of this form emerged in the nineteenth century: the German historical school, of Kantian pedigree; and the Hegelian school, whose principal figure is Croce. Both schools, however, can be traced back to Vico. Both emphasize liberty, rather than necessity, and hence, as their modern successors Dray, Scriven, and others do, they emphasize the decisions and values of historical agents. In both cases, philosophy, and in particular some ethical conception of social reality, takes precedence over empirical explanation. Whereas the Marxist form of historicism does not renounce scientific explanation, the second form embraces humanism: it denies the scientific character of historical studies and, in effect, rejects the theory of unity of scientific method. In place of the latter, it proposes a method of interpretation which wholly dispenses with the notion of causal laws. Since this idealist form is the one most often referred to as historicism, and because Croce exerted considerable influence on Gramsci, it will be necessary to explore in some detail both the main claims put forth by historicism and their relation to Gramsci's thought.

Any interpretation of the *Prison Notebooks* is faced with two difficulties. First, the scope of Gramsci's thought is far too wide for any specialist to assess his contribution. He writes on philosophy, history, politics, and even grammar. Second, the *Prison Notebooks* consist of 2353 pages of unfinished notes, with no apparent order or overall structure. These notes, most of which are very short, are often cryptic. Many inconsistencies were left, as Gramsci died only two days after being released from prison before he could revise and organize his prison labour into several monographs, as he had intended to do. Although some notebooks are devoted to more or less defined topics, Gramsci's thought tends to range over several interrelated areas. Given, then, both the scope of the notebooks, and their unfinished and inconsistent character, the interpreter is put in the difficult position of evaluating the relevance of many passages whose meaning is obscure and of dealing with topics of

3

which he or she knows little. This is nevertheless necessary because one never knows where a revealing statement will be found. Above all it is of fundamental importance to read the complete text so as to obtain some insight into Gramsci's general outlook, as well as the weight he placed on different topics.

The contradictions present in the *Prison Notebooks* make it difficult, if not impossible, to give a consistent interpretation that can account for every single relevant statement. This means that any interpretation will have to leave out some statement; that is, if one tries to verify one's own reconstruction of the *Prison Notebooks*, one will inevitably find statements that falsify that interpretation. The difficulty faced by any commentator, then, will be that of choosing which statements to ignore; that is, one will have to be prepared to defend some view of the 'real Gramsci', as opposed to the mistaken Gramsci. This process, however, can be an arbitrary one. In what follows, an attempt is made to present one such real Gramsci, one that, it is hoped, will not be a totally arbitrary construction.

In view of the difficulties noted above, it is necessary to give some reasons for the choices made in this work. The method chosen to select texts and interpret them is quite a simple one. First, an attempt has been made to analyse Gramsci's use of the term 'historicist' and its cognates. Surprisingly enough, this has not been done by previous commentators. Fortunately, Gramsci gives some useful hints with regard to his intended meanings of 'historicism', meanings that, as we shall see in Chapter One, fall into four distinct, but interrelated, senses.

Second, care must be taken to interpret the meaning of fundamental terms such as 'immanence' and 'transcendence'. These terms have long standing in philosophical writings; Gramsci uses them in his philosophical analysis of historical materialism. Because these terms are laden with philosophical content that is often extraneous to Marxism, there is the possibility of carrying those contents into Gramsci's reconstruction of Marxism, thus giving rise to Husserlian variations, Crocean variations, etc. Again, fortunately, Gramsci provides some interesting hints about language, hints which remind one of Althusser's concept of 'symptomatic reading', and which allow the interpreter to avoid some too easy traps. Gramsci asserts that words are often used in a metaphorical sense, metaphorical because, although the word is the same, the concept is not: 'Often when a new conception of the world follows a preceding one, former language continues to be used, although it is precisely used only in a metaphorical sense'.[3] This is not to be taken to mean that all 'discourse is metaphorical regarding the thing or sensible and material object indicated (or the abstract concept)' but that today's language 'is metaphorical with respect to the meaning and ideological content that words have had in preceding periods of civilization'.[4] He then adds that historical materialism uses the term 'immanence' in a precise sense, a sense that is concealed 'underneath the metaphor' and whose definition is theoretical.[5] Thus 'immanence', Gramsci contends, is not to be taken as expressing a form of pantheism, or in any other metaphysical or traditional sense. Historical materialism 'purifies the metaphysical apparatus of the concept of immanence and brings it to the concrete terrain of history'.[6] As we shall see, the suggestion is that the meaning and function of the concept of immanence is not that of a speculative philosophical concept, but a historiographical one.

Furthermore, idealist philosophers, such as Croce or even Vico, use explanations of concepts such as 'Providence' or 'fortune', concepts that are speculative, but which point to real processes that must be clarified and understood.[7] The methodological principle we must draw from these reflections is that Gramsci uses many of the terms commonly used by speculative philosophers, but he uses them to express different concepts. Identifying these new concepts is a necessary condition for interpreting Gramsci's philosophy. Gramsci's general procedure, one can infer from some of his remarks, is to take those fundamental terms as indications of real problems, to which he intends to give a real solution. At any rate, this is, for instance, his approach to some of Croce's theories, theories that point to real methodological problems, to which Croce only gave verbal, not real, solutions.[8]

Third, Gramsci's uses of 'historicism' will be taken as areas of interpretation. This means that each separate use will be correlated with other relevant material in the *Prison Notebooks*. The result, it is hoped, will be an integrated reconstruction of Gramsci's concept of historicism, one that can serve as the philosophical basis of Gramsci's thought. By filling in the meanings of 'historicism' with the writings on historiography, sociology, and politics, some light will be shed on the structure of Gramsci's thought.

This method will permit us to discard as slips or confusions some of Gramsci's texts. Since the point of departure is Gramsci's own intended meanings of 'historicism', and since these meanings are specified in terms of his own writings on history and politics, the result will be a definition of 'historicism', and with it his most basic philosophical thesis, that is most consistent with the *Prison Notebooks* as a whole.

In the first chapter of this work, and after a brief description of various forms of historicism, the four main uses of 'historicism' in the *Prison Notebooks* will be elucidated. The contrast with both the German historical school and Croce will be immediately obvious, for Gramsci not only espouses (not without grave confusions) philosophical realism, but also a conception of historical laws, the necessary forms of transition of social forms, and the denial, described by him as humanism, of the transcendent origin of thought and of history. Because philosophical realism is a theory most often thought to be rejected by Gramsci, it will be necessary to emphasize his arguments in this respect. It is in this area that many of Gramsci's texts will have to be discarded as mere confusions or slips.

In Chapter Two, the four uses of historicism previously elucidated will be given some specific content. Hence, Gramsci's critique of what he calls 'sociology', as well as his writings on history and politics, will provide all the necessary materials. As it happens, his critique of sociology, apart from some general remarks, can be neatly fitted into four areas of theory that correspond to his four senses of historicism. Little will be added on the question of realism. The emphasis will be laid on his theory of the transience of social forms, which will uncover a general, though not always unambiguous, theory of historical necessity and a corresponding theory of historical time which bears some resemblance to that of Fernand Braudel.

The elucidation of Gramsci's notion of historicism brings to the fore a number of other important issues, issues which have already been amply discussed in the literature and to which little will be added in these pages. To the extent that Gramsci's historicism deals with some conception of the law-like process of social transformation, his contribution to the old questions of Marxist theory are prefigured by his general philosophy. In the third and final chapter a brief sketch of his theory of history and politics will be offered. Some of the questions that have focused debate on the Left today, such as the relevance and importance of class-analysis and the primacy of politics, will be reviewed in so far as they are pertinent to the analysis of Gramsci's *Prison Notebooks*. Although in some socialist circles the concept of final determination by the economy, and hence the importance of classes in history, has become a suspect theory, Gramsci continues to think of history within this model. He offers, however, some theory of the relative autonomy of politics, and hence of the possibility of political intervention in forms that are not exclusively class-bound, though they are generally subject to long-term determination by class-structure. For this reason, Gramsci remains a Marxist, though he offers a number of important insights and fruitful suggestions for the study of complex social wholes. Opposed to economism as he is, he is not opposed to a multi-causal conception of history in which classes are determinant in the last instance.

The effort to present a general interpretation of Gramsci's historicism and the consequences of this concept for Gramsci's theory of history and politics does not, and perhaps cannot, result in a reconstruction free from ambiguities. Gramsci's general thought seems clear enough; its details and implications, alas, are often a matter of conjecture. Given the unfinished character of his work, it is not always possible to offer more than sketchy outlines of the general arguments that can be culled from many disparate statements. Often, one has to find possible solutions to the problems of interpretation in the work of historians, political scientists, and sociologists, as well as philosophers. Thus Gramsci's thought will be clarified by translating it into a more modern language provided by the thinkers to whom reference will be made. This exercise in translation, however, must not be taken as an analysis of modern historiography nor as a history of Gramsci's ideas; its purpose is merely that of providing an interpretation of confusing terms and statements in the *Prison Notebooks*. It is, at any rate, useful to familiarize oneself with the language and modes of thinking of historians, for they speak the language closest to Gramsci's idiom.

Gramsci's dislike of philosophical speculation often led him to pose all problems as historical problems. This has sometimes led to the conclusion that even statements' truth-values are a function of their historical conditions. Our interpretation of Gramsci denies this. In so doing, a conclusion must be reached rejecting the view that Gramsci's historicism is absolute, as Croce's was, or that it subsumes every truth under the general category of historical truth, or that, for Gramsci, truth is simply a matter of the historical function of truth-claims. If there is anything absolute about Gramsci's historicism it is his claim that to explain history we need not have recourse to extra-historical entities such as Providence. The activity of human beings, their relations with nature and among themselves are all that is required to explain the process of social transformation. That Gramsci thought as a historian faced with the task of explaining socio-economic formations, from the mode of economic production to the process of the production of knowledge, does not entail that he denied truth-value's independence of history.

CHAPTER ONE

HISTORICISM

INTRODUCTION

In the *Prison Notebooks*, Gramsci claims that Marxism is an 'absolute historicism'. [1] There are several possible interpretations of this claim, for the term 'historicism' has been used in different senses. Often, historicism is associated with epistemological or moral relativism. In general, historicism is thought to be essentially an idealist philosophy. There is no doubt that the origins of historicism are idealist; they are to be found in the works of Vico, Kant, and Hegel. Moreover, most historicists, such as Croce, Dilthey, Rickert, or Windelband, are clearly associated with either Hegelian or neo-Kantian philosophical schools. Thus, taking Gramsci's claim at face-value, as Althusser seems to do, one would be obliged to conclude that Gramsci is either a neo-Kantian or a Hegelian Marxist. In general, Gramsci is thought of as a member of the Hegelian Marxist group of thinkers which included Lukács and Korsch. His Marxism, like western Marxism in general, is an attempt at reinterpreting Marxism with the aim of transcending economism, the theoretical positions of the Second International and, above all, of absorbing the lessons of Lenin's contribution as well as the events of the Russian revolution.

The western Marxism that originated out of those experiences seems to have emphasized the subjective element of historical materialism: class consciousness in Lukács, hegemony in Gramsci. As Alex Callinicos has pointed out, Hegelian Marxism, especially that of Lukács, attempted 'to reintroduce the concept of a transcendental subject into Marxism'.[2] Of course, this subject became a class, rather than a pure ego. Nevertheless, the Hegelian interpretation of Marxism, with its emphasis on the concept of the identity of subject and object, proved unable to overcome idealism for it reduced social relations 'to forms of consciousness', at the same time that it gave primacy to ideological struggle in the strategy for overthrowing capitalism.[3] Clearly, Gramsci seems to fit this pattern quite well. His historicism might be interpreted as the doctrine that asserts 'that scientific theories ... have not truth-value independent of the circumstances of their formulation'.[4] The transcendental subject, in Gramsci's case, is historicized, but it nevertheless acquires the status of a philosophical category. Seen in this light, Gramsci's theory of hegemony is the equivalent of Lukács' concept of class consciousness. Gramsci's other general claim, namely, that Marxism is an absolute humanism,[5] seems to confirm this interpretation of his thought.

If we take this interpretation of Gramsci as a credible one, then the emphasis commentators place on his philosophy of praxis as the activity of the will to solve historical problems seems justified. In this case, Gramsci's Marxism is rightly construed as the theory of the primacy of political action, and in particular, a theory of the cultural aspects of that action. In short, seen in this light, Gramsci's reconstruction of Marxism is an anti-determinist, perhaps volun-tarist, reduction of Marxism to a humanism in which the political action of groups to preserve or to assume hegemonic status takes the form of the activity, both theoretical and practical, of a historicized transcendental subject. His 'historicism', in essence, is no more than the recognition that the transcendental subject is not a fixed, immutable entity, and that, as a consequence, all activity, both practical and theoretical, will reflect the historicity of the subject. One could go further than that, and claim, as Gramsci does at one point, that the object of both practical and theoretical activity is not independent from the subject.[6]

This historicized transcendental subject, however, poses a con-undrum, for how are we to understand the process of the historicization of the subject of history? Does the subject have an essence that is itself historical and whose development determines the historical process? If this is the kind of theory of history that Gramsci espoused, how could he have maintained the primacy of the transcendental subject and claim at the same time that 'human nature is the ensemble of the historically determined social relations, which is an ascertainable historical fact'?[7] An analysis of

Gramsci's use of the term historicism suggests a very different theory. Gramsci uses 'historicism' in several senses; one can, however, isolate four distinct, but interrelated, uses of this term in the *Prison Notebooks*. It seems that many interpretations of Gramsci emphasize but one such use, that of historicism as humanism. In the following pages I shall attempt to present the groundwork for a new interpretation of Gramsci's historicism. To do this, I shall first give a descriptive account of the roots of historicism and its two main schools, the German historical school on the one hand, and that of Croce on the other. Second, I shall analyse Gramsci's use of the term 'historicism'. This analysis will immediately disclose the vast differences between Gramsci's thought and the philosophy of other historicists.

VARIETIES OF HISTORICISM

Today, due to the great influence of logical positivism on the social sciences, historicism is not a popular theory. Even within western Marxism, historicism seems to be firmly rejected by such influential writers as Althusser.[8] It has been conceived, by both its defenders and its detractors, as an anti-scientistic theory of history. Its origins are to be found in the reaction against both rationalism and empiricism as it developed during the Enlightenment and after. More recently, it has also been opposed to some aspects of positivism, as is well exemplified by Croce's thought as well as that of Collingwood, William Dray, and Michael Scriven. The philosophical seeds of historicism, or rather, of the various currents which are usually referred to as historicism, were sown by Vico and Kant.

In his *Principles for a New Science*, Vico set out to establish the foundations of a scientific history that would investigate 'the common nature of nations'.[9] The nature of nations, however, was not understood in terms of some immutable elements or final essence that would underlie the variety of existing nations, but in terms of their genesis. 'The nature of things', Vico wrote, 'is none other than their origin in a certain time and in a certain manner'.[10] The method of the new science could not be thought of as a geometry of nations, taken as aggregates of simple natures; rather,

11

this method had to establish the principles for the study of 'nations in their progress, states, decadence, and end'.[11]

The foundation of the genesis and development of nations, Vico contended, was to be found in the human mind. His principles were intended to produce a history of human ideas which in turn would provide the elements for a 'metaphysics of the human mind'.[12] To fulfil this project, Vico proceeded to study myths and legends, which he believed contained real descriptions of the past cast, however, in the language of imagination. Myths are the first form taken by the human mind; they contain 'civil truths, and for this reason they are the history of the first people'.[13] Myths are cast in what Vico called 'imaginative universals',[14] which are precursors of the true universals of philosophy and science. The interpretation of myths would therefore furnish the first materials for the study of 'modifications of our own minds'.[15]

The results of the history of the modification of the mind would in turn furnish the materials for a deeper study. The aim of the new science is to unravel the apparent disorder and to penetrate the amorphous mass of historical detail in order to bring to light 'an ideal eternal history'.[16] Vico's grand design, then, was aimed at understanding history, in particular at understanding the thread of necessity underneath the apparent accidental occurrence of historical events. In a passage that anticipates Adam Smith's concept of the hidden hand, or Hegel's cunning of reason, Vico argues that 'men love mainly their own utility', but Providence uses the self-interest of individuals to preserve human society.[17] The deeper sense of history, the ideal eternal history, is the history of Providence which 'so ordered things human according to this eternal order'.[18] It is appropriate, then, to think of the new science of history as 'a rational civil theology of divine providence'.[19]

The science of history, is, for Vico, superior to any other science, including geometry.[20] The reasons for this claim are to be found in his epistemology. Both in his *Della Antichissima* and in his *New Science*, Vico stresses the identity of *verum* and *factum*. This identity is based on a distinction between *intelligere* (understanding) and thinking, where the former is far superior to the latter. Vico compares *intelligere* to 'reading perfectly', for in the same way that reading is the gathering of words and the ideas signified by them, 'understanding is the gathering of all the elements of a thing in order to form a perfect idea of the thing'.[21]

12

But gathering the elements of things is the same as making the things, and hence the perfect knowledge of a thing can only be had by he who makes it, or, what is the same, by he who constructs the thing out of its elements. Hence, the truth of things is known by their maker and it is to be found in the making or genesis of them.

For Vico, this means that God alone, as creator, can understand the nature of all things. Human beings must be satisfied with thinking about the world. Thinking is also a gathering of the elements of things, but it is considerably limited. As maker of things, God can understand both the internal and the external elements of things,[22] whereas human beings can only read the external elements and cannot hope to gather the internal ones. For this reason, human beings cannot attain understanding of the nature of the universe, they cannot have a science of nature. Unfortunately, Vico does not give any precise analysis or definition of the external and internal elements of things. However, in the *New Science*, he claims that understanding of history is possible because man makes history or, more precisely, because the genesis of history, its internal elements, are to be found in the human mind.[23] This allows the historian to penetrate beyond the appearances, the manifold events and accidents of history, and to tap the modifications of the mind that are the inner essence, the creative power which alone explains history. Vico's claim to the scientific character of his historiography is based on this contention that the historian can know the modifications of the mind which are the inner aspects of history. Knowledge of them is clearly superior to knowledge of the external aspects, and since the study of nature cannot ever reach the inner aspects of natural things, historical knowledge is superior to the natural sciences. In this, we can already see the beginning of what was to become a crucial point for a school of historicists, namely, the distinction between *Naturwissenschaften* and *Geisteswissenschaften*.

There seems to be an inconsistency in Vico's thought between his claim for human agency in history and the metaphysics of Providence he espouses. Nevertheless, three essential points of his thought played an important role in the development of historicism: first, the distinction between the internal and external elements of things; second, the belief in the ideal nature of history, with the consequent emphasis on cultural and intellectual history;

third, the doctrine that the nature of things is to be found in their genesis. Support for the first two theses was drawn from the philosophy of Kant. The distinction between noumena and phenomena, and the analysis of the third antinomy, provided an interpretation of the distinction between the internal and external elements of history that proved essential in the development of German historicism.

On the traditional interpretation, Kant's solution of the third antinomy, the conflict between freedom and causality, relies on his distinction between the intelligible world, or noumena, and the spatio-temporal world, or phenomena. Causality is the category that regulates the temporal succession of events, hence it belongs wholly to the phenomenal world. Freedom, or the causality of freedom as he calls it, is the sphere of spontaneous action, and it is intelligible in this creation.[24] Freedom belongs to the world of noumena. An action, seen from the point of view of its effects in the sensible world, must be 'in conformity with all the laws of empirical causality'.[25] But from the point of its origin, it 'is not to be looked for in the causally connected appearances',[26] for it 'has in its *noumenon* certain conditions which must be regarded as purely intelligible'.[27]

Kant himself, in his writings on history, considered human action from this double perspective. He considered human actions to be determined by universal laws in so far as they were the appearances of the freedom of the will.[28] History, in so far as it is the narration of these phenomena, seeks to find the laws of human action. However, in so far as the actions themselves are an expression of freedom, the drama of history is time charged with moral significance. This conception of history became the basis of the anti-naturalist doctrine of the separation of the method of the natural sciences from that of the cultural sciences. The historicist's emphasis on the distinction between *Naturwissenschaften* and *Giesteswissenschaften*, which Iggers thinks is 'the core of the historicist outlook',[29] is thus the culmination of a process of thought whose essence is the understanding of history as a moral rather than a natural process. The German historical school tended to ignore Kant's dual analysis of history, as both noumena and phenomena, and to emphasize the inner meaning, or the noumena as the essence that historical knowledge was to capture.

Two main features characterize the German historical school:

the first is the critical method developed by Ranke; the second is historicism. The critical method, which Ranke taught in his seminars at the University of Berlin, was essentially a canon for rigorous empirical research. The emphasis of this method lay in the careful study of documents, their authentication and criticism, and the interpretation of the findings. Its motto is to be found in the Preface to Ranke's *Histories of the Latin and Germanic Nations.* He wrote that the task of the historian is not to judge the past, but to show how it really was (*wie es eigentlich gewessen*). This aspect of the German historical school has constituted a positive contribution to historiography. At times, however, it has been interpreted as the view that history should dispense with philosophical or theoretical considerations, and focus on the narration of a carefully researched and well established mass of details. The temptation of empiricist narrative was always close to the German historicist.

The second characteristic of the German historical school was historicism. From Humboldt to Dilthey, Rickert and Meinecke, the painstaking accumulation of facts was viewed as a necessary but external aspect of historical writing: it was concerned with the phenomena of history. Interpretation, understanding or hermeneutics was to penetrate the inner core of history. The inner core was, for most historicists, constituted by moral values, often conceived as a metaphysical reality which manifested itself through the drama of individuals, nations, cultures, etc., of the historical process. The narrative would set out the details of this drama, while understanding would fathom the inner meaning of history. In Dilthey's words, the phenomena of history become 'the subject matter of the human studies when we experience human states, give expressions to them and understand these expressions'.[30] The phenomena perceived by the senses, the description of events, are merely the signs of an inner content. This conception of history is clearly connected to both Vico and Kant, although it focuses on moral values rather than Vico's notion of the development of the mind.

Since the real subject-matter of history is the inner meaning, not the phenomena as perceived by the senses or described in documents, historians must develop a proper method for understanding or interpreting this inner meaning, a method that would not be subject to the 'new bondage' of science.[31] Their arguments centred on what they perceived to be the essential

15

difference between natural science and history. Rickert was perhaps the most successful in formulating this difference. Natural science, he argued, is nomological, that is, it is primarily concerned with establishing regularities, patterns, or laws in events. Individual natural events are taken as instances of general concepts, but not as expressions or signs of an inner meaning. Consequently, no value is attached to them. In contrast, the human sciences are ideographical: they must seek to understand the uniqueness, the value or meaning of historical phenomena. Historians, then, must proceed to interpret the evidence culled from documents so as to arrive at an intuitive understanding of the historical past. In short, intuitive understanding 'must recognize some inner content from signs received by the senses'.[32]

But how is this intuitive understanding possible? How can the historian of the present penetrate into the inner reality of the past? The best answer was probably the one provided by Dilthey. He conceived historical reality as the objectification of the mind, such that one could look at historical events as 'a manifestation of the mind in the world of the senses'.[33] Hence, 'what is around us helps us to understand what is distant and past'. For this to be possible, however, the experience we transfer into the events of the past 'must be permanently and universally valid for man'.[34] Historical understanding, then, is seen as the 'rediscovery of the I in the thou'.[35] In short, it is because of the identification between the mind of the present, embodied in the mental structure of the historian, and the mind of the past, objectified in the phenomena of history, that historical understanding is possible.

One of the consequences of this approach is that, in general, historicists deny the existence of historical laws. Because laws, they contend, are regularities concerning types of events, they can only be formulated where events are repeatable. The inner aspects of historical events are not repeatable, hence no laws applying to them can be formulated. The actions of human beings, as opposed to physical events, are not subject to causal laws; they are, if anything, the expression of freedom'. In this vein, Ranke asserted that 'historical writing traces the scenes of freedom'.[36] Necessity is not denied; it is identified with 'that which has already been formed and cannot be overturned again' by Ranke,[37] and with the natural aspects of human life by Dilthey.[38] According to the latter, the historian may use scientific laws to establish facts, that is, to

16

accumulate and describe the external details of human history. In this, as Rickman points out, his argument is not unlike Popper's[39] who argued that because the whole historic process is a unique event, no laws of historical development can be formulated or tested, though other laws, such as those of psychology and biology, can and must be applied to the study of history.[40]

Along with the conception of historical laws, historicists rejected the conception of a constant human nature and, in particular, the rationalist version of this conception. For them, it was history, not some inherently rational human nature, that was to be taken as 'the only guide to an understanding of things human'.[41] Furthermore, they also dismissed natural law theories that played such an important role in the intellectual upheavals of the eighteenth century. As a consequence, historicists rejected any claim to absolute or trans-historical values based on some conception of either human nature or reason. Instead, they stressed the need to understand the value and meaning of historical deeds and to judge them in terms of their own inherent values, rather than from the standpoint of standards external to the context of their origin.[42]

This stress on the inherent value of all historical deeds, coupled with the rejection of absolutist thinking, leads to the conclusion that it is not possible to judge historical epochs or cultures, or to attribute a higher value to any of them. In general, most historicists tended 'to approach ideas and values not in terms of absolute norms of truth or good, but as expressions of a specific age, culture, or people'.[43] The paradox of this view is that while it may be more tolerant than views based on a conception of absolute values, it can also lead to hardly defensible extremes. For instance, Meinecke held that 'nothing can be immoral which comes from the innermost, individual character of a being', and therefore, 'the seeming immorality of the state's egoism for power can be morally justified'.[44]

This view, as many came to recognize, is itself, or easily leads to, moral and epistemological relativism. Some historicists, however, attempted to avoid it with the argument that all individual values are partial manifestations of a metaphysical reality from which they derive their meaning. Thus, the apparent chaos of actual historical phenomena was, for them, the revelation 'of a fundamental and meaningful unity that unfolded itself in history'.[45] The meaning of any specific event is a function of that unity. For Dilthey, 'the category of meaning designates the relationship, inherent in life, of parts of a life to the whole'.[46] This may seem to avoid relativism. However, the emphasis on the experience of individuals and on the ability of the historian to relive this experience in the present may very well bring relativism in through the back door; for there will be as many pasts as historians' experiences of past deeds, with no universal criteria for assessing competing claims. This theory, which Croce was to reformulate in his concept of 'contemporary history' is one of the essential methodological claims of the German historical school, and perhaps also one of its fatal flaws.

The unravelling of the meaning of history, it was hoped, could in turn provide the foundation for a rational politics. This, as Iggers claims, was a reversal of the Enlightenment's views on the relationship between history and political science.[47] Now history was to be the queen of the sciences, as metaphysics had been before. It was both the study of the past as it had really been, and the main source of ideas for the active politician, aloof and engaged at the same time.

Politically, the majority of German historicists were liberal moderates. Most of them were deeply interested in the German question of the nineteenth century, and some participated in political organizations that shaped the unity of Germany. Generally, they disliked Bismark, but in the end most of them were not too opposed to his policies, as they tended to be suspicious of the value of democracy.

It is possibly in the conception of the state that German historicists came closer to Hegel. As Iggers argues 'German historians and political theorists from Wilhelm von Humboldt to Friedrich Meinecke almost a century later were willing to view the state as an ethical institution',[48] consequently they tended to view history as 'the interplay of great powers'[49] and they neglected the social and economic issues as well as the mass organizations whose importance must have been quite evident in the age of industrialization and revolution. Historicism then, showed a double face, for on the one hand it had attempted to establish historiography on a more solid foundation, while on the other it became an ideology. Its dependence on a metaphysics of moral value and its denial of historical laws, as Cruz has argued, made it impossible to periodize history. As a consequence, the capitalist system could no longer be seen as one more period whose end would necessarily come.[50] More specifically, 'historicism provided a theoretical foundation for the established political and social structure of nineteenth century Prussia and Germany'.[51]

In its distrust of sociological generalizations and historical laws, its rejection of both abstract theories and of natural law, German historicists proposed what in reality amounts to an approach for the study of all social phenomena: the historical or genetic approach. As Ortega y Gasset put it in his study of Dilthey, it is because 'human reality is evolutionary and its knowledge must be genetic',[52] that social phenomena must be studied with the historians' methods. However, the historicists' appeal to a metaphysical reality meant that the very substance of the historical process itself, the order of values whose partial manifestations constituted the inner reality of history, was beyond the historian's grasp. This betrayed the historical approach, for ultimately, history had to be subordinated to metaphysics or to ideology. To avoid relativism, German historicists had to appeal to a supra-historical reality, and thus subordinate history to metaphysics, a predicament that denied their aspirations for history as the master science. On the other hand, if they gave up the supra-historical moral world, they easily fell into ethical and epistemological relativism, casting some serious doubt on the validity of their works.

As we saw earlier, Vico's conception of history was also based on a metaphysical reality, namely Providence. The difference, however, was that Vico conceived of Providence in developmental terms. The emphasis on development was in reality more in tune with the historical nature of social reality than the appeal to a supra-historical order of values. This emphasis on process and development was taken up by Hegel who conceived of history as essentially a dialectical process. Although German historicists rejected Hegel's conception of history because it was too determinist for their taste, it can be argued that, in fact, some features of Hegel's view of social reality are historicist.

As we have seen, German historicists viewed values as expressions of an age or culture. In a similar vein, Hegel took all forms of consciousness, including religion and philosophy, to be subject to a dialectical process of development. The *Phenomenology of Spirit* can be understood as an ambitious attempt to understand

19

ɔcess of history as the dialectical unfolding of forms of
ousness. The process is dialectical in that it is impelled by
mitations and contradictions with which each stage in the
ss is fraught. Thus, in order to understand a philosophical
ɔ̄ ̄ept it must first be placed in the context of its historical
genesis as well as in relation to the totality of concepts. These two
notions, the historicity of consciousness and the concept of
totality, are central to Hegel's thinking.

Marx can also be said to be a historicist thinker inasmuch as he
stresses the historical character of forms of consciousness and
social forms, at the same time as that he denies their natural or
absolute character. The conservatism inherent in the German
historicists is explicitly rejected by Marx. His conception of
dialectics is directed against speculative conceptions of a
metaphysical essence of history, at the same time as it attempts to
theorize the necessarily transitory character of social processes. In
the 'Afterword' to the second German edition of *Capital*, Marx
stated his view of a rational dialectical in opposition to the
mystified form which glorified the existing form of society. He
wrote that his dialectic 'regards every historically developed social
form as in fluid movement, and therefore takes into account its
transient nature no less than its momentary existence'.[53]

This view has important consequences for the social sciences.
Marx often criticized the analysis of social phenomena of other
thinkers on the grounds that their methodology was faulty. For
instance, in the *Grundrisse*, Marx advanced some revealing
criticisms against Malthus' theory of overpopulation

His conception is altogether false and childish (1) because
he regards *overpopulation* as being *of the same kind* in all the
different historic phases of economic development; does not
understand their specific difference, and hence stupidly
reduces these very complicated and varying relations to a
single relation, two equations, in which the natural reproduction of humanity appears on the one side, and natural
reproduction of edible plants (or means of subsistence) on
the other, as two natural series, the former geometric and the
latter arithmetic in progression. In this way he transforms the
historically distinct relations into an abstract numerical

relation, which he has fished purely out of thin air, and which rests neither on natural nor on historical laws.[54]

Marx is rejecting sociological abstractions that relate two series of phenomena without attempting to trace their relationships to the totality of the historical process. This form of sociological abstractions ignores that overpopulation is 'a historically determined relation' and that the same phenomenon, over-population, can have very different causes, as well as very different effects, in different historical periods. Looking merely at the two series – geometrical progression of population and arithmetical progression of food – without taking into consideration 'the inherent conditions of population',[55] is simply looking at the phenomena externally. Marx's own wording, by contrasting 'inherent conditions' to Malthus' 'external checks', reminds us of the internal/external distinction made by Vico and by German historicists. The meaning of this contrast, however, could not be more different. Marx does not trace the distinction on the basis of the meaning or value inherent in every social event, but rather on the basis of the network of historical relations and laws that explain concrete historical situations. In Marx's case, the meaning of over-population is to be understood in terms of its relations to the whole of a historical period, in terms of its origins and its effects, and its occurring in a given economic structure.

Similar considerations can be found in other works by Marx and Engels. For instance, in a footnote in *Capital*, Marx argues that Smith and Ricardo give little importance to the form of value, not only 'because their attention is entirely absorbed in the analysis of the magnitude of value' but because of a reason that lies deeper: they fail to understand, fail to take into consideration 'its special historical character', in other words, they treat this (the capitalist) mode of production as one eternally fixed by Nature for every state of society and overlook that which is the *differentia specifica* of the value form.[56] In short, they are guilty of producing abstract theories, that is, theories that are not grounded on the historically determined structure of a society. The meaning or value, that is its origin and effects, its relations to the whole of the concrete society, is different in different historical epochs. Marx's analysis is an attempt to grasp the concrete, the historically specific, not the

gical abstraction based on the relations between isolated
mena.

rx's methodological injunction has as its necessary basis a
of reality which is well summarized by Engels in his overview
egel: 'All that exists deserves to perish'. That is, all reality, and
social reality in particular, is becoming a process. On these
grounds, Engels argued that all successive historical systems are
only transitory stages in the endless course of development of
human society from the lower to the higher. Furthermore, 'each
stage is necessary and therefore justified for the time and
conditions to which it owes its origins'.[57] The significant point in
Engels' and Marx's view is that the various stages of development,
the different social phenomena, are not just viewed as filled with
value in themselves, but as being rational (the real is rational) in
so far as they accord with historical necessity. Thus, knowledge of
society is at its best when it can place the phenomena under study
in the line of development that makes it necessary. This means that
sociological abstractions such as those given by Malthus have very
limited value. Furthermore, the historical knowledge proposed by
Marx and Engels rejects the historicist view of the individuality of
historical events and hence their ultimate unintelligibility other
than in terms of a metaphysical reality that confers value on them.
The study of history is not the study of the inner value of social
forms, but the study of a natural process; 'natural', that is, in the
sense that it does not depend on a transcendent sphere of being.
Rejecting transcendence, Marx and Engels proposed a theory of
history that would begin with a real premiss, that is, 'the existence
of living human individuals'.[58]

The concept of historical laws on which Marx and Engels'
historicism depends is essentially different from the positivist
concept of law as the regular conjunction of discrete events. For
historical materialism, historical laws are founded on the existence
of social structures rather than on the regular conjunction of
similar events. The latter is a consequence of the former; for this
reason their capacity to explain is rather limited. Because Marx
takes the view that society is a totality or system regulated by
structural relations, he is not committed to the empiricist atomism
for which necessity is a function of the constant conjunction of
events. For Marx, necessity arises out of the relations that
constitute the social system. On this account events are system-

22

dependent; their full description is not possible without reference to the system. Understanding the concrete, then, requires not only knowledge of the specific features of a phenomenon and the circumstances that surround it, but also its function in the set of relations in which the phenomenon occurs. From this point of view, the question of the typicality or uniqueness of events is a false alternative. Marx insists on the need for a clear understanding of the historical specificity of social phenomena, which may have different significance under different historical conditions. This means that historical events are both of a kind and unique at the same time. From an abstract point of view, overpopulation is overpopulation, a phenomenon of a certain type. From Marx's point of view, overpopulation is assessed in terms of its insertion on a network of historical relations. The typicality of an event, then, is not given by its intrinsic properties; rather, it is determined by both its intrinsic properties and its function within a system.

The principle of the transience of all entities implies that mental constructions, forms of consciousness, are also transient. Writing on the categories of political economy, Marx stated that 'the same men who establish their social relations in conformity with their material productivity, produce also principles, ideas and categories in conformity with their social relations'.[59] As the social relations change, so do the forms of consciousness. The implication is that ideas must be analysed in their historical circumstances. They are not, as they are for idealist thinkers, independent of material reality or manifestations of some transcendent order of being, but a necessary aspect of the material process of history.

To summarize, historical materialism is a form of historicism in so far as it asserts the transient character of reality, both material and spiritual. The study of social formations must be founded on a methodology and a conception of laws and causal relations that are appropriate to a process of change. Furthermore, an important aspect of historical materialism is its conception of the relation between material reality and ideas, as well as the concrete manner in which this relation affects the historical process itself. In *The German Ideology*, Marx and Engels conceptualized this relation as one of reflection: the ideas of an epoch are the reflection of its material reality. However, the theory of reflection can be understood in at least two different ways. First, it can be conceived as an epistemological theory which proposes that

23

reflection is a causal relationship between matter or material processes and ideas. Complementing this theory, the claim is sometimes advanced that all matter is characterized by a property akin to reflection. Second, the theory of reflection can be taken as a historical hypothesis concerning the correspondence between socio-economic formations and forms of consciousness. In this second sense, the hypothesis is a methodological principle for historical investigation, and it can be said to apply to the long-term relationship between structure and superstructure, but not necessarily to short-term fluctuations of the superstructure. Incidentally, Gramsci is mainly concerned with developing this second view, although he often refers to theories as reflections of reality.

We have so far reviewed various forms of historicism that emerged in Germany during the nineteenth century. It was in Italy, however, that a non-Marxist historicism found one of its most able exponents. Benedetto Croce, whose thought exerted considerable influence on Gramsci, endeavoured to elaborate a thoroughly historicist philosophy both in his philosophical work and in his historical work. Croce's thought, like the thought of German historicists, was a reaction against the dominant positivism of the end of the nineteenth century, a positivism that in the words of Rossi was interpreted 'as the naturalist reduction of man and of his world to his biological environmental conditions, and as the negation of the methodological autonomy of historical research'.[60] However, whereas German historicism originated in Kantian philosophy, the absolute historicism of Croce relied on Hegel.

Like the German historicists, Croce at first emphasized the unique character of historical phenomena. This was the reason, he argued in an essay written in 1893, why history could not be a science and should therefore be classified under the general concept of art. However, in developing his system of philosophy, Croce found it necessary to modify his conception of history. The basis for this new conception was laid in his *Logic*. He argued that 'all features of History are reduced to the definition and identification of history with individual judgement'.[61] The judgement is a synthesis of the individual subject and the predicate, which is a universal concept. In other words, the judgement is a synthesis of representation (narrative) and concept (philosophy), or intuition and thought. For this reason, history is more than narration; in so far as it necessarily employs concepts, it is also philosophy. As he put it in his *Theory and History of Historiography*, the true subject of history is not the individual subject; it is the predicate, the universal. The historical judgement 'determines the universal by individualizing it'. Hence, 'the subject of social and political history is *Culture, Civilization, Progress, Liberty*. . . that is, a universal'.[62]

Although the starting points of German historicism and Croce's absolute historicism differ, there is nevertheless an important similarity. Both place ideas, rather than real human beings or social relations, at the centre of history. Croce's history of the predicate, brings to mind a passage in Marx's *Critique of Hegel's Philosophy of Right*. Hegel is taken to task for giving the idea 'the status of a subject'.[63] As Marx puts it, 'the important thing is that Hegel at all times makes the Idea the subject and makes the proper and actual subject, like "political sentiment" the predicate'.[64] The universal predicates that, for Croce, constitute the subject of history, are not simply partial manifestations of a transcendent order of values, as they were for the German historicists, but the essence of a dialectic whose development is the historic process. Thus, whereas for Dilthey, for instance, meaning is constituted by the 'relationship . . . of parts to the whole',[65] in Croce the whole itself is defined by an essential moment, a centre that unifies the dialectical process. The consequence is that history is not seen as the individual development of unique cultures, but as the ordered process of the unfolding of a fundamental universal. As Rossi observes, whereas 'for Meinecke the recognition of individuality implies . . . the impossibility of reducing history to rationality, for Croce it results in the thesis of the immanent rationality of historical development'.[66]

However, this 'immanent rationality' of the historical process does not mean that causal laws are applicable to history. Croce rejects causality in history just as much as German historicists did. The search for causes, he argues, leads to an infinite regress, which he finds unacceptable. The infinite regress can be stopped in two different ways. (1) By restricting our search to the sphere of proximate causes. This, however, is not satisfactory, for it is not always easy to determine where to stop the search; that is, the chain of causal links must be arbitrarily cut. (2) By seeking a transcendent end of history. This is also unsatisfactory to Croce, for he sees history as being immanently rational.

Croce's theory of the real subject of history coupled with his theory of pseudo-concepts, already entails the negation of historical causation. For Croce, a pseudo-concept is a general concept, whose 'content is furnished by a group of represent-ations, or even by a single one'. As a consequence, the concepts of the natural sciences are not pure concepts: they are pseudo-concepts. Since the real subject of history is the universal pure concepts that are individuated in particular subjects and events, and since these concepts are 'ultrarepresentative',[67] that is, they are not grounded on groups of representations, it is impossible that causation could be applied to what Croce considers to be the real subject of history. Causation belongs to the realm of individual objects, or in theoretical terms, types of objects. Its application is limited to the realm of Croce's pseudo-concepts. Natural science, Croce argues, is a science of phenomena or facts, philosophy is the science of noumena, or values. Hence, science cannot know what Croce calls pure phenomena; but it does not deal with mere facts either. Natural science elaborates 'representative concepts, which are not intuitions or concepts, but spiritual formations of a practical character'.[68]

The pure concept, in contrast to representative concepts, is one that has no basis in existing objects, although it can be exhibited in them. Croce's arguments, at times, come very close to Plato's. Indeed, perhaps the best example he offers is taken from Platonism. A pure triangle, he argues, is not to be found in reality; the concept of a 'triangle' then, is not a representative one, but a pure one. We do find in actual reality forms that approximate that of the triangle, or which exhibit the general shape of the triangle. They are understood as triangles because the pure concept is already in our possession, prior to the observation of such forms. The identification of the historical subject with pure concepts introduces an element that is pre-experiential, although it can be observed at work in the phenomenal world. For Croce it is the pure concept, the philosophical aspect of history, that renders history rational, something more than the haphazard flow of events. Nevertheless, history is not pure knowledge, precisely because in it the pure concept is always embodied in institutions or in human beings who have practical needs and who are often motivated by passion. Real history, then, does not exemplify the pure concept perfectly; it is, rather, a dialectic of the practical and the ideal.

The unifying concept of all human production and experience is, for Croce as it was for Hegel, the concept of spirit. It is a unity which exhibits four distinctions. There are two basic forms of the spirit, the theoretical and the practical.[69] These two forms, or activities, yield the four-fold distinction of reality into the true, the beautiful, the good, and the useful. The unity of these four is what he calls the circle of the spirit, which should not be taken as a dialectical unity, that is, a unity of opposites. In his essay on *What is Living and What is Dead of the Philosophy of Hegel*, Croce takes Hegel to task for having 'conceived the link between these degrees dialectically'.[70] A dialectical connection is, for example, the relation between true and false, but not that between false and good.[71]

These distinctions are important for the understanding of history, because 'the human mind cannot think of history as a whole without distinguishing it, at the same time, into the history of deeds and the history of knowledge; into the history of practical activity, and the history of aesthetic production, of philosophical thought, and so on'.[72] On an empirical basis, by introducing empirical concepts into its study, history may be divided into the history of the state, of the Church, of society, etc.[73] But Croce stresses that it is a grave mistake to suppose that these pseudo-concepts have a 'constitutive character', an error that results in 'the positivist fixation to reduce history to a science (a natural science, that is)'. Historical pseudo-concepts, or empirical concepts, have only a 'subsidiary character', they are helpful, for instance, to 'divide the mass of facts and to regroup them for the use of memory'.[74] The task of the historian, as opposed to the task of the chronicler, is to go beyond the mass of individual facts and to grasp the dialectic of the pure concepts. In a passage reminiscent of Vico's thought, Croce remarks that the philosopher, considering the spirit *sub specie aeterni*, will grasp an 'eternal ideal history'.[75]

The basic pure concept that Croce offers as the essence of the historical process, is the concept of liberty. He came to believe that the best definition of history that could be given is that history is 'the story of liberty',[76] as was common with liberal historians of the period. It is as story of liberty that Croce conceived his *History of Europe in the Nineteenth Century*. In this work, Croce traces the struggle of the religion of liberty[77] against other religions: absolute monarchy, radical democracy, communism, and Catholicism. In keeping with his theory of the historical judgement, the subject of his history is not the various parties that took part in the struggle, nor the victors and the vanquished, but liberty itself, liberty as the immanent force of history that, through the secular labour of philosophy, has finally become a permanent acquisition. This history, then, is an account of what he saw as the lessening of the distance 'between heaven and earth, God and the world, the ideal and the real'.[78] The Hegelian shadow in this passage is quite evident, for Hegel, in the *Phenomenology*, also envisioned the descent of God to earth or the emergence of the 'universal divine man, the community'.[79]

In his *History of Italy*, however, Croce presents a somewhat different historical dynamics; here, the two main conceptual poles are ethics and politics, or the ethical ideal of the creation of a unified Italy and the practical needs of building a country. These poles become personified in the historic Right and Left, and in the ruthless Sicilian prime minister Crispi and the liberal Giolitti. The theoretical basis of this dialectic is found in an essay entitled 'State and Church in their ideal sense and in their perpetual struggle in history' first published in 1931. In this essay, Croce argues that Ranke's dictum that 'history is always the history of the relations and of the struggle between the Church and State', is profoundly true.[80] The truth in the dictum, however, is not about the institutions that bear the names of Church and state: these are two different forms of the state. It is, Croce argues, the opposition between 'consciousness and political action on the one hand and consciousness and moral action on the other'[81] that constitutes the inner dynamic of history. This conception of 'ethico-political history' is what enables the historian to construct a history of 'full humanity'.[82] It is indeed this conception of history that, for Croce, enables the historian to grasp the significance of the actual events in terms of the struggle to incarnate liberty, a struggle that is often embodied in the form of the antithesis between practical concerns and ideals.

As it has already been mentioned, this theory of history entails the unity of history and philosophy. This is so for several related reasons. First, in so far as the universal concept or the predicate of the historical judgement is the real subject of history, real historical knowledge will be attained by the analysis of pure concepts, i.e., by philosophy. Second, philosophy is itself history for it offers an analysis of the pure concepts whose dialectic is the historical process. Philosophy, then, is self-consciousness of the progress of ethical ideals, and it becomes the spring from which history flows. The identity of philosophy and history thus presents two aspects. Epistemologically, 'history is not possible without the logical element, which is philosophy; philosophy is not possible without the intuitive element, which is history'.[83] Ontologically, the real ground of historical development, the real motor of history, is a dialectic of ethico-political concepts; consciousness of these concepts, as well as their analysis, is philosophy.

In so far as the 'intuitive element' is said to be historical, and furthermore, in so far as scientific concepts have a mere practical significance, natural science itself is subsumed under history. This is one of the most fundamental aspects of Croce's absolute historicism. As Rossi argues, 'this absorption of nature by history, and the consequent affirmation that historical knowledge is the only authentic form of knowledge, was . . . foreign to the development of contemporary German historicism'.[84] Whereas the German historicists attempted to make a clear cut between the natural sciences and the cultural sciences, thus denying the positivist doctrine of the unity of method, Croce insists that all sciences are unified in history. This is not to be interpreted as a form of the doctrine of the unity of method. Croce is not claiming that the methods of history should be applied to physics or biology. His claim is that natural science does not count as a theoretical activity because its concepts are not pure concepts. Science can attain certainty; truth, however, can only be attained 'with the help of the principle of historical interpretation'.[85] Because 'thought always thinks history',[86] the full comprehension of reality by means of universal concepts, or truth, is made possible by taking scientific activity, and through it nature itself, as part of the spirit. The all-encompassing reality, then, is spirit, and true knowledge is the knowledge of the dialectic of the activity of the spirit. It is, as Rossi argues, Hegel's influence that 'leads Croce to interpret spiritual activity as an all-inclusive process, in whose circle the individual and the universal can coincide'.[87]

A final note on the spirit and its activity. It seems fairly obvious that for Croce the subject of history is not, and cannot be, any individual human being or group of human beings. As he puts it, 'history, in this conception, as it is no longer the work of nature or of an extramundane God, so it is not either the work of the powerless, empirical, and unreal individual, whose work is interrupted at any moment; it is rather the work of that truly real individual that is the eternally individualizing spirit'.[88] In short, it is not real, empirical, active men and women who make history; they, in fact, play out a history prescribed for them by the dialectic of spirit. The spirit is the subject of history, but it is not a transcendent being. It is rather an idealized version of humanity itself, which in practical terms reduces itself to, or incarnates itself in the great intellectuals, the men of vision, who can transform ethico-political ideals into practical institutions. Neither transcendent God or idea, nor empirical humanity, spirit lives in the vision of an elite of intellectuals; it is they, not the masses, who create history.

From the point of view of the writing of history, Croce argues that all history is contemporary history. The historian must be rigorous in his examination of documents. However, a document 'separated from life, is nothing but a thing'.[89] What brings documents to life is the soul of the historian, the problems and interests he brings to the documents. These problems and interests are contemporary ones: they originate in the life of the present. For this reason, all history is contemporary history.[90] In this sense, contemporary history is conceived as 'the crucible of interests by means of which certainty is transformed into truth',[91] that is, the evidence culled from documents, certainty, is given an interpretation, the truth, whose philosophical basis originates in the life of the present. This is perhaps best exemplified in Croce's histories. In the Preface to his *History of Italy*, Croce claims that it is not written with a purpose.[92] Nevertheless, in reading it, one feels that Croce is attempting to show that Mussolini's attempt to revive a heroic age is a futile attempt, as empty as the exaggerated verbosity and sensualism of D'Annunzio's poetry. Similarly, in his *History of Europe*, Croce is clearly defending a liberal conception of society, a conception that he sees threatened by both the fascists and the communists.

However, the contemporaneity of history may mean more than this. As Badaloni points out, there is a second sense of the term 'contemporary' to be found in Croce's thought. In this second sense, contemporary refers to the 'integral acceptance of the past as it realizes itself in the eternal present of the spirit'.[93] In this second sense, the task of the historian is seen as one of under-standing, not of judging the past. Indeed, history cannot discriminate between good and bad facts, progressive and regressive epochs. All facts and all epochs are productive in their own way, and 'the past does not live except in the present, as force in the present'.[94] This living of the historical past in the present is a consequence of Croce's conception of the dialectic of the spirit as an eternal ideal history, which has been mentioned above. Indeed, the spirit is an eternal present so that its ideal history is not in time.[95] This being so, it is difficult to see how human thought, which always thinks history, could grasp what is essentially beyond history, and how, for that matter, an eternal present could produce the fleeting life-and-death drama of history. Whereas in the first sense the temporal dimension of history is not denied, in this second sense Croce seems to affirm that the past is either non-existent or unimportant, for what really matters is the present life of the spirit.

This conception of history as philosophical truth to the extent that it reveals the pure concept of the spirit originates with Vico, but is not really different from the metaphysics of the German historical school. In both cases, the attempt to historicize all reality finds its limit in an eternal present. The major difference between these two forms of historicism is that Croce, under the influence of Vico and Hegel, paid more attention to the developmental aspects of history. Whereas for Dilthey, meaning was a function of the relation of parts to the whole, in Croce meaning is a function of a dialectic of the ideal and the practical in which liberty grows. In his later work, which is not considered here for it was not known by Gramsci, Croce began to question his former philosophical historicism. As Rossi notes, World War II and fascism made it very difficult for anyone to believe in the rationality of history.[96] This questioning had a two-fold result: first, Croce began to develop a methodological historicism that would eliminate the Hegelian influence; second, he began to look at the human dimension of historical development.[97]

Finally, Croce's historicism is quite evidently anti-democratic. As Kahn points out, Croce's philosophy does not 'escape from the realm of the mental cogitations of an intellectual elite'.[98] Hence, in so far as philosophy is both epistemologically and ontologically primary in the historical process, no importance is accorded by

31

Croce to the activities of masses of people. The ethico-political ideal of liberty, as it is consciously appropriated by philosophers, rather than classes or masses, is for Croce the substance of history as well as the source of its movement. In theory, the idea of liberty, as Croce warns, should not be confused with economic liberalism, for the latter is a proper economic principle, but not a proper ethical principle.[99] The ideal of liberty is not to be confused either with the liberal party, which is a party among parties, without any prerogatives.[100] In reality, however, Croce first supported the fascist movement until the murder of Matteoti in 1925, and then he became the soul and life of the liberal party. He wrote in his diary that the struggle for the liberation of Italy should follow the example of Garibaldi, thus implicitly rejecting the democratic republicanism of Mazzini.[101]

In the broadest outline, the various historicist theories from Vico to Croce, attempted to offer an alternative to empiricist and rationalist approaches to the study of human reality. What they held in common was the need to give historical explanations for social phenomena; however, their conceptions of what constitutes a historical explanation were vastly different. The German historical school accepted a positivist conception of scientific law, but denied that history is governed by causal laws. The interior of history, the real substance of history, is the meaning that derives from a moral metaphysical reality, which is a reality beyond history. This noumenal reality is expressed or signified in the phenomena of the human world; partial knowledge of it is possible only by means of the hermeneutical method or understanding. Croce also rejected the conception of causal law in history, and, like the German historicists, emphasized the ideal meaning of history. The eternal life of the spirit, which only philosophy can grasp, albeit inadequately, is the real substance of history; it manifests itself in dialectical opposition to the practical needs of human beings, a process that is identical with the progress of liberty.

These idealist forms of historicism are characterized by the rejection of the unity of scientific method and by their anti-naturalism. In contrast, Marxism, which also seeks to understand the underlying realities of the historical process, is a realist and materialist theory of history. These underlying realities – the inner aspect of history – are not moral values or pure concepts; they are social structures whose base is to be found in the process of production. Marxism emphasizes the transient nature of all social forms, and seeks to understand specific phenomena on the basis of the social structure in which they occur; it does not deny the applicability of concepts of causality and of law to human phenomena, but it espouses a conception of them that contrasts with the empiricist view.

Because of the emphasis given to the historical explanation of all social phenomena, historicists have often been considered to fall into epistemological and ethical relativism. If values and ideas are functions of the historical conditions in which they emerge, then they change with changes in those conditions, and no possible evaluation of their value or truth in general is possible. However, not all historicists have been willing to accept this conclusion, and they have had to seek some way out of this predicament. It would seem, however, that idealist historicists, in confusing the conditions of knowledge or experience with the conditions of reality, have been unable to distinguish between the conditions under which knowledge or values arise and the justification of such knowledge or values.

Historicism, in its various and often vague senses, constituted Gramsci's intellectual background. We must now turn to his *Prison Notebooks*, first to analyse his use of the terms 'historicism' and 'historicist', and later, in Chapter Two, to develop a general *interpretation* of what he meant by this term. The use of the term 'historicism' alone will already suggest a marked contrast between Gramsci, on the one hand, and Croce, Hegel, and the German historical school, on the other.

GRAMSCI'S HISTORICISM: A PRELIMINARY ANALYSIS

The first issue that we must deal with is that of Gramsci's awareness of the development of historicism from Vico to Croce. There is no doubt that he knew Marx as well as Hegel and that he had read Croce extensively, as his frequent references to his work attest. In fact, the *Prison Notebooks* could be characterized as a sustained dialogue with Croce as well as an attempt to purge his own thought of Crocean influences. Croce's ascendancy over Italian culture, Gramsci felt, had to be opposed with an anti-Croce. Gramsci notes two main reasons why it was necessary to 'write a new *Anti-Duhring*': (1) Croce's historicism was too speculative, not immanentist enough;[102] (2) Croce was too obstinate in his opposition to historical materialism.[103] Such a critique of Croce would be the first step towards the transformation of Italian culture; hence, besides its theoretical interest, the anti-Croce was conceived as having great practical significance.

Gramsci's knowledge of the German historical school was not as extensive, or as deep, as his knowledge of Croce or Marx. Apart from a few references to Weber, whose interpretative sociology is linked to the German historical school, there is only one work related to German historicism used by Gramsci. This is Ernst Bernheim's *Lehrbuch des Historischen Methode und der Geschichts- philosophie,* first published in Leipzig in 1903. This work became a widely used textbook to teach the critical method of historical research initiated by Ranke. Essentially, it deals in great detail with historical methodology, authentication and critique of sources, and interpretation. Although Gramsci's direct knowledge of German historicism is limited, his indirect knowledge must not be ignored. For Croce's knowledge of German historiography was considerable, and he often wrote about, or commented on, indivi- dual German historicists. Thus we can take Gramsci's concern with the problem of the uniqueness of historical events and the possibility of theory,[104] and with the question of the unity of scientific method,[105] as evidence of his indirect knowledge of German historicism.

However, apart from Gramsci's knowledge of German and Italian historicism, the question that really matters is that of the extent of the influence that these theories had on his thought and his interpretation of Marxism. On this point, commentators are not in agreement. On the one hand, the most widespread interpretation of Gramsci maintains that he is a Hegelian Marxist. A variation on this theme is found in Finocchiaro's essay on 'Gramsci's Crocean Marxism' whose 'proof lends support to the Crocean character of Gramsci's thought in general'.[106] On the other hand, a recent interpretation of Gramsci argues that 'what Gramsci calls "absolute historicism" is precisely the radical rejec- tion of any essentialism and of *a priori* teleology'.[107] On this view, Gramsci would reject the theory that there is an element, such as the social relations of production, that determines all the other social elements; he would also reject the theory that history has any particular direction in, or end to which, it tends. Since Laclau and

Mouffe maintain that 'all identity is relational',[108] it would seem that they place Gramsci closer to Dilthey than to Croce.

For Dilthey the 'category of meaning designates the relationship inherent in life, of parts of a life to a whole',[109] the various elements of reality have a unique and equal value. In contrast, for Laclau and Mouffe, the various elements are 'floating signifiers, incapable of being wholly articulated to a discursive (i.e. social) identity', so that the meaning or identity of elements is partially fixed by a 'practice of articulation';[110] different practices will produce different meanings. Despite what appear to be fundamental differences between Dilthey, or German historicism in general, and Laclau and Mouffe, they seem to agree in one thing: there is no privileged element, no essential feature that would confer identity to the whole by its relationship to the rest of the elements of that whole. The conclusions, both theoretical and practical, of this position are of great importance for social theory, and particularly for Marxism. For if there is not a privileged element, then history cannot be explained by appealing to any one particular element, be it classes, technology, or whatever. This demise of class-centred history, the rejection of class reductionism, has signalled, perhaps more than any other critique of Marxism, what is now widely claimed to be the crisis or even the death of Marxism.

Let us now turn to the analysis of Gramsci's *Prison Notebooks* in order to define his own brand of historicism. The aim of this analysis is to lay the groundwork for the general thesis that Gramsci attempts to interpret some of the essential theories of Croce in a realist and materialist sense. In this, he did not always succeed, and thus we find in his *Prison Notebooks* many passages that are still locked into the idealist view. Nevertheless, his historicism makes no sense unless one takes it as a form of dialectical realism. However, this alone does not account for Gramsci's thought. His Anti-Croce and with it the Crocean influence accounts for only a portion, albeit an important one, of his re-interpretation of Marxism. Other important elements must also be considered. In what follows, an attempt will be made to clarify some of the fundamental theoretical questions that are linked to Gramsci's historicism.

A cursory analysis of Gramsci's use of the term 'historicism' and related terms, shows that he consciously attempts to define the term in opposition to speculative thought and to abstract rationalism; consciously, because in many instances he associates terms or expressions with the word 'historicism' which show the meaning he intended. This will allow us to identify four areas, as well as four theoretical positions, where the analysis of Gramsci's 'absolute historicism' is to be sought.

Historicism as transience

One of the terms most frequently associated with 'historicism' is 'transience'. In an argument that closely follows Marx, Gramsci states that whereas the pure economists speak of the determined market and its automatism as natural and eternal elements, the critique of political economy begins with the concept of the 'historicity' of the determined market.[111] It is clear that in this passage Gramsci uses 'historicity' as transience, that is, he affirms the temporary character of economic institutions. Even the 'automatism' of the capitalist economic system, that is, the logic of capital or the laws of capitalist production, is said to be afflicted with transience.

Thought, or consciousness in general, is also said to be transient. This is not to be taken as a denial of the value of past philosophical systems: 'their transience is considered from the point of view of the whole historical development of the life-death dialectic; that they deserved to fall is not a moral judgement or one of objective "truth", but a dialectico-historical one'.[112] Ideology, forms of social consciousness, are thus said to be influential within a defined historical time, which is not to deny that they have any value. The transitory character of forms of consciousness affects the philosophy of praxis itself. Gramsci states that it is implicit in Marxism as a whole, and in particular in the doctrine of the passage from the realm of necessity to the realm of freedom, that 'the philosophy of praxis conceives itself historicistically, that is, as a transitory phase of philosophical thought'.[113]

It is important to stress that Gramsci's approach is that of the historian. He is interested in understanding the forms of development of a social whole, including science and philosophy. It is not an attempt at providing an epistemology. Confusion on this point may lead to some form of subjectivist interpretation of Gramsci. Alas, this sort of confusion did sometimes cloud Gramsci's own thinking. Some interpretations of Gramsci's theory take his historicism to be an epistemological theory or at least to contain 'a formidable epistemology'.[114] There are, indeed, some epistemological theses in Gramsci's thought as we shall see presently, but one should not take as a defence of a general epistemological theory about what counts as knowledge or about what can be known, Gramsci's attempts to offer actual historical or political explanations from within a supposed epistemological framework never fully developed, much less defended, by him.

This aspect of Gramsci's historicism is in fact the rejection of all permanent elements in history. History is life and death, it is change. The social is ephemeral. As he puts it, movement 'is the organic mode in which historical reality manifests itself'.[115] This implies that the study of social phenomena must always take into account their fleeting nature; or that the study of society is a study of a temporal process. The problem that one needs to address is that of the forms of this temporal process, that is, the shape of transience itself. The second characterization of historicism that Gramsci gives provides us with some clues about the manner in which the historical process takes place.

Historicism as historical necessity

In discussing the adoption of the Spanish constitution of 1812 by the Neapolitans, Gramsci argues that the constitution was 'the exact expression of the historical necessity of Spanish society', and he suggests that the Neapolitan conditions may not have been very different from Spanish ones, and therefore the adoption of that constitution was not due to political mimesis or mental laziness, for it was 'more historicist than it seems'.[116] In this context, it would seem that 'historicist' is equivalent to 'corresponding to historical necessity'. Other texts by Gramsci confirm this interpretation. True historicism, Gramsci writes in a critical note on Croce and Gioberti, cannot be equivalent to an arbitrary act of the will in choosing the elements of the present that will survive in the future. Whatever survives, as well as what may be generated in the dialectical process of history, 'will result from the process itself, it will have a character of historical necessity'.[117] It is only through an adequate conception of historical necessity, which takes into consideration both the material premisses and the cultural level of society, that a 'historicist conception (and not a speculative–

37

abstract one) of "rationality" in history can be attained'.[118]

This meaning of historicism is the ground for the distinction between arbitrary acts or ideologies, and those that correspond to the movement of history. Thus, an ideology that does not 'correspond to the exigencies of a historical period' will 'more or less rapidly be eliminated from historical competition', although, due to special circumstances, it may become popular for some time.[119] This distinction between 'historicist' and 'arbitrary' phenomena results in a distinction between what is historical and what is ahistorical. The distinction itself is entertained by some historians. For instance, Pierre Vilar refers to suicide as 'an ahistorical fact *par excellence*, because it cannot, even within a society in a very grave crisis, exceed certain limits, take the character of typicality, become the cause'. It is a 'marginal fact' which does not become part of the 'causes–effects of the dialectic of history'.[120] This distinction implies a conception of history in which certain types of phenomena have a fundamental causative, as well as explanatory, character. Historical necessity is, for Gramsci, the complex set of relationships that account for the historical process as a whole, but not necessarily for everything that happens in a society.

This use of 'historicism' as historical necessity contrasts with the anti-naturalist historicisms of both the German historical school and of Croce. First, it asserts that both actions and ideologies depend on some as yet unidentified elements which necessitate them. Second, it is necessity, rather than liberty or values, that defines Gramsci's historicism. Whether historical necessity can be interpreted in terms of causal laws will be discussed in Chapter Two. Also, we must consider whether the grounds on which historical necessity arises commit Gramsci to some form of essentialism such as the one discussed above.

Historicism as realism

Closely connected with the previous definition of 'historicist', Gramsci offers a third use of term. According to this, 'historicist' is synonymous with 'realist'. In a critique of Croce's and Gentile's interpretation of Hegel, Gramsci wonders whether they eliminated 'the most realist, most historicist part' of Hegel's thought, which constitutes the origins of Marxism.[121] Again, on the relation between 'effectual reality' and what 'ought to be' in the thought of Machiavelli, he points out that in the creation of a new form of society, considerations about what ought to be are not founded on 'abstract and formal thought', but on the 'realist and alone historicist interpretation of reality'.[122]

The first passage quoted above can be construed as a distinction between speculative elements in Hegel, emphasized by Croce and Gentile, and the elements based on a sound analysis of historical reality. The second passage points to 'political realism' in the sense that no major change in society is possible when the conditions for such change are not present. In this sense, 'realism' is in fact similar to, if not the same as, respect for what is 'in accordance with historical necessity'. However, there are still doubts as to whether this is to be interpreted as a realism in the philosophical sense. Nevertheless, in rejecting speculative thought in favour of sound historical analysis, and arbitrary actions in favour of those actions whose conditions are supported by historical necessity, Gramsci clearly rejects a conception of historical reality as dependent on a transcendent world as well as the view that the will can arbitrarily impose itself on reality and create a new world. This would indicate that Gramsci subscribes to the view of the stubborn independence of reality from consciousness, as well as to the view that the origin of ideas is to be found in the real historical world, not a supra-historical or a transcendental consciousness.

This interpretation of Gramsci may be surprising to many. It seems to be a widely accepted view that Gramsci was a subjective idealist, an anti-realist. I have already quoted a passage by Callinicos which supports this view. Similar views are expressed by Gregor McLennan. He is prepared to accept Gramsci's account of the historical conditions of philosophy, but he claims that this 'does not commit us to his notion of *absolute* historicism, especially when we recall Gramsci's idealist notion that the existence of the external world is dependent upon human cognition'.[123] It must be admitted that one can find some passages in the *Prison Notebooks* which justify this statement. However, one can also find passages that contradict it. Because this is a crucial philosophical issue, I am going to attempt to settle it now, before we proceed with further analysis of the term 'historicism'.

A clear indication of Gramsci's realism is found in a note devoted to the physics of infinitely small phenomena. He argues that if these phenomena 'cannot be considered as existing independently of the subject that observes them, they are not really "observed but, created"'.[124] And he adds that this theory is not only solipsism, but witchcraft.[125] He also states that 'it is difficult to imagine that reality changes objectively with changes in ourselves, and it is difficult not only for common sense but also for scientific thought to accept this'. Given that knowledge is not definitive, 'it is difficult to avoid the thought of something real beyond this knowledge, not in the metaphysical sense of a "noumenon" or an "unknown God" or of "an unknowable", but in the concrete sense of a "relative ignorance" of reality, of something as yet "unknown", but which will be known some day when the "physical" and intellectual instruments of men are more perfect'.[126] Although this passage might be taken to imply the non-realist theory of the identity of knowledge and reality, the previous quotation, as well as his belief that a theory such as the theory of the atomic structure of matter, although not definitive, is 'the reflection of an unchanging reality',[127] suggests that objects of knowledge exist independently of the beliefs (desires, etc.) of knowing subjects and that it is possible for the latter to discover truths about such objects. On this interpretation, the difficulty in imagining that reality changes with us, which would include its changing with changes in our knowledge, could be taken as grudging surrender to realism, perhaps in a moment of weakness, on the grounds that it is difficult to admit the dependence of reality on cognition, however desirable that position may be. On this view, Gramsci's opposition to realism would be a kind of prejudice rather than a well-thought-out disagreement with it.

However, another interpretation of the text is also plausible. On this other view, Gramsci is performing what could be called a *reductio-ad-absurdum* argument: it is not any contradiction involved in the negation of the independent existence of the external world, but rather the difficulty for both science and common sense to grasp such a world that shows the realist thesis to be true. In other words, cognition itself is contingent upon the independent existence of the external world. This argument, which is merely adumbrated by Gramsci, has recently been made by Bhaskar, who argues that 'it is a condition of the possibility of science ... that such objects exist and act, as what may be termed the *intransitive* objects of scientific inquiry, independently of their identification'.[128] Besides this argument, Gramsci refers to Engels' claim that the materiality and objectivity of the world are proven by the history of science and technology,[129] although it is questionable whether he understands such a proof in the same way as Engels.

In effect, Gramsci for the most part does not offer, nor was he too concerned to offer, a justification for realism. The point, however, is that at least some texts suggest a realist position. In those texts Gramsci's thought fulfils two conditions for philosophical realism: (1) the independent existence of the real; (2) the conception of knowledge as reflecting that reality, which involves a correspondence theory of truth. Further evidence for this interpretation is Gramsci's belief that historical materialism is 'the historical methodology most fitting to reality and to truth',[130] which implies that our effort to know must be adequate to something distinct and independent from that knowledge, rather than reality having to fit knowledge.[131] Gramsci thought that the historicist realism of Marxism, as opposed to the speculative ideology of other systems, was decidedly superior. It was the weakness of speculative philosophy which prompted bourgeois intellectuals to appropriate elements of Marxism in order to 'strengthen their conceptions and to curb their overwhelming speculative philosophizing with the historicist realism of the new theory'.[132]

Although the texts analysed above strongly suggest that Gramsci was a realist, other texts, often quoted by commentators, point to a very different Gramsci, a non-realist Gramsci. It is useless to deny that such passages exist; they often appear within the same paragraph in which realist statements are found. The point that I wish to make is that Gramsci's intention was not to deny realism, but dogmatism, and that he was confused or misled by ambiguities in his use of terms such as 'objective'. We shall return to this below. The objection may be raised that there is no way of knowing Gramsci's intention other than by analysing his writings; but since his writings are unfinished and inconsistent, his intentions remain unclear at best. However, in a passage that refers to the genesis of historical materialism, Gramsci asserts that the only element of French materialism that the philosophy of praxis has kept is philosophical realism.[133] Although the accuracy of this statement may be questioned, it is clear that Gramsci approved of realism. In the absence of any denial of this assertion in *Prison Notebooks*, there is the strong presumption that, in spite of his inability to argue consistently with realism, he believed it to be a sound philosophical position to take.

A number of reasons may account for his confusions and inconsistencies. To begin with, the conditions under which Gramsci wrote his notes were not the most conducive for serious, consistent work. More important, however, Gramsci's inconsistencies may be the result of his attempt to avoid both empiricist materialism and idealism. In this respect, he assumed different positions against one or the other of the views he objected to for polemical reasons. In any case, he did not completely succeed in formulating an independent Marxist view of these problems. We have to interpret Gramsci, then, as undergoing a process of intellectual maturation which was interrupted by death soon after being released from jail, a process that, had it continued, might have resulted in a more consistent and clear argument for realism.

We must now turn to the anti-realist statements in the *Prison Notebooks*. It is important to note that these statements are often polemical, directed against empiricism, and that, for this reason, he often writes as if he were attacking the realist epistemological foundations some attribute to empiricism. One of the main claims made by Gramsci in these criticisms is that the concept of the objectivity of the external world has its origin in religion. Religion, he writes, has always taught that 'nature, the universe was created by God before the creation of men' and so human beings found it already 'defined once and for all'.[134] Gramsci's main concern is not so much with the concept of objectivity itself, or more precisely, with the independent existence of external reality, as with the conservative and dogmatic use of this concept due to its articulation in a religious discourse. For religion, in particular the Catholicism that Gramsci knew, was not only conservative in its political practice, but in theory it posited a world made by a divine will superior to any human will, and hence unchangeable by human beings. In this conception of reality, men and women were reduced to actors playing their roles with no possibility of consciously overcoming oppressive inequalities. In fact, any rebellion against social reality was characterized as ungodly, as sinful, for it was said to be a transgression of divine law.

Gramsci's argument, then, is designed not so much to reject realism, as to understand it critically in order to dislodge it from any extraneous ideologies. To do so, Gramsci may have questioned, as a sort of exercise in methodological doubt, the conception of objectivity that is implied by realism, and may, furthermore, have been confused about his own procedure. That this is so seems to be suggested by his questioning the belief in, but not the fact of the reality of, the external world: 'What is the origin of this "belief" and what critical value does it have "objectively"?'. Since in this passage Gramsci is concerned with questioning Bukharin's discussion of the question of the objectivity of the external world in a popular manual, a question that only elicits laughter from the general public,[135] it cannot be taken to constitute a doubt on objectivity. Rather, it doubts its value in the effort to educate a public for whom the question is settled by religion. If anything, then, that question might reinforce, rather than weaken, religious beliefs. This, however, is not a denial of realism.

His attack on objectivity must be seen as a rejection of prevailing forms of culture, of a level of common sense which he feels is an impediment to progress. In fact, he sees that in 'common sense the "realist", materialist elements predominate, that is, the immediate product of crude sensation. This is by no means inconsistent with the religious element, far from it'.[136] At the same time that he rejects this dogmatic and religious conception of reality, it is clear that, as the previous quotation indicates, Gramsci also objected to the empiricism prevalent in that conception of objectivity. The reason for this exercise is to be sought in what Gramsci thought about the unity and independence of Marxism. Following Labriola, Gramsci argued that Marxism is an original philosophy with no need of support from other philosophical systems. For him, orthodoxy is 'the fundamental concept that the philosophy of praxis is self-sufficient and contains in itself all the fundamental elements to construct a total and integral conception of the world'.[137] Hence Gramsci's arguments must be understood as the attempt to sever philosophical questions both from religious ideology and from other philosophical systems, with the intention of developing a coherent and independent philosophy.

An independent philosophy need not deny whatever true theories other philosophical currents may have. But Gramsci thought that Marxism had to be developed systematically, not as an eclectic aggregate of truths. The importance of this is not merely theoretical, but above all practical and didactic. If Marxism had to 'give life to an integral, practical organization of society, that is, to become a total, integral civilization',[138] it had to pose philosophical questions not merely in a way that could be shown to be objectively true, but in a way that could succeed in dislodging people's beliefs from ideologies or philosophical doctrines that were to be rejected. In other words, posing questions, developing theories, and making them assume the character of social forces is an exercise that must begin with the actual culture of the people to be persuaded. Failing to pose the questions in an appropriate manner may result in emphasizing undesirable elements of the old culture, thus subverting the new one. Marxism is not, nor was Gramsci, immune to extraneous influences. What in effect Gramsci argues for is an appropriate treatment of questions for educational purposes. Marxism must reject the commonsense approach to the question of the existence of the external world, even if they reach the same conclusions.[139]

Extraneous influences, Gramsci thought, had resulted in a 'double revision' of Marxism. On the one hand, a number of pure intellectuals, such as Max Adler, had been 'absorbed by and incorporated into some idealist currents'. On the other hand, those thinkers in close contact with the masses had sought to overcome religious transcendence with 'the most crude and banal materialism'.[140] In an attempt to regain the intellectual independence of Marxism, as well as the capacity to present an alternative hegemony, Gramsci embarked on his reinterpretation of Marxism. Hence his interest in the origin of philosophical concepts such as that of objectivity.

Gramsci's use of the word 'objective' is fraught with ambiguity. Because of this, he often produces fallacious arguments concerning the objectivity of the external world. There are at least five meanings of the word 'objective' in the *Prison Notebooks*: (1) 'being in itself'; (2) 'permanent being'; (3) 'common to all men'; (4) 'independent of any point of view which is particular'; (5) 'definitively true'.[141] Sense number one involves an ontological concept of 'objective', as meaning that which exists in itself and is, therefore, independent of its being perceived or known. Gramsci's concern with sense number two stems from his views of the transitory nature of social phenomena, to which he opposes the permanent existence (or permanent relative to history) of natural laws. In this sense, 'objective' is used in a similar sense to 'natural'.

It is important for Gramsci to distinguish these two forms of existence, as it was for Marx, because he wanted to avoid any reductionism of social to physical phenomena, or any form of biological determinism. Not only was it necessary for him to reject any conception of capitalism as being natural or determined by physical or biological laws, but he was also concerned with some racist overtones of those social theories. It was argued by some Italian sociologists, including socialist ones, that the backwardness of the south was due to the natural inferiority of the southern peasants. Gramsci rejected this sort of explanation, as he did biological theories of crime, pointing out that they ignored the historical conditions for the backwardness in the south.[142]. Against the sense of 'objective' as 'permanent' Gramsci sometimes writes of 'historically objective', by which he means that social conventions are not natural or God-given; they are objective to the extent that they are appropriate for a given society.[143] Senses number three and number four together are synonymous with 'impartial', as opposed to prejudiced by interests that could not be universally accepted. And finally, in sense number five, objectivity is a property of truth, the correspondence with what is real; Gramsci argues that, in fact, what we take as true or objective knowledge is not definitive, it is always subject to revision.

For our own purposes, it may suffice to distinguish two senses of the word 'objective'. 'Objective' can mean: (1) what exists as an object, be it a substance, property, fact, etc., independent of its being perceived or known, or ontological objectivity; (2) the veracity of thought, its correspondence with what exists objectively in sense number one, or epistemological objectivity.

Some of Gramsci's arguments, which provide the basis for Crocean and subjective-idealist interpretations of his thought, are based on ambiguities and confusions in his use of the term 'objective'. For instance, he affirms that reality is known through its relation to men, which, assuming that human beings are the only knowing subjects, is trivially true. Since human beings change through history, so does knowledge – that is, knowledge is an accumulative process, and its objectivity improves with improvements in both intellectual and practical tools. It follows that the objectivity of this knowledge is subject to a historical process. The conclusion Gramsci draws is that there is no reality outside man.[144] In this argument, Gramsci switches from the

45

empirical conditions of the production of objective knowledge ('objective' in our sense two), to the objective conditions of the existence of real objects ('objective' in our sense one).

In the same note, Gramsci asks whether 'an extra-historical and extra-human objectivity' can exist. Although he does not provide an answer at that point, in asking whether anyone could judge such objectivity or whether anyone could assume the 'point of view of the cosmos itself', a point of view that only God could attain, it seems that what Gramsci has in mind is not the formal possibility of objective knowledge of all reality, but rather, whether human beings can ever acquire such knowledge.[145] It would seem that Gramsci thinks of two limitations to that possibility: (1) the vastness of reality and the indefinitely complex interconnections among things make it impossible as a matter of fact to know everything about any non-trivial object of study; (2) the institutional and intellectual conditions of the acquisition of knowledge are not, and may never be, sufficiently adequate for knowledge perfect to its subject matter. His doubt about the possibility of an 'extra-historical and extra-human objectivity' is then a doubt about the possibility of complete and absolute knowledge for human beings: all knowledge, all objectivity in our sense two, is limited or imperfect, it is rooted in the intellectual and practical activities of historical agents and it is conditioned by those activities. Specifically, the instruments of science, both technical and conceptual on which the advance of knowledge depends, are the result of historical development.[146]

This is a thesis about the history of knowledge, not about truth-conditions, though at times it is stated as if it were an epistemo-logical claim. It is in fact an optimistic thesis about progress in science. Gramsci points out that scientific progress was greatly facilitated by the abandonment of Aristotelian and Biblical conceptions. This change in turn was due to the general progress of modern society.[147] The conclusion Gramsci reaches is that science is not independent of the general development of society, and inasmuch as basic philosophical concepts that spawn scientific theories are often linked to general cultural and political develop-ment, the objectivity of scientific theories will depend, at least indirectly, on the adequacy of the latter. Nevertheless, Gramsci does not write, as for instance Kuhn does, of incommensurable scientific paradigms; he writes that progress in science is linked to the historical progress of humanity, and that it is measurable in terms of the ability of a new science either to solve the problems posed by the old science or to show that they are false problems.[148] The solutions to new problems, however, cannot be arbitrary constructions: the difference between the empiricism of common sense and science lies in the fact that the former cannot 'establish the real links of cause and effect'.[149]

Gramsci's interest, it would seem, lies in the interrelationship between knowledge and society. At times, however, he made truth a function of that relation, so that truth is what is 'universally subjective' or accepted by all,[150] which is certainly incompatible with realism. But, if that relation is seen as an aspect of the process of production of knowledge, then his analysis is compatible with realism. Admittedly, a number of statements in the *Prison Notebooks* point to the anti-realist position. Gramsci's thought is directed to this double aspect of science: (a) as a superstructure, that is, as ideas about reality, often tinged with ideology; (b) in its influence on the development of the forces of production. From this perspective, science is conditioned by the needs of the economy as well as the intellectual attitudes of a society. Gramsci's arguments concern mainly the first aspect, namely, the relationship between ideologies and science.

This historicized view of science is based on the premiss that knowledge of nature is conditioned by the relationship between human beings and nature. Although to the scientist, scientific activity may seem to be a purely contemplative exercise, in reality 'science is tied to the needs, life, and activity of man'. The peculiarity of science is that, as a form of consciousness, it is part of the superstructure, although it has a privileged position because its reaction on the structure has 'greater extension and continuity of development'.[151] Because of this influence, in particular because of the development of scientific instruments which are 'closely linked to the general development of production and technology',[152] science can also be conceived as forming part of the structure, together with labour and class.[153]

The disappearance of distorting points of view is dependent on the disappearance of social contradictions, so that one of the conditions for the acquisition of objective knowledge is the unification of the whole human species in a unitary cultural system. For this reason, the acquisition of objective knowledge is seen from a historical perspective as an on – going struggle: 'there is a struggle for objectivity (for the liberation from partial and fallacious ideologies) and this struggle is the same struggle for the cultural unification of the human species'. There are some respects in which humanity is more unified than others. The natural sciences have provided 'the terrain in which such cultural unity has reached the maximum extension'.[154] As a consequence, the experimental sciences have been able to reach a higher level of objectivity than the social sciences. The 'universal subjectivity' of which Gramsci writes is but a condition for objectivity, namely, the condition that knowledge must not be tinged with fallacious ideological elements. The unification of humanity, however, is not a sufficient condition for the highest objectivity; this unification must also include freedom from ideology, from distorting points of view. Because Gramsci thinks that such distortions are at least in part due to the contradictions that rend societies, the condition of cultural unification and that of the disappearance of distorting points of view are thought to form a single historical process.

There is, however, a related interpretation of this theory of objectivity, one that complements the above remarks. In his critique of modern physics quoted above, Gramsci is concerned that the subjectivity exhibited in some formulations of the new physics entails that science will become 'a series of acts of faith in the assertions of single researchers'. Objectivity as 'universal subjectivity' requires that experiments and theories be open to analysis and verification by anyone. Furthermore, scientific progress depends on this open character of scientific theories in so far as new theories correct and expand previous ones.[155]

Besides textual evidence for realism, Gramsci's writings in general assume a realist position. In general, the concepts he uses, such as 'hegemony', 'relations of forces', 'passive revolution', etc., are conceived as theoretical concepts derived from historical reality and reflecting real social entities. For instance, paraphrasing Marx's 1859 Preface to his *Contribution to the Critique of Political Economy*,[156] Gramsci writes that the first level in the relations of forces is closely connected to the structure and it is 'objective, independent of the will of men, and can be measured with the systems of the exact or physical sciences'.[157] The subject matter of history is social groups conditioned by economic and other circumstances that are the result of past historical development. The mode of explanation offered by Gramsci is always founded on actually existing conditions, tendencies, ideologies, etc. We do not find in the *Prison Notebooks* concepts such as reason or consciousness, spirit, or, as in Croce, the concept of liberty. He does not write about man in the abstract, or about universal values whose incarnation is human history. Nor does he seek to re-enact the past in some mode of historical experience, as some historicists did. In short, the tone of his historical and political writings suggests that he considers his concepts and his hypotheses as reflecting a reality that exists in itself, or independently of its being thought. This would suggest that Gramsci is not only a realist but a materialist. We shall return to this in Chapter Two.

The concept of 'reason', moreover, one of the fundamental concepts of idealist philosophy, is hardly present in Gramsci's writings. The word 'reason' itself is seldom used, and when it is, it appears mostly in the adjective form 'rational'. By 'rational', Gramsci usually means one of two things: (1) linked to historical necessity, or historicist;[158] (2) adequate to an end, useful or functional.[159] And, at least in one passage, rational is used in both senses.[160] The conclusion that must be reached is that, for Gramsci, the content of reason does not originate in reason itself, be it due to its structure or to its own life or dialect, which would allow it to formulate problems or concepts outside any relation with the material world. It is for this reason that Gramsci praised Croce for asserting 'that the problems that philosophers must solve are not an abstract offspring of previous philosophical thought, but they are posed by the actual historical development'.[161]

In spite of Gramsci's realist intentions and of the preponderance of realist elements, especially in his political and historical writings, it might be argued that his choice of the expression 'philosophy of praxis', as a substitute for 'historical materialism' indicates that he did not approve of philosophical realism. Gentile, in his book on *Marx's Philosophy*, used the same expression to characterize the theory in which 'subject and object are two purely correlative terms . . . such that their effective reality is the result of their relation in the organism'. The nature of this relation, Gentile continues, 'is the activity of knowing'.[162] This version of the philosophy of praxis is rejected by Gramsci, who argues that it is the impure act, the material activity of human beings, not Gentile's pure act, which is the concern of historical materialism.[163]

However, two years before the publication of Gentile's monograph on Marx, Antonio Labriola wrote that 'the philosophy of praxis [he wrote 'praxis', not the usual Italian version *'prassi'*] is the "marrow of historical materialism"'. It seems more likely that Gramsci followed Labriola rather than Gentile. Labriola, although inconsistent or ambiguous in his epistemology, seems to define the philosophy of praxis as the realist process 'from life to thought', and not the other way around.[164] It is this view that Gramsci echoes in his critique of Gentile. In a note devoted to Machiavelli, Gramsci suggests that he was also developing a philosophy of praxis or a neo-humanism 'in so far as he does not admit transcendental or immanent (in the metaphysical sense) elements, but is wholly based on the concrete action of men who work and transform reality for their historical needs'.[165] Since the note deals with such issues as constitutional law and the state, it would seem that, on this occasion at least, Gramsci used 'philosophy of praxis' to characterize theories of history which seek to understand the social process on the basis of the activity of real men and women, and which reject explanatory frameworks that appeal to divine intervention, Providence, or world spirit. We shall return to this in the next section, when we deal with humanism.

Finally, Gramsci used the terms 'Marxism' or 'historical materialism' until some time in 1932. After that date, the expression 'philosophy of praxis' replaces both Marxism and historical materialism. Since the names of Marx and Engels are also replaced by expressions such as 'the founders of the philosophy of praxis' after the same date, it would seem that Gramsci was concerned with hiding the real identity of his theories, rather than with a theoretical issue. Given, then, that his definition of the 'philosophy of praxis' is concerned with the subject matter of history, not with knowledge, and that he replaced both the names of Marx and Engels with expressions that could be easily associated with Gentile, who became Minister of Education under Mussolini, it is plausible that Gramsci's main concern was avoiding the jail censor.

The analysis of Gramsci's arguments seems to yield three different theories. First, a realist theory of knowledge and a realist ontology; second, a theory about the social conditions of the production of knowledge, the effect of those conditions on the knowledge thus acquired, and the function of knowledge in society; third, a non-realist account of objectivity as the consensus of a community, complemented by the subjective-idealist thesis that nothing exists outside history. Since the first and the third theses are incompatible, one must either choose one of them or, alternatively, conclude that Gramsci confusedly held two contradictory basic epistemological theories. Given the fallacies that he commits and the ambiguities that he cannot unravel, the second of these two alternatives is clearly plausible. However this may be, it seems more interesting as well as useful to choose between realism and anti-realism. The anti-realist Gramsci would be a Crocean Gramsci; in that case, 'historicism' would signify a theory of the identity of truth and the historical conditions of truth-claims. The realist Gramsci, on the other hand, would keep those two aspects separate, the first as an epistemological theory, the second as a sociological or historical one. If we take his statement to the effect that the philosophy of praxis retains philosophical realism from French materialism as a kind of basic programmatic statement or statement of intention, it would not be arbitrary to reformulate Gramsci's theory in a realist fashion, and we could discard any anti-realist statements as mistakes or slips that he would have corrected, had he realized that he had committed them.

To conclude, there are good reasons for a reconstruction of Gramsci's *Prison Notebooks* on the basis of a realist epistemology. First, he uses 'historicism' as signifying a sort of realism. Second, he contends that the philosophy of praxis surpasses French materialism while retaining its philosophical realism as a programmatic statement. Third, he writes that scientific theories change, but they reflect a 'permanent' nature. Fourth, his writings on history and politics provide some evidence for a theory of truth as a reflection of an independent reality. In view of this, one can dismiss his anti-realist statements as confusions. If this is accepted, then we must reach the conclusion that Gramsci's thought was different from Croce's in important respects, for Croce's absolute historicism encompassed truth.

Given the preponderance of statements in support of realism as well as the realist tone of his historical and political analysis, it is, I think, proper to conclude that Gramsci's historicism is indeed a species of realism. If we take into consideration Gramsci's own statement that the true philosophy of thinkers may not be found in their occasional philosophical reflections, but that it is to be sought in their dominant activities,[166] then we must give more weight to Gramsci's historical and political thought, for these were the areas in which he felt more at home. It seems, then, that the evidence of realism found in his writings on politics and history should be given more weight than his philosophical statements. If this is accepted, we must conclude that for Gramsci, historicism means a species of realism. Whatever anti-realist elements we find in his *Prison Notebooks*, and there certainly are some, can be attributed to the lingering influence of Croce, an influence that Gramsci was trying to leave behind. As both his work and his Anti-Croce were left unfinished we cannot know what direction his thought might have taken. Nevertheless, it is both proper and in keeping with Gramsci's project, to reconstruct the *Prison Notebooks* on a realist basis.

This conclusion has been half-heartedly accepted by some commentators, although some do not attempt to make their theory consistent with the kind of realism that Gramsci was beginning to develop. Nemeth, for instance, states that 'the philosophy of praxis *does* ultimately agree with the realist conclusion of common sense'.[167] However, Nemeth, by means of considerable stretching of concepts, links Gramsci's philosophy of praxis to Husserl's transcendentalism. It is true that Gramsci emphasizes the historical conditions of the production of knowledge, including needs and the relations of individuals to nature. Whether this can be called a transcendental condition of knowledge in a Husserlian sense is doubtful. The weakest point in Nemeth's argument, however, is in his conception of 'objectivity'. He argues that 'objectivity itself must be redefined in terms immanent to consciousness – this is the legacy of modern philosophy, especially of Marx'.[168] He then cites Gramsci's arguments on the limits of epistemological objectivity and his rejection of transcendent explanations of history, to conclude that Gramsci's philosophy is a historicized version of Husserl's phenomenology. The real basis of the transcendental conditions of knowledge is, according to Nemeth, the area of 'transcendental needs'. These are not empirical needs, although 'they have a mundane correlate'.[169]

There are two problems with this interpretation. First, Gramsci's rejection of transcendence and his emphasis on immanence have nothing to do with consciousness or with the constitution of objectivity. For Gramsci, transcendence and immanence are historical concepts, not epistemological ones. For instance, he uses the term to differentiate theories of the extra-historical origin of history, which he terms transcendent, from those theories, such as historical materialism, which seek to understand the 'worldliness and earthliness of thought'[170] or the historical origin of statistical generalizations.[171] Thus, Croce's 'speculative historicism' and 'idealist speculation' which are rooted in the theory of an eternal ideal history are said not to be really immanent,[172] although in Nemeth's use of the term, Croce is an immanentist to the extent that all knowledge and truth depend on their place in history. In brief, Gramsci rejects speculative historical philosophy which conceives history as the result of supra-historical deities, values, or laws. His historicist realism, as a guiding principle for historical research, consists in the injunction to explain history on the basis of historical phenomena and historical necessity and that none of this has a transcendent, religious, or speculative meaning.

Second, the concept of transcendental needs is too speculative for Gramsci's taste. Perhaps one of the most valuable qualities of Gramsci's thought is his avoidance of unnecessary conceptual complexity and his efforts to produce concepts that could be given a historical content. That Nemeth is on the wrong track is shown by what he thought was Gramsci's shortcoming, namely, that he 'failed to see how crucial an adequate account of time is for the completeness of the philosophy of praxis and therefore its self-sufficiency'. The *Prison Notebooks* show that Gramsci was preoccupied with the concept of time. It was not, however, with 'consciousness of time itself' or with 'the constitution of objective time',[173] but with historical time or with the rhythms and forms of transience of social phenomena. This is the cornerstone of Gramsci's philosophy of history as will be seen in Chapter Two. Nemeth's interpretation of Gramsci is flawed in that he did not take into consideration Gramsci's writings on history and politics. As I suggested above, it is in these writings that the structure of Gramsci's thought is to be sought, and consequently they are of the utmost importance for interpreting his philosophy.

Historicism as humanism

Gramsci's use of 'historicism' as 'humanism' has received a lot of attention; it is generally the use that most commentators stress to the neglect of the other three. This one-sided emphasis on humanism often leads to voluntarist interpretations of Gramsci. In this fourth sense, historicism is a philosophy that 'does not recognize transcendent or immanent elements (in the meta-physical sense) but is completely grounded on the concrete actions of man who works and transforms reality for his historical needs'.[174] It is in this sense that we must interpret Gramsci when he asserts that the philosophy of praxis is an 'absolute historicism' or an 'absolute humanism'.[175]

It is evident that Gramsci's main concern is the rejection of transcendent metaphysics that would account for the historical process, such as is found, for instance, in the German historicists. Against that sort of metaphysics, Gramsci conceives Marxism as 'the absolute worldliness and earthiness of thought, an absolute humanism of history'.[176] From this perspective, Marxism is seen as having a twofold significance, theoretical and practical, for historicism is 'the liberation from any abstract "ideologism", the real conquest of the historical world, the beginning of a new civilization'.[177] At the same time, however, Gramsci also rejects reductionist varieties of materialism which desire to be ultra-materialist, and attempt to explain social phenomena by appealing to the laws of physics.[178] Similarly, he rejects biological determinism, in particular any theory that biological differences among men, such as race, the colour of skin, or the shape of the head, have a causal significance in the historical process.[179]

If we can give a general meaning to Gramsci's humanism, it must be that history is to be understood as a human process, as opposed to a divine, or biological one; as a consequence, social scientists must look for explanatory frameworks in the relations among human beings and between humankind and nature. The definition does not specify how the process is to be understood, or what kinds of explanations are to be framed. As Althusser recognizes,[180] Gramsci's stress on humanism, more than a positive theory about the subject of history, is a negation of idealist theories according to which history is the dialectic of reason, liberty, moral values, etc. Nevertheless, Gramsci's identification of Marxism with absolute historicism or absolute humanism, which in fact appears only twice in the *Prison Notebooks* has become an object of some interest in the debate between humanist Marxism and structuralist Marxism. In general, Gramsci would seem to support humanist Marxism; in reality, however, the issue is more complex.

Although it is difficult to provide a single definition of humanism that would cover all humanist Marxists, it seems that three main assumptions underlie humanist interpretations of Gramsci's thought: (1) Marxism is not a science; its purpose is not to explain historical phenomena by appealing to general laws, but to transform society. (2) Primacy is given to the ethico-political aspect of society. (3) Emphasis is placed on human liberation from alienation and on the free development of the individual. A humanist interpretation of Gramsci, such as Salamini's, would tend to emphasize Gramsci's guarded rejection of statistical generalizations; it would oppose historicist Marxism to scientific Marxism;[181] and finally, it would conclude that hegemony is the primary element in a social whole. In doing so, Gramsci's historicism is linked to the historicism of the German historical school in its denial of the possibility of scientific history.

Emphasis on humanism brings to the fore the importance of human agency, and hence the will, in historical development; on this interpretation, Gramsci, often said to be a voluntarist, would tend to dismiss the existence of historical or social laws or would, at least, advocate the study of history simply in terms of the organized will of individuals and groups of individuals. Thus, when Gramsci writes that the main problem of historical materialism is to determine how the historical movement originates on the base of the structure,[182] he seems to be making a sharp distinction between history and some underlying structure which would always remain beyond history, beyond human agency.

Some interpretations of Gramsci, notably that of Badaloni, seem to come close to this conclusion. Badaloni seems to interpret Gramsci as posing a distinction between the forces of production, on the one hand, and the relations of production together with the superstructure, on the other.[183] The structural, or as he puts it, the 'logical' elements are conceived as being essentially outside the historical movement. This, of course, is so by the definition of the terms used by Badaloni. The result, however, is that history is seen as a drama whose actors are classes rather than individuals.

Hence, Marxism has been split in two; political economy and drama (history). This split has had profound consequences for the development of historical materialism in the west, as is attested by the debates between structuralist Marxists and humanist Marxists. Whereas the former emphasize the determinist character of social relations, from economic to personal ones, the latter tend to emphasize the creative aspects of human praxis, especially at the level of political intervention.

According to Badaloni, Gramsci's historicism contains two essential elements. The first one is defined as 'actualization of utopia'.[184] On this view, the will becomes the fundamental element of history and, as a consequence, the interpretation of history must be based on the concept of the 'ideas-will'.[185] The second element is defined as critical realism, which consists in giving a realist foundation to the revolutionary will.[186] But in describing Gramsci's historicism as a theory of revolution, Badaloni neglects the other aspects of historicism I have outlined above. The result of this narrowing of perspective is an interpretation of Gramsci as merely a theoretician of the superstructures. This is true, however, in so far as Gramsci dealt mostly with superstructural matters; but it is not true if this is accorded a philosophical significance, that is, if it is asserted, as Bobbio has, that Gramsci carried out a double inversion of Marx's theories, so that the superstructure, rather than the structure, would have the primary role, and more emphasis would be given to civil society than to the state.[187]

Badaloni does not claim that the logical and the historical form two separate realms. In fact, he presents Gramsci's concept of the 'historical bloc' as an articulation of the logical and the historical, affirming that 'the determining element is that of production',[188] but avoiding economic reductionism inasmuch as 'the starting point is now the domination of the economic by the political'.[189] However, this formulation of the question is not very satisfactory, unless it is admitted that the economic is also historical. The problem with Badaloni's interpretation is that he takes the structure, production, or the economy, as the forces of production which is just one step away from speaking of the economy as the realm of technology. Gramsci rejects this view of the economy and he rejects any historiography that is not based on a deeper understanding of both the structure and historical necessity.

From Gramsci's point of view, the distinction between the

logical or structural and the historical, or superstructural, is not a real one, but a didactic one. Describing the material forces as the content and ideologies as the form, he argues that 'the material forces would not be historically conceivable without form, and ideologies without material forces would be individual whims'.[190] Clearly, the material forces are to be conceived historically, which means that they must be taken as an integral part of the network of historical necessity. Gramsci, in fact, attempts to formulate a theory of the identity of politics and the economy, an identity that is manifested in the permanent organizations that 'originate in the "permanent and organic" terrain of economic life'.[191] It is from this perspective that Gramsci objects to Croce's view that historical materialism separates the structure from the superstructure and reinstates a form of theological dualism in which the structure becomes a hidden God. Gramsci's answer to Croce is clear: the structure 'is conceived in an ultrarealist manner', and the development of the structure and the superstructure is thought of as being 'intimately connected and necessarily interrelated and reciprocal'.[192] We shall return to the analysis of the relation between structure and superstructure in Chapter Three, where a non-reductionist view of the determining role of the economic structure will be suggested.

Gramsci's humanism, then, must be taken first as a philosophical theory which understands human agency as a necessary condition of historical development and which rejects any explanation which is grounded on such entities as God or Providence, which are not themselves human, or the result of human activity. Hence, history is the development of human societies as well as the development of the relationship between human beings and nature. But it must not be concluded that, for Gramsci, history is the result of the process of transformation of a transcendental human nature. Dilthey, for instance, conceived of the objective world of history as the materialization of the human mind, and Vico viewed history as essentially the development of the human mind. Gramsci, following Marx, argues that human nature is the ensemble of social relations, and hence he asserts the transience of so-called human nature.[193] Human nature is not prior to history, it 'is a historical fact that can be verified, within certain limits, with philological and critical methods'.[194]

Gramsci's emphasis on hegemony or moral intellectual

leadership, on the role of intellectuals, and on popular culture would seem to place him in that rather vague category known as humanist Marxism. It cannot be denied that Gramsci's thought largely focused on those issues. Perhaps it was out of personal interest, or because of the perceived need to fill a gap in Marxist theory, that he devoted most of his thought to the process by which the structure is transformed into a superstructure, a process that he sometimes characterized as 'catharsis'. Catharsis is, according to Gramsci, the 'passage from the merely economic moment (or egoistic-passional) to the ethico-political moment'. This is a passage from the objective to the subjective, in which 'the structure is transformed from an external force that crushes man. . . to a means for freedom, to an instrument to create new ethico-political form'.[195] This passage from necessity to liberty is a process in which the role of human agency is much more obvious than in structural processes, which are often perceived by the historical agents as external or imposed by the past. As Texier observes, in this process the historical movement is here presented as the struggle of implacably opposed classes, and the result of the conflict depends 'on the intelligence and energy of men'.[196]

The question of the 'humanism' of history depends largely on the perspective from which history is viewed. Gramsci chooses to look at the moments of history in which the cathartic passage is realized, and hence, moments in which human agency is more obvious. This, however, must not be construed as a theory of history; it is possibly a theory of revolution. But Gramsci does not ignore that the depths of history are hardly fathomed by a theory of revolution. In the larger view of history, Gramsci is concerned with the process of integration and disintegration of historical blocs, and this, of course, is far more than a merely humanist theory of history, for it must not only understand humanity as it is expressed in folklore, culture, art, etc., but also in the general structures that condition human activity. Thus, Gramsci's analysis presupposes and supplements the results of the analysis of political economy; it does not replace them.

CONCLUSION

Commentators on Gramsci's *Prison Notebooks* have generally agreed that historicism is central to his interpretation of Marxism. Some, like Althusser, have rejected both historicism and humanism. Many have shown a positive attitude towards historicism. In general, they have assumed that Gramsci's historicism is a form of humanism and they have proceeded, quite uncritically, to treat Gramsci's thought as a form of humanism. Since, as Salamini observes, Gramsci gives no definition of humanism,[197] commentators have been free to use whatever definition of humanism they deemed appropriate. A link between humanism and an anti-scientific theory of history which stresses the creative role of the will has been the favoured interpretation of Gramsci's *Prison Notebooks*. As we have seen, Badaloni's analysis of Gramsci takes this route, although he is careful enough to speak of realism, that is, the need for the will to conform to the general pattern of historical causation.

A case which clearly exemplifies this interpretation of Gramsci is provided by the work of Leonardo Salamini. He argues that Gramsci's historicism is a rejection of scientific Marxism as well as the rejection of eternal truths. Basic to Salamini's defence of this humanist Marxism is the thesis that 'the admission of the existence of objective reality outside human will is a blatant historical error'.[198] Although his statement is somewhat ambiguous in so far as we do not know whose human will or what reality is concerned, it seems, nevertheless, that if I am not wrong in my interpretation of Gramsci's historicism, this is not a correct analysis of Gramsci.

The emphasis placed on the role of the will in history, activism, and culture, provide the basis for Salamini's definition of humanism as 'an anthropocentric vision' in which

> the reduction of knowledge to historical social relations entails the reduction of the *relations of production*, political and ideological social relations to *historicized* "human relations", to inter-human, intersubjective relations, to use Althusser's precise characterization of Gramsci's humanist conception.[199]

The relations of production to which everything is reduced, or 'which are considered to be objective socio-economic categories within orthodox Marxism, are subordinated by Gramsci to man, the centre of the cosmos.[200] This vision, however, according to which human beings are the measure of all things, is never seriously contemplated by Gramsci, who was painfully aware of the fact that his existence was not the measure of very much while he was in jail. In fact, Gramsci, perhaps unfairly, chastises Bukharin for his acritical endorsement of a common sense which has remained 'Ptolemaic, anthropomorphic and anthropocentric'.[201]

Salamini, like many other commentators, offers but a few general remarks by way of definition of historicism. They are mostly based on Gramsci's definition of Marxism as an absolute historicism and absolute humanism, thus ignoring the many passages in which Gramsci uses the term 'historicism' in some other sense. The result is that they provide only a vague, uncritical, and often shallow account of what they consider the marrow of Gramsci's thought.

This narrow perspective has led to what I consider serious errors of interpretation of Gramsci's thought in general. Perhaps the most important error is to give his studies of culture and politics a theoretical significance that they do not have. The conclusion that Salamini, Bobbio, and others reach, is that Gramsci 'ascribed to superstructural activities a primary role in Marxist Theory'.[202] However, the fact that Gramsci was interested in culture, perhaps because he felt that this was the least developed aspect of Marxist theory or that it was the most urgent task in the development of communism at the time, is not to be construed as a statement about the primacy of culture. One must look at the theoretical framework within which Gramsci sought to analyse culture; and to do this, a fuller and more precise account of his conception of historicism is necessary. The first step towards this end must be an analysis of the main uses of 'historicism' in the *Prison Notebooks*. This enables us to understand the structure of Gramsci's thought and to establish the main lines of contrast between his thought and that of previous historicist thinkers.

A number of preliminary conclusions can be drawn from a comparison of Gramsci's historicism with the other historicist thinkers we have studied. Perhaps the most significant contrast between Gramsci on the one hand and Hegel, the German historical school, and Croce on the other, is Gramsci's rejection of the concept of an ideal, eternal history. This concept, first formulated by Vico, but traceable to St Agustine's idea in *The City of God*, found various formulations in nineteenth-century German thought and in that of its Italian followers, such as Croce. Their attempt to see in history more than a narrative of discrete events was positive in so far as it was a critique of empiricism. But the speculative method led them to posit such explanatory concepts as transcendent moral values, the Idea, etc. which Gramsci clearly rejected. In this respect, his realism as well as his critique of transcendence, must be seen as the attempt to develop a non-empiricist theory of history which would grasp the totality and complexity of the historical process, from the tendencies of the economic structure to the forms of popular culture that shaped the consciousness of the masses. Of vital importance in this theory was the analysis of the revolutionary process, the moment at which organized masses break the seeming regularity of history to create new forms of civilization. But this analysis must always be understood in the larger context which Gramsci called integral history.

From Gramsci's perspective, the error of speculative theories is not so much their lack of empirical content, for they often contain sound historical observations, but their attempt to explain this real content as a necessary consequence of metaphysical, i.e. transcendent concepts. Gramsci's relation to Croce must be seen as an effort to take advantage of Croce's acute analysis and to put whatever was living in his thought on a sound realist foundation. Gramsci's approach to speculative philosophy is not entirely different from Marx's. Speculative philosophy, Marx wrote of Hegel, 'makes the Idea the subject and makes the proper actual subject ... the predicate'.[203] Thus, the predicates become independent of the real subjects,[204] with the consequence that human activity appears 'as the activity and result of something other than man'.[205] In the case of Croce, despite his attempts to eradicate transcendence from his system, historical agents, as we saw, are not real, empirical men and women, but some abstract conception of a universal humanity, a 'truly real individual' which, nevertheless, succeeds in inverting the subject and predicate.[206]

This conception of history is clearly rejected by Gramsci. His use of historicism as realism, his use of the concept of reason, and the conceptual framework he proposes for historical explanation, suggest that for him the actual subject of history is the real, empirical subject, not ideas. From this perspective, his humanism, as a rejection of speculative transcendence, is an echo of Marx's criticism of Hegel. Both Gramsci and Marx are opposed to a theory of history in which the predicate, be it reason or liberty, is transformed into the active subject of history.

In what concerns the concept of historical necessity, speculative theories advanced a conception of ideal necessity, or a logic according to which the course of history is an objectification or manifestation of the dynamic inherent in concepts. It is the 'ideal eternal history' of Vico rather than a material process governed by material necessity. This inversion of terms is well characterized by Colletti as 'the distortion of fact into a metaphysical axiom'.[207] The German historical school, however, differs substantially from both Hegel and Croce in this respect. Their positivist conception of law as invariant relations between events, together with their conception of the uniqueness of historical phenomena, led them to the conclusion that there are not any historical laws. History, for them, is the realm of freedom, not of necessity. As we saw, this implies that the writing of history should be concerned with the inner aspects of history, not with the events themselves, but with the values, reasons, and ideals of historical agents, or with the ethical substance of the state.

Historicists in general have been concerned with the transitory character of social phenomena. Their reflections often broached this theme. The German historical school advanced the thesis that the past was relived by the historian, and that its meaning, recreated in the historian's mind, depended on its relation to a universal moral reality of which each system of values was a partial manifestation. The present as experience of the historian, and with it the system of values which he shared, was of crucial importance for interpreting history. In this sense, the present as experience was dominant. Similarly, Croce's concept of the contemporaneity of history emphasized the present as the focus of the past's meaning, and at times, as the only existing historical reality. Gramsci, in sharp contrast, writes of the transience of all social forms as being subject to a structure of necessity. The meaning or identity of social phenomena does not depend on the timeless life of the spirit, the ideal eternal history, or any transcendent reality, but on its occurrence in a determinate net of relations, the causal link or nexus, as he often refers to it. And this is the greatest difference between what Gramsci calls 'historicism' and those forms of historicism that emphasize the uniqueness of historical phenomena.

Gramsci's historicism, taken both as a commitment to historical necessity and as realism, suggests that historians must look beyond the fleeting drama of events, beyond the empirically visible, to the inner aspects of history, to its 'generative mechanisms', as Bhaskar appropriately designates them.[208] Thus, in Gramsci, historicism is a rejection of a history that is 'externally descriptive, without bringing into relief the necessary and the causal links'.[209] The problem that Gramsci consciously faces is the need for a theory of history even if historical events appear to be unique.[210] Although he seems to be perplexed about the issue of historical necessity and the uniqueness of events, it is obvious that his historicism, as outlined above, requires a theory of material historical necessity which would avoid both positivism, on the one hand, and the idealism of Hegel, Croce, and the German historical school on the other. Although no fully developed theory of historical necessity is found in the *Prison Notebooks*, there are indications that he had thought a good deal about it.

It will have been observed in my account of Gramsci's historicism, that I have not dealt with the issue of freedom of the will. I have stressed historical necessity, but have so far ignored Gramsci's well-known statements against determinism and fatalism. The main reason for my proceeding in this manner is simply that Gramsci uses 'historicist' as a synonym for historical necessity. However, there is still pending the matter of the agent in historical activity, or in particular, the political agent. In so far as history is viewed as a result of human activity, the question of freedom of the will must be conceived as the possibility of choice within a network of historical necessity. Suffice it to say at this point that Gramsci was primarily interested in the possibility of effective political intervention by organized groups.[211] He was not concerned to address the abstract philosophical question about whether in general causal determinism is compatible with freedom of the will.

In conclusion, Gramsci's use of 'historicism' suggests that his thinking is radically opposed to all previous historicist thinkers except Marx, with whom he shares a number of views. Furthermore, it appears that the four uses outlined above form a coherent foundation for the social sciences. In simple terms, Gramsci's historicism is the view that all social phenomena exist as aspects of a process, and hence the historical method is the only scientific one. But the historical method is not merely a narrative of events. It is rather the study of the transience of social forms according to a network of necessity. These structures of necessity are not simply logical constructions that fit the events, but real forms of social life. Furthermore, they are ultimately the work of real men and women, even when they appear as external chains that crush them. Gramsci, then, can be seen as rejecting both the historicism of Croce and that of the German historical school because they involved a search for a metaphysics of history, and often fell into relativism; he also rejects the poverty of empiricism, its incapacity to search for historical laws, other than statistical generalizations, as well as the lack of historical specificity of rationalist thought.

Gramsci's historicism is not to be taken so much as a concrete theory of history, in the sense that it specifies his thinking on concrete social phenomena; but rather as a foundation for the social sciences in general, in the sense of a set of guiding principles for social research. These are not *a priori* principles or a transcendental schema. They are based on the observation that social life is human activity conditioned by the structures inherited from the past; in other words, that social life is history. Consequently, full understanding of social phenomena can only be attained if they are studied from a long-term perspective. As Marc Bloch observed,

> In the continuum of human societies, the vibration between molecule and molecule spread out over so great a span that understanding of a single moment, no matter what its place in the chain of development, can never be attained merely by contemplation of its immediate predecessor.[212]

As should be obvious now, Gramsci's historicism, in particular his objections to transcendence and his acceptance of immanence, should not be taken as an epistemology, although, as we have seen, it contains a realist one. Nemeth tends to interpret Gramsci's statements on immanence as if they had a Husserlian transcendental significance, where 'objectivity itself must be redefined in terms of immanent to consciousness'.[213] As we have seen, Gramsci stresses that his comments on the function of ideas and their transience is a historical judgement, not a judgement of value or truth.[214] It is easy to distort Gramsci's thought by attributing to some of his statements an epistemological meaning, when they are in fact intended as, or related to, historical explanation and interpretation. They concern the specific process of the origin of social phenomena and of ideas in so far as they are superstructural elements, not the conditions for truth and assessment of empirical claims.

In so far, then, as Gramsci's historicism is intended as a foundation for the study of society, one could say, for a science of history, it is not to be construed as a denial of objectivity in the ontological sense. Although there are lapses into subjectivism in Gramsci's arguments, they are due to the fact that he was not always able to distinguish between 'epistemological' objectivity and 'ontological' objectivity, and that he confused empirical descriptions about the process of producing knowledge with normative theories concerning truth, as well as with ontological objectivity. Serious as these errors are, it is still possible to accept his theory that knowledge is produced under specific historical conditions which have an effect, positive or negative, on its validity, while preserving a realist epistemology and a realist ontology. However flawed Gramsci's arguments are, it seems that some of his commentators, notably Salamini, have not even attempted to see the missing but suggested element in Gramsci's thought, namely, the distinction suggested above. This, of course, results in the construal of an idealist Gramsci. Nor, for that matter, have they realised that Gramsci's writings on science are not about the methods of science, or its philosophical presuppositions. On the only occasion on which Gramsci approaches the philosophy of science, his analysis leaves no doubt about his realist epistemology, as I have shown above.

When Gramsci writes about the concept of matter, it is not to deny the scientific concept of matter, nor its independent existence, for Gramsci clearly accepts that natural phenomena, such as electricity, existed even before they were known.[215] It is to point out that it is not the business of historical materialism to judge the theories of scientists; its business is to understand how a natural phenomenon is 'historically active, not as mere natural force ... but as an element of production mastered by man and incorporated into the ensemble of material forces of production'.[216] And to the extent that scientific ideas shape the culture of an age, historical materialism will study them as an element of the superstructure. This clearly means that Gramsci did not attempt to reduce science to the philosophy of praxis, as some have suggested;[217] a move that would make Gramsci hardly distinguishable from Croce. It means that he had an understanding of society as an interrelated whole and that its study must reconstruct all its elements, including science, and their interrelationships in the movement of history.

If for the 'philosophy of praxis "matter" is to be understood neither in the sense that it has come to have in the natural sciences . . . nor in that of the meanings that it takes in the diverse materialist philosophies', clearly science has a dimension that is beyond the reaches of historical materialism. The 'diverse physical properties' which together 'constitute matter itself'[218] are the object of scientific investigation. This distinction may seem trivial; it shows, however, that Gramsci did not deny the independent existence of the material world or its existence outside history. That science itself is always shaped by the needs of human beings[219] certainly is both historically and theoretically significant; it does not entail, however, that matter or nature depend on history or on human will, though it entails that science does so depend.

A careful reading of Gramsci's writings show that his historicism is a far more complex theory, a much richer and also less extravagant one, than some commentators have suggested. I have attempted to bring out a fuller sense of Gramsci's historicism and to point out two main sources of errors of interpretation, namely, to construe as an epistemology what is a theory of history, and to reduce all aspects of Gramsci's historicism to humanism. In Chapter Two, the four senses of 'historicism' will be given a general interpretation, one that takes into consideration Gramsci's *Prison Notebooks* as a whole. Such an interpretation, it is hoped, will shed some light on the inner structure of Gramsci's thought.

CHAPTER TWO

A GENERAL INTERPRETATION
OF GRAMSCI'S HISTORICISM

INTRODUCTION

In the preceding chapter four main uses of the term 'historicism' in the *Prison Notebooks* have been identified. However, that analysis alone does not provide a definition of Gramsci's historicism: it is merely an attempt to lay the groundwork for such a definition, as well as to give a warning that historicism is more complex, and probably more interesting that a cursory reading of the *Prison Notebooks* might suggest. This preliminary work of analysis allowed us to detect some errors of interpretation of Gramsci's work which have seriously flawed some commentaries on the *Prison Notebooks*.

We must now attempt to elucidate the meaning of the four senses of historicism so that a general interpretation of Gramsci's thought can be given. Fortunately Gramsci deals with all of them in the *Prison Notebooks*, which suggests that his often brief, almost causal definitions of 'historicism' were not unthinking slips of the pen, but part of his deeper interest in historiographical and philosophical questions. And this is the reason why, in Chapter One, I used the expression 'the structure of Gramsci's thought' to refer to his brand of historicism. Unfortunately, as is the case with most questions in the *Prison Notebooks*, Gramsci's treatment of the issues that concern us here is but sketchy. Hence, only the general outline of his historicism can be drawn with any certainty.

Because it seems to be the cornerstone of Gramsci's historicism, I shall emphasize the notion of transience. Little will be added to the analysis of realism and humanism given in Chapter One. The most difficult part by far is that of the concept of historical

67

necessity and related issues, of which only a tentative interpretation can be given at this point. Gramsci's critique of sociology will
provide the backbone for this general interpretation of his
historicism.

GRAMSCI'S CRITIQUE OF SOCIOLOGY: SOME PRELIMINARY REMARKS

Perhaps the most revealing passages in the *Prison Notebooks* are
those in which Gramsci discusses sociology. In this section I shall
discuss those passages, not so much to clarify Gramsci's view of
sociology, but so as to shed light on his historicism. It is important
to keep in mind that, as Gallino explains, Gramsci's knowledge of
sociology derived mainly from Italian sociology, which was
dominated by the evolutionist thought of the last quarter of the
nineteenth century. Gramsci's objections, it would seem, were
addressed not so much to positivism as to a primitive, substantially
backward [1] form of positivist sociology. Nevertheless, as we shall
see, he managed to address some of his concerns to fundamental
tenets of positivism. In addition to this, Gramsci often discusses
Michels and Pareto, and he refers to Weber on six occasions; not
to be discounted, as Gallino points out, is the influence of
Durkheim through the work of Sorel. Nevertheless, sociology is
normally associated by Gramsci with the positivist and theoretically
underdeveloped forms of evolutionism prevalent in Italy at the
time, and it is in this restricted sense that the term will be used in
this text. In effect, Gramsci uses the term 'sociology' not so much
to indicate the discipline as to characterize a specific approach to
the social sciences.

A number of social scientists have studied Gramsci's critique of
sociology, often giving accounts of that critique that are mutually
incompatible. Thus, Salamini, while acknowledging that 'it would
seem paradoxical at first glance to search for a basic structure of
Marxist sociology in the anti-sociological writings of Gramsci',
reaches the conclusion that his 'rejection of bourgeois sociology
does not entail a rejection of the possibility of the existence of
sociology within a Marxist perspective'.[2] And yet, Razeto and
Misuraca, in an excellent account of some aspects of Gramsci's
thought, argue that Gramsci rejects all sociology, whatever its
philosophical basis may be.[3]

In their reconstruction of Gramsci's critique, Razeto and Misuraca argue that there are two kinds of reasons, theoretical ones and historical ones, why Gramsci rejected sociology, not just the Italian brand of positivist sociology. Theoretically, sociology was a response to Marx, an attempt to supersede Marxism which was closely linked to the need to contain the dissolution of capitalism.[4] Historically, sociology is the specific mode assumed by ideology, and in this, sociology plays the role formerly played by political economy. Whereas the latter was the science of the origins of bourgeois society, the former is the science of the established bourgeoisie which must now contain its dissolution, it 'anomie', and its disfunction, rather than justify its origins.[5]

Razeto and Misuraca argue that sociology also became the official state doctrine of the Soviet Union when it was confronted with the task of reorganizing the economy.[6] The result was that sociology, developed according to a model borrowed from natural science, became a technique: 'sociological efficacy – assumed as the criterion and guarantee of "scientific objectivity" – is the operational efficacy typical of any science. It manifests itself in the "experimental" character that sociology tends to acquire as a technique of adaptation and of social control'.[7]

Sociology has become the theory on which the decision process of the state is based. The institutional framework on which this process takes place is bureaucracy. The two pillars of the modern capitalist state are, according to Razeto and Misuraca, sociology and the bureaucracy. As they write, 'the organic character of the relationship between bureaucracy and sociology in effect constitutes one of the fundamental characters of the organization of contemporary states'.[8] Accordingly, they analyse Gramsci's notes on sociology and on the nature of bureaucracy to find the foundations of Gramsci's social theory, and in particular, of his analysis of the modern state.

The brief outline of the book by Razeto and Misuraca cannot do justice to their analysis of Gramsci's thought. They reveal, however, two aspects of Gramsci's thought that are particularly interesting for us. First, sociology is an attempt not so much to understand society, but to manipulate it bureaucratically so as to preserve its present irrational state. Hence it is an undemocratic and conservative discipline. Second, at least part of the problem with sociology is said to be that it is modelled on the natural

69

sciences; its foundations are external to itself. This seems to entail one of the central theories of German historicism, namely, the radical distinction between the method of the historical sciences and that of the natural sciences, albeit that no specific form of, or grounds for, this distinction is given.

Let us now turn to Gramsci's own critical remarks on sociology. These can be seen to fall into two main categories. The first one contains the general political and theoretical reasons for his rejection of sociology; the second provides a number of more detailed objections which cover the four aspects of historicism previously analysed. I shall begin with the general comments, and I shall incorporate the detailed ones in the interpretation of Gramsci's historicism that will follow.

Gramsci links the rise of sociology to 'the decadence of the concept of political science and political art that took place in the nineteenth century'. This decadence, Gramsci suggests, results in the reduction of politics to 'parliamentary politics' or 'personal cliques'. The assumption on which sociology is based is that 'with constitutions and parliaments an epoch of "natural" "evolution" had begun, that society had found its definitive because rational foundations'. This assumption about the definitive, rational organization of society makes it possible to study society with the methods of the natural sciences.[9] On this basis, sociology can look for regularities, for statistical laws, assuming that no change will transform them. And, in return, it can use its findings to buttress the capitalist system.

Sociology is not the only discipline to assume the naturalness of capitalism; classical political economy was sharply criticized by Marx for doing so. This assumption of the definitiveness of the present state of society entails a view of history as either a series of fumbling attempts undergone by societies to reach their rational forms, or as the development of inner possibilities that culminate in the modern state. According to the first view, the whole of history is irrational, hence it is not really worth studying; according to the second, the origins must already contain the possibilities of all future changes, as the acorn contains the future growth of the oak tree, which raises the ahistorical question of the cause of that essence. Hegel is sometimes thought to have held the second model. In any case, the sociology Gramsci had in mind seemed to make it impossible to understand the possibility of fundamental

70

change. For this reason, Razeto and Misuraca are right in their view that sociology is a modern form of bourgeois ideology. Gramsci's historicism is first of all a rejection of the assumption of the naturalness and rationality of capitalism common to classical political economy and sociology; hence, Gramsci objects to sociology for its anti-historicism as well as for its political conservatism.

The problem that Gramsci had to face on the ideological front, it seems, was that of breaking the circle of sociology and degeneration of politics, which support each other. As a practical question, then, Gramsci's historicism was conceived as the attempt to dethrone both the influence of Croce and that of positivist sociology on Italian culture. At the same time, the degeneration of politics that resulted in the relegation of all political life to the parliamentary game, with the consequent impoverishment of democracy, had to be reversed. A broader understanding of politics was thus necessary; consequently, Gramsci attempted to introduce the notion that all of life is politics.[10] We will later discuss the two senses that politics came to have in the *Prison Notebooks*.

Gramsci's analysis of the relationship between politics and sociology brings to light an important aspect of his thought. Some commentators have observed that Gramsci rejects determinist conceptions of history because they result in the passivity of the masses.[11] Gramsci himself might seem to agree with this view, although he is in fact concerned with fatalism and mechanical determinism.[12] This is, in a sense, a strange thesis, for it assumes that a theory of history will have a major impact on the way the masses think and act, which is itself a determinist thesis. This is of course quite questionable, although it must be admitted that a fatalist theory of history might reinforce certain conceptions of common sense.

A closer look at the *Prison Notebooks*, however, reveals a different aspect of this issue. First, in the passages analysed above, it is quite obvious that it is the degeneration of politics that produces sociology, not the other way around. Second, in his analysis of the various forms of revisionism in Marxist theory, Gramsci notes that vulgar materialism and the fatalist view of history associated with it emerged not only as a result of the primitive corporatism of the masses[13] but also because of their subordinate position.[14] It is the fatalism present in their common sense which is reflected in vulgar

71

.aaterialism; the latter, of course, gives support to the former and in this sense becomes an impediment to active politics. Nevertheless, Gramsci notes that this conception of history has not been totally useless. Recalling Weber's analysis of Calvinist theories of predestination and the development of capitalism, Gramsci argues that the fatalist conception of history played a useful role in given historical conditions.[15] For, 'when one does not have the initiative in the struggle and the struggle itself becomes identified with a series of defeats, mechanical determinism becomes a formidable force of moral resistance, of cohesion, of patient and obstinate perseverance'.[16]

Let us now turn to some of the theoretical objections levelled by Gramsci against sociology. According to Gramsci, 'sociology is the attempt to create a historico-political methodology dependent on a philosophical system already elaborated'. The problem with this approach is that the methodology developed does not respond to the problems posed by the subject matter itself; it is designed to solve problems that are alien to it. The point Gramsci makes is that by assuming the positivist doctrine of scientific method, sociology becomes a 'subordinate fragment' to a conception of the world, and hence, one could conclude, its autonomy as well as its scientificity is impaired. Furthermore, because it is dependent upon an extraneous logic, its coherence is not the coherence of a general theory developed on the basis of original research problems, but an imposed coherence, a mechanical coherence.[17]

At the methodological level, then, the problem with sociology is that it uses the methods of the natural sciences, and attempts to structure the study of society according to those methods, without first critically examining whether they could grasp that subject matter adequately. The task of general theory is not that of elaborating concepts and models applicable everywhere, but rather to develop within each discipline the appropriate concepts and models. This would imply that Gramsci rejected the theory of the unity of scientific method. Furthermore, carried to its extreme, Gramsci's position is far more radical than that of the German historicists, for it entails that each individual discipline would have its own method. I shall return to this question later on.

The second point Gramsci makes regarding sociology is that one must not substitute conjectures or, as he puts it, 'hypothetical history' for 'historical history' that is, for the analysis of documents.[18] For instance, the principle of correlation between the organic parts of a body may be useful, but it cannot take the place of the analysis of documents, without which there is no real historiography. Although it may be useful to begin with the assumption that individuals and groups always act coherently and logically, they do not always act thus; hence, there is the risk of arbitrariness if we allow analogies to take the place of the documents.[19] Clearly, Gramsci thinks that sociological generalizations, in so far as they are attempts to import conceptions or methods from the natural sciences, can easily turn into arbitrary or facile conjectures about the development of societies or the behaviour of individuals. In his critique of Bukharin, Gramsci clearly states that Marxist sociology is an 'incentive for facile journalistic improvisations of the pocket-genius'. And he links sociology to the tendency criticized by Engels in his letters to J. Block and H. Starkennburg.[20]

The uncritical appropriation of the methods of the natural sciences results in what Gramsci considers to be the tendency of sociology to construct abstract schemas. The charge of abstraction, of neglecting the concrete facts, is the one most frequently found in the *Prison Notebooks*.[21] This brings to light one of the basic features of Gramsci's historicism, namely, that knowledge of social phenomena cannot be produced by inductive generalizations based on apparent similarities of events or, in the language of historicism, on external resemblance. For instance, in a note on the work of Michels, Gramsci contends that he has not developed 'any methodology intrinsic to the facts'; his work is flawed by 'the pure descriptive character and external classification of the old positivist sociology'.[22] Gramsci's charge that sociology produces abstract schemas which do not correspond to concrete facts can be restated as the failure of sociology to meet the criterion of adequate description of social facts.

The question of the specification of facts is of crucial importance in determining the character of Gramsci's historicism. For, as we saw in Chapter One, German historicists have maintained that historical facts are unique and hence no laws of history can be discovered. It seems, then, that the issue of the adequate description of facts is connected with the theory of historical necessity. In what follows I shall take the rest of Gramsci's objections to sociology in the context of the specification of the four meanings of 'historicism' previously outlined. With this, the specific character of Gramsci's historicism, as well as its marked contrast with idealist forms of historicism, will become evident. In this chapter it will be necessary to reformulate Gramsci's thought, to translate it as it were, in terms of the language used by historians and philosophers who have reflected on similar problems of the methodology and philosophy of history. Because Gramsci at times remained close to the language of Croce, such procedure will allow us to penetrate to what is his thought. Because identity of terms does not mean identity of concepts, certainly not in the case of Gramsci's use of Crocean language, the introduction of the problematic of a number of modern thinkers will help us avoid some easy errors of interpretation.

GRAMSCI'S HISTORICISM

Transience

In its most complete form, the theory of the transience of all social phenomena holds that even the most durable structures change: history, as Pierre Vilar insists 'is the *change* of the rhythms, the change of structures. And it is the search for an explanation of these changes'.[23] From this standpoint, then, the study of any society must include the study of its origins as well as that of its dissolution. Gallino has observed that, for Gramsci, the first subject of social science is real history, whereas society in general is never the object of study.[24] This does not mean that history is merely a narrative of change without the attempt to discover the structural causes of change. Gramsci in fact often suggests that history cannot be studied merely as a succession of events; for, after all, the study of change is not possible without the adequate description of what changes. Gramsci is concerned with avoiding a conception of society in general; such a conception would lack specificity and would lead to the kind of empty generalizations that he thought were typical of sociology.

Two main issues are related to the transience of social phenomena. On the one hand, we must understand their temporality, the patterns and rhythms of historical time; on the other hand, the reasons for the change, or historical causation must also be explained. Historical time is in itself an important issue, for it gives a sense to the events occurring at a specified epoch. One of the reasons why Gramsci rejects sociological schemas is that they neglect the conditions of time and place[25] or they are conceived as 'abstract universals, outside time and space'.[26] It is clear that two important aspects must not be neglected in specifications of historical events: (1) their geographical setting, which is a complex of natural and social conditions; (2) their historical time. It is the latter that interests us at this point.

The relevance of historical time is two-fold. On the one hand, as we shall see, there seem to be social processes of different duration; they exhibit different tempos. Second, time in history often takes the character of an index which denominates variations in social systems. Thus, one speaks of the Age of the Reformation, the Middle Ages, or the Roman Empire, as descriptive terms for complex social systems. The adequate description of social phenomena requires, Gramsci suggests, both knowledge of their intrinsic properties and the properties of the system in which they occur, inasmuch as the character of such phenomena varies with systemic variations. A case in point is Gramsci's , as well as Marx's definition of 'human nature' as the ensemble of social relations. The freezing and consequent cracking of a car radiator – the example used by Hempel to illustrate his theory of scientific explanation[27] – will not really differ whether the event takes place in the Arctic in 1946, or in the Alps in 1986. But a social event such as a wedding, may have a very different significance whether it takes place in the twelfth century or the twentieth century, whether it occurs in a rural setting or in a modern city. The wedding of Isabel and Ferdinand in 1469 in effect resulted in the creation of the absolute monarchy of a united Spain, whereas a similar event today is almost unthinkable.

Thus, although under a certain description both weddings are events of the same type, a fuller description (one that includes systemic concepts) results in a different evaluation of their significance and their typicality. The question, then is, how far must one go in describing social events? Marx, in the *Grundrisse*, as I have already noted in Chapter One, chastised Malthus' conception of overpopulation for being 'altogether false and childish because he regards *over population* as being of the same

kind in all the different historical phases of economic development; does not understand their specific differences, and hence
stupidly reduces these very complicated and varying relations to a
simple relation . . . .'[28] Both Marx and Gramsci concur in their
criticism of generalizations that fail to recognize the different
significance of similar social phenomena in different historical
circumstances.

The political consequences of this theoretical question did not
escape Gramsci. Deficiency of description may be the theoretical
aspect of the equation of social democracy with fascism, for they
are regimes of the same kind, that is, bourgeois regimes. Yet, as
Gramsci saw, there is a world of difference between them.

Although Gramsci does not give any well-developed historical
examples to buttress his arguments, he certainly has two in mind.
First, he refers to the different forms of universal suffrage that
prevailed in France according to changes in economic and
political relations between Paris and the provinces, that is, between
the urban and rural forces.[29] Gramsci suggests that universal
suffrage cannot be understood except by relating it to the relations
of forces and to the temporary defeats and victories, the goals and
the tactics of these forces. The second example refers to what he
calls Caesarism. He argues that Caesarism is the expression of a
situation in which the political forces in struggle are in
equilibrium, so that neither can dominate the other. It is in such
circumstances that Caesarist solutions are usually found. However,
the simple formula of two forces, A and B, in equilibrium is too
abstract; Caesarism cannot be understood with such sociological
generalizations because its concrete significance varies with the
historical circumstances in which it emerges. There can be, he
argues, progressive and regressive Caesarism, depending on which
element prevails in the dialectic of revolution or restoration. As
examples of progressive Caesarism, Gramsci mentions Caesar and
Napoleon I; he mentions Napoleon III and Bismarck as examples
of regressive Caesarism.[30]

The second example may be thought to introduce evaluative
elements in the description of social phenomena. This may be
thought to be inappropriate in so far as it is often thought that
descriptions should be kept separate from valuations. However,
there are two sorts of reasons why Gramsci may have proceeded in
this manner. First, the philosophy of praxis, as he often described

Marxism, is not only interested in understanding the world, but also in changing it. The political activity of those who are engaged in changing the world must be based on both true descriptions and evaluations, for their attitude towards a progressive force must be very different from that towards a regressive force. As a consequence, Marxist theory, in so far as it aspires to the unity of theory and practice, must, from time to time, evaluate the degree of progressiveness of social forces. This does not mean that such value judgments are arbitrary; for the actions of the parties concerned can be seen to promote universal interests or to inhibit them. And this brings us to the second sort of reason; the evaluation of the degree of progressiveness of a ruler or an institution must be based on the results of his or her actions or its consequences. It is the effects of the situation in which Caesarism emerges that will indicate what kind of situation it is. And this is not a question of value, but a description of effects, a causal judgement. Hence, even if we refuse to evaluate a type of Caesarism, its specific character will be known not from some generalization about Caesarism, but about the effects that any one case will have at a given historical period.

This is one of the crucial aspects of Gramsci's historicism. An historical phenomenon is not fully known until its effects can be described. This is in fact a view held by some historians. For instance, Hexter argues that 'History is a becoming, an ongoing, and it is to be understood not only in terms of what comes before but also of what comes after'. For this reason, as more of the effects of an event are known, the history of that event has to be rewritten.[31] In a similar vein, Randall and Haines argue that 'the meaning and significance of the past is continually changing with the occurrence of fresh events'.[32]

This view of the historical process implies that understanding the present is important for understanding the past. In Gramsci's words, the present is 'in a sense the best document of the past', because 'every real historical phase leaves traces of itself in the successive phases'. The present, hence, contains the past, but not all the past; only those aspects that were essential, or viable, survive.[33] These considerations led Gramsci to infer the 'research canon' that 'subsequent events shed light on the preceding ones'.[34] Failure to apply this canon, Gramsci maintains, often results in sociological schemas instead of historical explanation.[35]

present, then, offers a principle of selection, a document of the meaning or significance of the past. Surely, many aspects of the past will be discovered, but one must avoid 'the dangers of sentimental antiquarianism',[36] as Christopher Hill puts it; the selection of sources, as well as our understanding of their significance must be directed by the present as document.[37]

Several issues are closely related to this theory of historical events. First, it seems that one of the important aspects of social institutions, such as Caesarism or hegemony, is their function. It is well known that functional explanations require the explanation of an event in terms of its effects, and in some cases, this might involve some form of teleological explanation. Gramsci does not accept teleological explanations. His 'functional explanations' do not involve the thesis that the future consequences of an event cause this event to take place. Yet Gramsci sometimes explains features of society in terms of their consequences. The point is merely that an adequate description of social phenomena requires knowledge of their consequences, for our knowledge of the significance or function of social phenomena depends on the kinds of consequences that follow them. It is in terms of the function of a phenomenon, more that in terms of its inherent properties, that comparisons between phenomena are possible. On this basis, for instance, Gramsci compares the use of Latin in the Middle Ages in Europe to the ideographical writing of Chinese culture,[38] for although the two phenomena are intrinsically heterogeneous, they performed 'the same function: that of transmitting the culture of a ruling class not rooted in the cultural and linguistic reality' of the national masses.[39]

Second, this theory of historical events entails that the present cannot be fully described, and hence not fully known, precisely because we lack knowledge of its eventual consequences. Gramsci argues that the structural phase of a social formation 'can be concretely studied and analysed only after it has completed all its process of development, not during the process itself'.[40] Unfortunately, this statement is ambiguous because Gramsci gives no indication of what a structural phase might be; it may indicate a whole era in which a mode of production is dominant, or it may indicate a stage within the life of a mode of production, say state capitalism, as opposed to other stages in the development of capitalism. Nevertheless, the significance of this passage for our purposes seems to be clear, that is, to reiterate, that knowledge of social phenomena requires that we investigate both its antecedents as well as its consequences, at least until its latent forces are spent or, what is the same thing, until its process of development is completed.

As Bhaskar has recently argued, 'the possibilities inherent in a new social development will often become apparent long after the development itself', which is why 'history must be continually rewritten'. The 'historical (transformational) character' of social systems implies that 'social scientific (unlike natural scientific) theory is *necessarily* incomplete'.[41] The incompleteness of all social theories, including Marxism, is one of the reasons for their historicity. Their limitations are linked to the objective process of social transformation, as well as the subjective process in so far as social theories are also a part of the process. Thus, their historicity can be said to be two-fold; first, as a social system unfolds, knowledge of that system is modified and second, theories also change to reflect the changes in the systems, that is, they are also, and to a certain extent, ideologies. This double historicity of social theories entails that, as we have seen in Chapter One, Gramsci's historicism is not a closed or an absolute one, for the truth of the theory, which depends on its correspondence to reality, is not necessarily the same as its function, or its character as ideology.

This brings us to the third point. Gramsci's language suggests that 'structural phases' undergo processes of change which come to an end; in other words, that the historical process at the structural level is not a continuous one. The breaks in continuity mark the completion of the process, the exhaustion of its possibilities. This is, in part, the sense that Gramsci extracted from the two principles he so often quoted, namely: 'No social order is ever destroyed before all the productive forces for which it is sufficient have been developed .... Mankind thus inevitably sets itself only such tasks as it is able to solve.'[42]

I think that at this point it is evident that the unit of historical research is, for Gramsci, not the event, and that history is not a narrative or a time series of discrete events. This implies that those philosophers of history who set as a basic example of a historical event 'Caesar crossed the Rubicon', or like Hempel, 'the car radiator cracked', are not engaged in studying the same sort of history that Gramsci conceptualizes. Establishing events as well as explaining the proximate causes, themselves prior events, is only the surface of historical research, the first step in the collection of evidence, but not the proper historiographical task of explaining historical phenomena. The kings of phenomena that form the material for historical explanation are, for Gramsci, structural, institutional, and functional phenomena, such as social groups, parties, hegemony, and, above all, social relations. It would appear that Gramsci's conception of what constitutes the subject matter of social theory is similar to that of Bhaskar, who argues that sociology is concerned 'with the persistent *relations* between individuals (and groups) and with the relations between these relations (and between such relations and nature and the products of such relations)'.[43] By way of analogy we can visualise Gramsci's concept of history as the constant friction of continental plates in their slow, but sometimes earthshaking motion, rather than the collision of two billiard balls. Again, a similar view has been defended by Bhaskar, who argues that 'the objects of experimental activity are not events and their conjunctions, but structures, generative mechanisms and the like'.[44]

Furthermore, Gramsci approaches historical research in a holistic manner, understanding by holism the view 'that in any given society we cannot understand the parts unless we understand their function and roles in relation to each other and in relation to the whole'.[45] This definition of holism, however, needs some qualification. In the first place, Gramsci holds that there are elements in a social whole that are causally primary; he subscribes to the view that the social relations of production are determining in the last instance. This claim will be further elaborated in Chapter Three. In the second place, it is not always obvious that Gramsci espouses holism, nor is his conception of this theory very clear. We cannot enter here into the debates between holism and methodological individualism; we can, however, propose a tentative interpretation of Gramsci's thought on this issue.

Gramsci affirms that, because 'every social aggregate is in fact something more than the sum of its parts . . . the law that explains social aggregates is not a "physical law"', in physics one does not leave the realm of 'quantity other than as a metaphor'.[46] The difference, then, between physical laws and laws of society is that whereas the former apply to objects whose aggregates are identical to the sum of their parts, the latter belong to wholes in which the sum of the parts result in the passage from quantity to quality. In this transformation, new properties or new laws emerge; these are not reducible to the properties, or the laws, that regulate the behaviour of the component parts outside the system or whole. For instance, the laws of society are not reducible to, or explainable in terms of, the laws of psychology, without remainder.

It must be noted that Gramsci may be wrong about his assessment of physical aggregates; the behaviour of a planet within the planetary system is different from what it would be in the absence of all the other solar bodies. Its actual behaviour is explained by the application of the laws of physics and a so-called rule of composition, such as the parallelogram of forces. This rule of composition, as Brodbeck argues, is not properly a rule; it is but an empirical law of the system.[47] Whether this law of the system is an emergent law, one not reducible to the laws of the component parts, is an open question. In any case, laws of composition are not foreign to physics.

Gramsci is defending two basic theses, theses that can be taken to constitute his definition of holism. First, social wholes do not exist apart from the activity of individuals. One must not hypostatize such wholes, as idealists do when they posit a spirit, or the state, as a being in itself; or as religion does, he suggests, in referring the earthly process of history to a transcendent being. Modern idealists, he continues in a reference to Gentile, posit a state that is superior to individuals. Whereas idealist and religious thinkers hypostatize the whole, and thus tend to neglect the individuals through whose activity it exists, positivist sociology is content with statistical analysis, that is, with the simple addition of parts. The most fertile and original contribution of historical materialism is that it takes quantity and quality as being closely connected.[48]

Second, and this cannot be too strongly asserted, Gramsci seems to think that what differentiates the mere addition of the parts from a social whole is *functional emergence* not *existential emergence*, that is, wholes differ from mere aggregates in that the former are subject to laws which cannot be reduced to the laws applying to its individual members separately, and not because of the emergence of a new object. The difference in the behaviour of a whole is a result of its organization, that is, its structural or systemic character.[49] In Gramsci's view, the social relations of production, hegemony, and, when necessary, coercion are the basic structuring principles of a societal whole, principles that account for the behaviour of individuals in accordance with the emergent laws of the whole. (Gramsci does not use the expression 'emergence'; his theory, as indicated above, is couched in terms of the basic principles of dialectics regarding the passage from quantity to quality.)

Gramsci rejects any attempt to reduce social laws, or laws of history, to psychological, biological,[50] or, as he thinks is done by those who deify hypostatized matter,[51] physical ones. If we accept Gellner's argument that methodological individualism is not different from psychologism, then Gramsci rejects methodological individualism. His argument is based on the premiss that values, dispositions, etc., are shaped by hegemonic forces – in Gellner's view, psychologism fails in that 'as a matter of causal fact, our dispositions are not independent of the social context in which they occur'. Incidentally, Gellner also contends that, as a matter of logic, dispositions 'cannot be described without reference to their social context'.[52]

However, in the same note, Gramsci also maintains that the 'something' hypostatized by idealist thinkers, is 'an arbitrary abstraction, not a procedure of analytical distinction practically convenient for pedagogical reasons'.[53] This, it would seem, points to a different kind of holism; one in which the laws of the system are, in principle, reducible to the laws of its component parts, though in practice it is difficult or even unnecessary to effect the reduction. Given, however, Gramsci's rejection of the causal import of statistical generalizations, as we shall see later on, his acceptance of an undefined link between quantity and quality, and his dislike for reductionism, his philosophy of social explanation is closer to holism than to methodological individualism. In short, Gramsci offers a guarded and partial defence of holism. He is anxious to avoid any metaphysical reality above the activities of individual human beings which would in any case be inconsistent with his humanism; at the same time, he suggests that the organizational complexity of social systems gives rise to laws which are systemic and not reducible without remainder to the laws of psychology, biology, or physics.

Given Gramsci's theory of transience, the relations between

parts and whole, their structures and functions must be seen not only as they obtain at any given moment, but, above all, in their development through time. This means that, as we have already seen, the process is best known when its development is completed, that is, when we have the evidence of its consequences as well as that of its causes. A methodological consequence of Gramsci's historicism is that the theoretical concepts proper to the study of society must be historical concepts. Proper theoretical concepts cannot be established by any model of society which merely seeks to capture its structure at any given moment; they cannot be conceived as a structural logic that can simply be abstracted from the totality of social phenomena, for the totality of social phenomena is never given in a single time, and hence no snapshot can adequately grasp it.[54] Theoretical concepts, such as class or hegemony, have a temporal dimension which defines them as much as their synchronic characteristics. They are, in short, each of them an abstraction that holds for a series of interrelated phenomena over a period of time, not simply a matter of series of properties in a static whole. This, of course, is not a denial of social theory, nor is it a rejection of the need to abstract from the empirically given. It is rather a conception of theory thought to be suitable for a type of phenomena, namely, social phenomena, which change rapidly.

The emphasis on the difficulty in knowing the social structure of the present is not intended as a rejection of any attempt to understand the present. But it certainly is a warning that any such attempt can only produce knowledge that is at best uncorroborated hypotheses.[55] In this regard, the expected or predicted outcome of the present situation is relevant evidence for understanding this situation. Consequently, if any trends can be identified in the present, they could be used to produce a fuller but tentative description of current phenomena. This, as is easily seen, involves a circle which seems to be theoretically unsolvable. I shall later return to the question of prediction.

In the context of Gramsci's conception of the present as 'document of the past', we must briefly remember Croce's theory of the contemporaneity of history. As we saw, Croce argued that it is the soul of the historian, steeped as it is in the problems of the present, that brings the available documents to life. A second sense of 'contemporary history' also seems to be present in Croce's work;

; to this second sense, the past only lives in the present,
n the eternal ideal history of the spirit. Gramsci, in
 does not deny the actual past existence of events, nor
claim that they only become alive in the present. Part of
n for this is that the significance of the past in relation to
the present is a causal one, not one of the preservation of life in an
atemporal, ahistorical spirit. In short, the relation between past
and present is seen in two related ways. First, as a relation of cause
and consequence; second, as a relation between historical reality
and the evidence for it. The present contains evidence of what was
necessary in the past. Necessity, then, is seen *post-factum*: we can
now identify the necessary features of the past in so far as they
produced effects that have survived to the present.

From a methodological point of view, one of the fundamental
components of Gramsci's historicism is that the rigorous
investigation of social systems is possible only from a long-term
perspective,[56] or a historical perspective. This involves two issues:
on the one hand, it is necessary to look at the long-term
development of social systems; on the other hand, the theoretical
concepts used to explain them must be abstracted from the long-
term processes of the system, in other words, they must be
historical concepts. Note that this does not mean that as
conditions change, the concepts and theories will also change. It
means, rather, that theoretical concepts must emerge out of the
complex abstraction of evidence ranging over a suitably long
period of time, not out of a synchronic analysis of a social system.

It is with this theory in mind that we can understand Gramsci's
comments on the periodization of the French Revolution. Noting
that historians generally do not agree on the date on which the
revolution ended, he argues that it 'was only in 1870 – 71 . . . that
all the germs originated in 1789 were historically exhausted'. The
reason for this is that only at that time was the victorious class able
to defeat both the old regime and the new groups that had arisen
in that period. This means that the French social structure was
finally settled, as later developments would show, and that allowed
the researcher to grasp the real character of the French
Revolution, to understand the necessary, vital, and lasting features
of that episode of French history.[57]

Given this understanding of social phenomena, it is to be
expected that Gramsci would provide some reflections on the

subject of historical time. Indeed, the first theme of Gramsci's reflection on the two principles by Marx quoted above, is precisely the various kinds of temporal processes to be found in history, their various rhythms, as well as their possible relationships in a more or less integrated whole. It can be said without exaggeration that Gramsci's reflection on the aforementioned principles provided the foundation for his historicism. Gramsci draws two main consequences from them. First, an organic theory of society which rejects the atomist conception of history as a series of discrete events; second, the rudiments of a theory of historical time, or more precisely, of a theory of the various tempos that criss-cross each other in history. It is this second issue that we shall now discuss.

The temporality of history has been the focus of reflection of historians and philosophers. Among others, Vico espoused a theory of the course and recourse of historical stages in a repetitive cycle of the age of Gods, the age of heroes, and the age of men; each age had its own characteristic mental structure. Comte also thought of history as the progress from the age of theology to the scientific or positive age. And of course Marx not only periodized history according to the various modes of production that succeed one another, but, most important, he called attention to short-term cycles, the five-to-seven-year business cycles, that produced crises in capitalist societies.

In the 1920s Kondratieff and Trotsky engaged in a debate on the condition of equilibrium in capitalist societies which was brought about by the studies of the former on what he called long-wave cycles. This type of cycle, lasting forty to sixty years, Kondratieff reasons, is linked to the 'wear and tear, replacement, and increase in those basic capital goods requiring a long period of time and tremendous investments for their production'.[58]

But the study of historical tempos is best associated with the work of Fernand Braudel and other *Annalist* historians. In 1949 Braudel published his influential work on *La Mediterranée et le Monde Mediterranéen à l'Époque de Philipe II*, a book also written in jail. In this work, Braudel produced a three-tiered analysis of the Mediterranean world in which each level represented a type of historical duration. The first part of the book, corresponding to the first level, was devoted to the analysis of 'an almost immobile history, that of man in his relationship to the environment'. The second part, corureponding to the second level, contained the study of 'social history, that of groups and their groupings' which exhibits a perceptible but very slow rhythm. The third part, corresponding to the third level, focused on the events and individuals, *l'histoire événementielle* as Simiand had called it, which is a history of 'brief, rapid, nervous oscillations'. Braudel called these three types of duration geographical time, social time, and individual time respectively.[59]

Braudel returned to this conception of historical time in an essay published in 1958 where he noted that socio-economic history places the concept of cyclical oscillation at the centre of its investigation. Whereas traditional, narrative history focused on the short duration, the drama of events and individuals, this new history looks at the conjunctures, that is, cycles, that may last 20 or even 50 years. He notes, however, that there are processes that last much longer; the concept proposed by Braudel to grasp this '*longue durée*' is that of structure. Structures 'are stable elements for an infinitude of generations',[60] such as for instance, the geographical determinants that put a constant pressure on the relations between humanity and nature. We must not think, however, that geography provides the only long-lasting structures, for, as Braudel notes, 'mental frameworks are also long-term prisons'. As an example of this kind of structure, he mentions the Aristotelian conception of the universe, which dominated astronomy until the age of Gallileo, Descartes, and Newton.[61]

Braudel's project, as indeed the project of the French historical school known as the *Annales* school, was a far-reaching attempt to enrich historical studies by introducing the theories developed by the social sciences in general. However, he thought that the lack of concern for duration, the emphasis on the immediate, the present, 'with its "volcanic" heat and teeming richness', detracted from their scientificity, for past and present explain each other, shed light on each other.[62] This is, precisely, the essence of Gramsci's critique of sociology, that is, its neglect of the canon of historical research according to which the present state of society is the consequence of the past and, for this reason, is the best document of the past.

The *Annales* school founded by Marc Bloch and Lucien Fevre in the 1920s, must be seen as part of the reaction against Rankean history and its emphasis on political history and the history of events. Simiand called this *histoire événementielle*. In order to develop a total history on a more solid foundation, he thought, one must begin with 'an attack on what he called the three "idols of the tribe" of historians: the idol of politics, the idol of the individual and the idol of chronology'.[63] In fact, this is an attack on the historicism of the German school. That attack was led by Lamprecht in Germany, J. H. Robinson and Charles Beard in the USA, Simiand himself and, later, the *Annalistes* in France. The *Annales* paradigm, as it has been called,[64] has become very influential, even among Marxist historians. Pierre Vilar, for instance, in his work on *La Catalogne dans l'Espagne Moderne* focused his research on the geographical milieu and the conjunctural process in an effort to provide not only an understanding of modern Catalonia, but also a theory of the nation.

It would seem that the new historiography in its sympathetic approach to geography, economics, sociology, and psychology is incompatible with Gramsci's historicism. However, on a closer look, Gramsci's historicism is not a rejection of social and economic theories in general, but a rejection of synchronic social theories; as we have seen, Braudel also complains of the lack of understanding of time among sociologists. Gramsci, in fact, often refers to economic theory to explain social phenomena; for instance, in his reflections on Italian society, he suggests that the broad role assigned to the state is linked to patterns of investment typical of a society with many investors and few producers.[65] Furthermore, the existence of a parasite group of middle-class investors, or the absence of 'a rational demographic composition', is given as one of the historically evolved conditions for the existence of a fossilized class of intellectuals typical of European traditions and civilization.[66] If demography and investment patterns are relevant to historical analysis, then the conclusion we must reach, at least tentatively, is that Gramsci was not opposed to theoretical generalizations, although he strongly rejected the kinds of abstract generalizations of the sociology he knew. Let us now turn to his reflections on the issue of historical time.

As I have indicated above, it was Marx's two principles which led Gramsci to think about historical time. In a note devoted to the 'crucial problem' of the relationship between structure and superstructure, Gramsci writes that 'one can draw some canons of

87

historical methodology' from Marx's two principles: the first such canon he draws is that 'in the study of a structure, it is necessary to distinguish that which is permanent from that which is occasional'.[67] He redefined this distinction as that between 'organic movements (relatively permanent)' and 'conjunctural movements (... which appear as occasional, immediate, almost accidental)'.[68]

It is the ensemble of forces of production which Gramsci thinks are 'the least variable element in historical development', and because of this they 'can be measured with mathematical exactitude, which can give rise to an experimental science of history, in the precise sense in which one can speak of "experimental" in history'.[69] Organic movements involve the structure of a social system and tend to last decades. Their long duration furnishes evidence that 'incurable contradictions' have matured and that the forces of conservation are attempting to prevent the dissolution of the *status quo*.[70] It seems, then, that Gramsci is affirming or asserting two propositions: first, that relative to the superstructure, the structure is permanent; second, that serious structural crises tend to last longer than other types of crises.

However, not all long-term processes are structural. Gramsci notes, as Braudel did with mental structures, that intellectual attitudes may last hundreds of years, spanning over different modes of production, with little change. Gramsci indicates his intention to embark on a 'double series of researches. One on the Age of Risorgimento and a second one on the preceding history ... inasmuch as it has created cultural elements that have had repercussions on the Age of Risorgimento'. As an example of the second type of research, Gramsci reflects on the origin of what he calls the cosmopolitan character of Italian intellectuals, that is, their failure to produce a national intellectual climate as well as a national popular literature. He indicates that the genesis of this intellectual phenomenon is to be found in the passage from the Roman Republic to the Empire. It was, he notes, the transformation of the 'equilibrium of the peninsula in the classical world' that was involved in the creation of the Empire, that resulted in the creation of a 'bureaucratic' centre in Rome and, with it, the de-nationalization of Rome and the peninsula, which became a 'cosmopolitan terrain'.[71]

Apart from the empirical accuracy of Gramsci's analysis, the methodological point he is making, as well as the remarkable similarity with Braudel's analysis, is clear. For the long duration of intellectual attitudes, such as the cosmopolitanization of Italian intellectuals, its persistence through centuries, is to be understood as a structure in the Braudelian sense, and that means that, as we have seen, historical phenomena are not simply discrete events, but long-lasting, slowly changing, relatively permanent determining factors – what Braudel refers to as prisons.

Absent from Gramsci's reflection is any reference to the temporality of geography. In Braudel's work the geographical structures are the slow-changing, long-term phenomena that underlie all social change, and in Vilar's work on Catalonia the regional aspects of nationality are conceived as forming the core of a way of living, of the psychology of a nation. This is not to say that Gramsci did not pay attention to regional differences. Such differences were so obvious in Italy that they had become the object of intense debate and analysis in which Gramsci himself participated. As I mentioned earlier, Gramsci not only rejected sociology for abstracting from time conditions, but also from space. That is, from the geographical conditions of social processes. In his analysis of Italian history, Gramsci took care to distinguish five 'forces' which were defined in terms of human geography, and which he thought of as a general outline for the study of city/country-side relations. These five forces were: (1) the northern urban force; (2) the southern rural force; (3) the northern/central rural force; (4) the rural force of Sicily; (5) the rural force of Sardinia. He then attempted to understand the relations between the different regions on the analogy of a train whose engine would be the northern urban force. The problem of the unity of the Italian state was, in part, the problem of the best arrangement to 'build a "train" that would advance the fastest through history'.[72] Nevertheless, Gramsci did not fully and explicitly develop his geographical insights, nor did he incorporate them into the analysis of transience he drew from Marx's statements.

The organic crises that Gramsci so carefully distinguished from conjunctural ones, seem to correspond to the exhaustion of the possibilities inherent in a social system. I do not think that the conception of crises that last for decades could be compared to Kondratieff's long wave, simply because Gramsci seems to be concerned with the deep contradictions whose maturation signals the end of a social system, not with the forces of equilibrium within the capitalist mode of production.

Conjunctures are defined by Gramsci 'as the ensemble of circumstances which determine the market in a given phase', and the process of ever new combinations of such circumstances 'as the economic cycle'.[73] In another note, he defines them as 'the complex of the immediate and transitory characteristics of the economic situation'. And he adds that the economic situation is to be understood as the 'more fundamental and permanent characters'.[74] Conjunctural crises, one can conclude, are the temporary crises linked to the business cycle, which in general do not appear to be catastrophic.

So far, we have taken Gramsci's definition of organic and conjunctural movements as being structural. Yet Gramsci's analysis of a situation in terms of relations of forces suggests that a situation also involves the superstructures. In effect, the distinction between conjunctural and organic movements can also be conceptualized from the point of view of politics. In political terms, Gramsci links the study of conjectures to 'immediate politics', or to short-term tactics, one could say, to the solution of day-to-day problems. The study of the situation, on the other hand, is tied to long-term strategy, to fundamental historical problems.[75] Hence, conjunctural problems, although 'certainly dependent' on organic movements, have little historical significance; they give rise to petty political critique, they involve small leading groups and personalities. In contrast, 'organic phenomena give rise to socio-historical critique, which involves the great groupings, beyond the immediately responsible individuals and beyond the leading personnel'.[76]

The distinction between structures and conjunctures, Gramsci maintains, is to be applied to all situations, not only to regressive ones or to crises. In general, it seems that Gramsci attempts to put what he calls the 'situation' as the unit of historical and political analysis. The Argentine sociologist Portantiero has clearly grasped the theoretical significance of Gramsci's analysis of situation. Suggesting that Gramsci should be called the "theoretician of conjunctures",[77] (in Gramsci's terms the modern use of 'conjuncture' is *his* 'situation') he argues that the situation is 'the concurrence of specific temporalities which results in the "event"'.

And he adds that Gramsci's historicism should be taken to mean that the relations of forces in each of the various levels 'express the rhythm of their own, irreducible histories'.[78] Structure, conjuncture, event: these are the elements of the situation, each with its specific rhythm, its temporality, and all linked together in a dialectical unity, a unity of contradictory forces.

It must be noted that Gramsci proposed his theory of historical duration as a principle for historical research. The significance of the principle is not to be taken as a hypostatization of time, time as a creative subject of specific rhythms. If Gramsci thought that that principle had great theoretical and practical significance, it is not because he gave particular attention to time in the abstract, but because he thought that temporal distinctions pointed to a crucial issue, namely, historical causation. He observed that a frequent error in historico-political analysis is that of not finding 'the right relation between that which is organic and that which is occasional: thus one manages to put forward as immediately operative causes that instead are mediately operative, or to assert that the immediate causes are the only effective ones'. These two errors lie at the core of economism and ideologism: 'in one case the mechanical causes are overestimated; in the other the voluntaristic and individual element is exaggerated'. The task of historical and political analysis is to find the right 'dialectical nexus between the two orders of movement', a task that, Gramsci acknowledges, is not easy.[79]

As Fontana, a Spanish historian, has observed with respect to Gramsci's interpretation of Marxism, historical materialism proposes a concept of determinism which refers to 'the "organic" variations that profoundly affect the structure and have important consequences for class-struggle, but not to the immediate, and conjunctural economic reasons of the struggle among groups, which fall in the sphere of traditional political history'. This of course implies that, although the economic structure, that is, the relations among classes, constitute the stage or the backbone of the historical process, not all social phenomena are immediately related to it. The economic structure, the long-term process of class relations, determines the general shape of the landscape of history as well as its fundamental changes, just as the continental plates determine the geography of the earth; but above it, the details of the landscape are autonomous in many ways. Thconclusion that one can reach is, in Fontana's words, that it is only with regard to organic changes that 'Marx's assertion according to which men take consciousness of the conflicts that appear in the economic structure in the terrain of ideologies' make sense.[80]

Unfortunately, Gramsci's theory of a situation and its various orders of movement was merely a sketch, not a well developed theory. The situation is the conjunction of structural and superstructural processes, each with its own dynamic, its own temporality. This implies that each process is autonomous to a certain degree, for otherwise the causal links between them would not allow for differences in their rhythms. However, as we have seen above, there are political processes that are organic, that is, linked to the long-term or 'strategic' process of change; and there are as well conjunctural political processes, or short-term or 'tactical' ones. There are also, as we have seen in the case of the cosmopolitanism of Italian intellectuals, superstructural elements of very long duration. One could suggest that other phenomena, for instance patriarchy, could be understood as long-term elements that play a causal role in the specific character of social wholes. In spite of these interesting insights, Gramsci does not give any precise theory of the relationship between these various elements, nor does he suggest how the interdependence on the one hand, and the partial autonomy of the various processes, on the other, could be conceptualized. Thus, as is often the case in the *Prison Notebooks*, we find a suggestive sketch of how one might approach a historical problem, but little else. This is not to say that the sketch in itself is without value, for it is certainly rich in possibilities.

Perhaps what is most interesting in it is Gramsci's cautious attitude; what is in reality a basic historical problem could hardly be solved by conceptual means alone. If anything, Gramsci wanted to avoid what he thought was one of the basic theoretical errors of economism, namely, to take as a historical cause what is a canon of research and interpretation.[81] This theoretical error, or perhaps it was a mental attitude, transformed 'the methodological principles developed by Marx and Engels into mere verbal, almost liturgical formulae, which are not used as analytical instruments to reach conclusions, but are merely enunciated as if they were an explanation'.[82] Today, Gramsci's caution should be taken as the rejection of the pursuit of pure theory without the support of historical documents; that is, it ought to be seen as a rejection of what E. P. Thompson called the kangaroo factor: 'gigantic bounds through the conceptual elements, with the most gracious curvatures of thought', and little contact with the ground of historical reality, the documents to which Gramsci often referred.[83]

The construction and analysis of situations is a fruitful, if difficult, approach to solving historiographical problems. In a sense, Braudel, Vilar, and many other modern historians, have attempted to develop our understanding of the articulation of structures, conjunctures, and events in the contradictory unity of a social formation. What is remarkable is that Gramsci's historicism as a conception of the transience of social phenomena, should transcend the narrative tradition in history and should begin to think in terms that today seem very modern.

I have suggested above that there are some similarities between Gramsci's and Braudel's thought. These similarities, however, should not be exaggerated, nor should they lead to the conclusion that Gramsci was a precursor of Braudel. My intention in this comparison was primarily to put in relief Gramsci's search for an integral history. In so doing, I neglected some aspects of Gramsci's thought that do not seem to match with Braudel's project. As Aymard has observed, 'the Risorgimento is the centre' of Gramsci's analysis, whereas the French Revolution was never the centre of historical research of the *Annales* school'.[84] The reason for this is that Gramsci's interest was primarily political, and this marks the great difference between Gramsci and those who followed Simiand in deposing the idol of politics. However, Gramsci's historiography was not political in the old sense of the historicists, as we shall see later on.

Gramsci's view of historicism as the theory of transience contains two related points. First, the principle that historical phenomena must be both described and explained not only by their antecedents but also by their consequences; second, that the unity of historical analysis is the situation, that is, the concurrence of processes of different duration. Both aspects point to the importance of an adequate understanding of historical time. Historical subjects must be studied both diachronically and sychronically; that is, both the sequence of causal links, and the interrelationships between elements at any given point in time are essential for historical understanding. Since Gramsci's analysis, as he explicitly stated, concerns the question of historical causality, I shall now turn to the second aspect of historicism, namely, historical necessity.

Historical necessity

The issue of historical necessity is probably the most crucial one for understanding the contrast between Gramsci's historicism and other forms of historicism, for it is closely linked to the fundamental themes of the nature of historical facts and unity of scientific method.

Salamini has suggested that 'all laws of necessity, causality and objectivity . . . disappear when the masses become politically and culturally autonomous'.[85] This would indicate that only subaltern classes are subject to laws, whereas ruling classes are free from them. If this were so, the cyclic crises of capitalism would only affect the masses, not the capitalists. In reality, however, such crises become the focus of conjunctural political and economic efforts to minimize losses. In other words, historical forces exist which exert considerable pressure on, or which restrict the freedom of, both leading and subaltern classes.

It may seem that Gramsci's critique of sociology is above all a rejection of the conception of laws in history. There are a number of passages in the *Prison Notebooks* which seem to argue that the organized will of the masses replaces laws in history. In his critique of sociology, to which we must now return, Gramsci argues that statistical generalizations, or laws of great numbers, are applicable to historical and political reality 'only in so far as the great masses of population remain passive'. And he adds that political activity precisely aims at changing the behaviour of the masses.[86] So far, Salamini's interpretation agrees with Gramsci's text. However, Gramsci develops his argument in a way that is as surprising as it is interesting. For he adds that, although a planned economy is 'destined to break up statistical laws mechanically understood, that is, produced by the fortuitous encounter of an infinite number of arbitrary individual acts', it nevertheless 'must be based on statistics'.[87] And one must suppose that statistical analysis would be used to ascertain generalizations of the very sort Gramsci denounces. Indeed, Gramsci thinks that in any social system there always is a 'conformism', a collective human being,[88] and that a hegemonic struggle in so far as it is a struggle between two forms of civilization, is also a struggle between two kinds of conformism. Each society engenders its own automatism, a conformism,[89] as each economic structure gives rise to its *homo oeconomicus*.[90]

The point that Gramsci makes against statistical generalizations is not that they cease to exist when the masses become active; it is rather, that the activity of the masses breaks up existing, oppressive, forms of automatism and substitutes a freely accepted conformism. It is not the existence of laws of great numbers, but their mechanical nature, that is, the fact that they are spontaneously accepted as natural, that Gramsci denounces. As he put it, the result of the activity of the masses is that 'human awareness replaces naturalistic spontaneity'.[91] What underlies Gramsci's argument is his theory of human nature as a historical fact, that is, as the ensemble of social relations. The *homo oeconomicus* is not a fixed entity, a natural essence with definite dispositions that allow for statistical generalizations.

In short, Gramsci believes that statistical generalizations have practical application, that is, they obtain within certain limits, but they are not historical laws. A prime reason why they are not historical laws is that they neglect change, and therefore they are of limited theoretical value. Politically, the assumption that these laws are 'essential laws, operating with inevitability, is not only a scientific error, but becomes a political one in action; it favours mental laziness and shallowness in programming'.[92]

A second objection raised by Gramsci against statistical generalizations is that they merely state a fact, but have no causal significance.[93] He writes that 'usually they are no more than a duplicate of the observed fact itself. A fact, or a series of facts, is described by means of a mechanical process of generalization, a relation of similarity is derived from it and it is given the name of law, which is then assumed to have a causal function.[94] Gramsci's objection is mainly to the lack of causal significance of these so-called laws. The conclusion we can draw is that Gramsci does not object to either laws or the concept of causality, but to empirical descriptions which are misrepresented as being causal laws.

Gramsci's rejection of statistical generalizations is not surprising, for it is implied by his ontology. Since events are, as it were, only the surface of the social process – the external aspect of history – they are not the most significant aspects of history. They need to be explained, generalizations themselves need to be explained; for a statistical generalization is after all no more than a kind of description. Gramsci's ontology, as we saw, is based on a holistic understanding of the object of study, and it emphasizes structures and functions rather than discrete events. The distinction between the external and internal aspects of history that had been used by historicists since Vico, is used by Gramsci to oppose what he calls 'external description' to analysis of the 'causal nexus'.[95] This distinction raises the issue of the 'right balance between the deductive method and the inductive method', which is the problem of determinate descriptions, or historical descriptions, that is, descriptions that take their subject matter as a specific historical subject, not as an abstract one devoid of temporal references.[96] Induction alone cannot solve the problem of constructing hypotheses, for one must first have a criterion for choosing the relevant facts or the relevant relations among them, and this 'presupposes a "concept" that allows one to distinguish the facts'.[97] As we saw earlier, this is precisely the problem of adequate description.

One must not think that Gramsci is following Croce in rejecting empirical concepts as 'pseudo-concepts', nor does Gramsci either explicitly assert or implicitly assume in his thinking, that the subject of history is the pure concept, or the predicate. Gramsci's critique of empiricism is not really different from Marx's; they both argue that the external aspects of history, the appearances, must be explained by the internal ones, the essence. The internal aspects are, for Gramsci, a 'causal nexus' and, as I have indicated before, social structures such as class-relations, and functions, such as hegemony, play an important role in shaping that causal nexus. The subject matter of history, then, is not the immediate events, although these are also considered and explained, nor is it the predicate, such as Croce's liberty. The subject matter of history is the complex interaction of sub-processes which is the ever-changing situation.

It is interesting to note that, as the expression 'causal nexus' suggests, Gramsci did not reject the concept of historical causality. In fact, he even asserts that the value of common sense is that it is not 'led astray by pseudo-scientific, or pseudo-profound,

96

metaphysical puzzles and quibbles'; it not only 'employs the principle of causality', but identifies 'the exact cause'.[98] What Gramsci rejects is the attribution of single causes to social phenomena.[99] For example, he questions the view that the 'technical instrument is the unique and supreme *cause* of economic development'.[100]

Historical causality, then, must be analysed in terms of what Gramsci calls the situation: it involves the concurrence of sub-processes, each with its own rhythm, its own duration, resulting in an event or a change in the overall pattern. A feature of this form of causality is the reciprocal action of concurring processes. Gramsci notes how sometimes a phenomenon is both cause and effect of another phenomenon. Such a form of causality cannot, of course, obtain between two momentary discrete events; but it is quite conceivable in the case of long-term structures, where there is a relation of mutual dependence as well as antagonism between the various structural elements, such that any change in either of them affects the overall structure and hence the terms of the relation themselves (in such wholes, the existence and properties of the terms are not independent of the relation in which they arise).

The specific manner in which historical causality manifests itself is not a question that can be determined *a priori*. From Gramsci's point of view, it is an empirical problem, one that requires the most thorough and careful analysis of existing documents. The attempt to give a detailed analysis of causality is, then, a metaphysical enterprise, one that can only fail. Gramsci's scant notes on causality, must be taken as indicating a principle for historical research.

One can distinguish two general types of causality: (a) linear causality, that is, causality which, whether simple or complex, relates a series of successive events or changes; (b) structural causality, or what Gramsci at one point calls dialectical causality[101] and Marx and Engels' reflection, which relates different sub-processes within a whole, that is, it involves the relation between structures and superstructures. In this second sense, the fundamental problem to be resolved is that of the relationship between economic structure and ideology. This distinction is, however, no more than an analytical distinction. In reality, the two forms of causality are not clearly distinguishable, for both account

97

for changes, which are generally temporal processes. The significance of this distinction, which is only hinted at by Gramsci, is that it underlies Gramsci's case in analysing both the linear development of social systems, as well as their social depth, that is, their structure. Gramsci's historicism is not merely an assertion about the importance of historical understanding; it is also the claim that mere narration of events without social theory is scientifically inadequate.

The concept of dialectical causality emerges in a note where Gramsci discusses Corce's theory of the four distinct moments of the spirit and poses the question of the autonomy of politics. 'Given the autonomy of politics', Gramsci asks, 'what dialectical relationship exists between it and other historical manifestations?'[102] Returning to the same issue at a later date (the first note is written in the period 1930–2, the second one in 1932–5), Gramsci writes that Croce's theory of distinct moments is a 'purely verbal solution to a real methodological requirement'.[103] He notes that a dialectic of distinct moments is a contradiction in terms, because dialectics is a relation that obtains between opposites, not between distinct moments.[104]

The question is unresolved by Gramsci, or so it appears. In fact, the problem of the distinction between different temporal processes, and the theory of distinct realms of Crocean origin are the same problem, the 'same methodological requirement' expressed in different terms. There is, however, one suggestion that Gramsci makes with respect to the concept of dialectical causation. He writes that the 'priority of the politico-economic fact, that is, the structure' is 'the point of reference and the point of dialectical, not mechanical, causation of the superstructure'.[105] The expression 'dialectical causality' is dropped in the second version of the note, as also is his reference to the primacy of the politico-economic fact. Nevertheless, the problem is an important one, and much of what Gramsci writes is in some way an attempt at defining and solving this problem. Again, as he often does, Gramsci warns that this is not merely a formal problem. Referring to Croce's conception of the unity of the spirit and to a relationship of implication between distinct moments, he asks rhetorically whether this problem can have a speculative solution or only a historical one.[106] It is obvious from Gramsci's insistence on the historical treatment of problems that he thought that the only adequate answer is a historical one, that is, one drawn from documentary evidence: a real, not speculative, solution.

Gramsci's sparse remarks on a theory of causality do not allow for a full reconstruction of any such theory he may have held. Although on occasion he refers to necessary and sufficient conditions, he does not offer any analysis of causation in these terms. One can conclude, at most, that Gramsci thought that a complex concept of causality was of some importance for the study of history, provided that one avoided a simplistic model of linear causality. Such a form of causality leads, he argues, to the question of the first cause, the prime mover.[107] More effective for understanding history is to unravel the causal nexus, the productive or effective aspects of the situation, without necessarily attributing temporal primacy to any of them. To illustrate with an example the kind of analysis Gramsci may have had in mind, a summary of Bloch's account of the relationship between types of plough and the shape of the fields in feudal France will be useful.

Bloch notes that the wheeled plough requires more space to turn, and, to reduce this problem, the fields tended to be shaped in thin, long strips, which affected the social organization of villages. However, Bloch warns, the temptation 'to trace the whole chain of causation back to a single technological innovation' is to be resisted, for there are many other factors involved in this phenomenon. Noting that wheeled ploughs required long fields, but not narrow ones, Bloch argues that peasant mentality and hence social custom, was responsible for the thinness of the fields, for in this way each individual's land was dispersed in the village land; this allowed for equal participation in the different qualities of land, as well as equal chances of avoiding any disasters that might hit upon a restricted area. Furthermore, communal habits of cultivation were a necessary condition for the adoption of the wheeled plough.[108]

It is the temptation to trace the 'whole development back' to a single cause, which Gramsci also wants to avoid. For in a process as complex as history, the 'single cause' is itself often dependent on some of the other contemporary conditions of the process, just as communal habits of cultivation were necessary for the adoption of the wheeled plough as well as the modifications in land tenure and organization of work that ensued.

The question that we must now turn to is that of historical laws.

For if statistical laws have no causal significance, and if causality is a viable concept in historical research, what kind of historical laws would be causally significant and acceptable to Gramsci? Gramsci's critique of statistical generalizations points to both a theory of causality and a theory of causal laws. Gramsci uses the expression 'laws of history' in several contexts, which leave no doubt that he thought that some forms of law acted in social processes. Thus he writes that intellectuals must link dialectically the passion of the masses to the laws of history.[109] This points to a view that what is felt is ultimately a result of one's relation to objective social circumstances, and presumably, knowledge of the latter is indispensable not only for self-awareness but also for political organization and action. In this context, the intellectual has the difficult task of politicizing the feelings of the masses, that is, of channelling the energy contained in those feelings to the right target.

Gramsci also argues that Fordism is the result 'of the immanent necessity' of reaching a planned economy.[110] This would indicate that there are tendencies in the structure of the capitalist mode of production which lead to a planned economy; the outcome of these tendencies, however, depends on the response of the organized forces, an outcome that, depending on which forces prevail, may either be Fordism or even a corporatist state, such as fascism, or a socialist one. There are other instances in which Gramsci seems to depend on some notion of law, or at least, the law-like behaviour of social wholes. An example of these is Gramsci's tendency to engage in comparing aspects of different historical epochs, as he does when he writes that a better understanding of Italian intellectuals might be gained from a study of European Jewish intellectuals.[111]

More important for our purposes are his notes on the stages of development of classes, which seem to have general application, independent of concrete historical circumstances. This form of abstraction, Anderson believes, led Gramsci to commit serious errors.[112] Whatever the consequences which might stem from misinterpreting the assumed similarities between the compared phenomena, the point is that Gramsci implicitly accepted the concept of regularity in historical development. Further evidence of this hypothesis is furnished by Gramsci's statement to the effect that any new hegemonic group is faced by the task of creating a new moral and intellectual order,[113] and by his belief that any newly formed state must go through a primitive, corporatist stage.[114] Finally, Gramsci thought that 'a general principle of political science and art' could be drawn from the fact that in the course of history 'almost always similar situations arise'.[115] It might seem that, after all, Gramsci engaged in some form of sociological abstraction such as the ones he so thoroughly rejected. It must be noticed, however, that Gramsci compares situations, not single events, which is consistent with his critique of positivist sociology as outlined above. The conclusion we can draw from these remarks is that Gramsci did not maintain that there are no laws in history. His negative comments on this respect are directed against simplistic sociological generalizations which, he felt, had no causal significance, were based on a faulty anthropology, and were merely descriptive, not explanatory.

It seems that in the light of what we have seen so far, the first condition that causal laws would have to meet is that they should not be conjunctions of events, such as that whenever A occurs, then B occurs. Events in Gramsci's ontology of history have little causal and explanatory value. It is social relations and the specific manner in which they structure social wholes that are causally primary. Implicit in the *Prison Notebooks*, we can conclude, is a distinction between patterns of events and causal laws, a distinction which Bhaskar has also noted.[116] These laws would clearly differ from the laws of great numbers which are merely the 'fortuitous encounter of an infinite number of individual free acts'.[117] Nevertheless Gramsci often speaks of individuals, such as Cavour, Mazzini, Croce, etc., in his historical and political analysis. Events themselves – uprisings etc., – are also discussed on occasion. Furthermore, he discusses group activities as examples of the free choice which takes place according to certain lines which are 'identical for a great mass of individuals or single wills'.[118] It would appear, then, that Gramsci is concerned with showing that all historical laws are reducible to patterns of events, a proposition that casts doubt on the holistic interpretation of his thought advanced above. If this were so, however, historical laws would be reducible to statistical generalizations, generalizations that Gramsci believes have no causal import. Gramsci does not analyse this question in full; he suggests, however, that the patterns of events are not the cause but rather the effect, or manifestation of a deeper causal mechanism.

An individualist explanation would consist in isolating the dispositions of individuals which account for their decisions and actions. The coincidence of decisions and actions which result in a more or less unified social whole has usually been attributed to a common human nature. Theories of the possessive nature of human beings, referred to as a 'possessive individualism' by C. B. Macpherson,[119] have often been adduced to explain the smooth functioning of the market as well as the form of the state most suited to social life. We find such theories in Machiavelli, who writes of the avaricious nature of man, as well as in Vico, Adam Smith, and others.

Gramsci, in the passage quoted above, also gives credit to the dispositions of individuals, to their wills. The difference is that whereas for the individualist the psychological explanation is ultimate, for Gramsci those dispositions are not uniquely determined by psychological laws. As suggested earlier, dispositions are themselves conditioned by social relations, hegemony, etc. At times, Gramsci's position on this issue is quite extreme. In a letter to his wife, where he discusses the progress of their son Delio, he goes so far as to assert that 'man is completely a historical formation, brought about through coercion (not exclusively understood in the sense of brute force and of external violence)', and condemns as metaphysical the theory that newborns already contain as potentiality or in a latent state their whole future development.[120] In the *Prison Notebooks*, however, he limits the historicity of human nature to some common element that can be described by statistical generalizations and is determined by social relations.

Historical laws would need to meet another criterion to be acceptable to Gramsci: they must not exist in an absolute or eternal way;[121] they are not determined by extra-historical causes; such as Providence or biology, and they are not unchangeable. Gramsci writes that historical laws must be understood in a historicist manner, that is, they exist to the extent that a climate exists which is 'organically alive and connected' in its development.[122] Although this classification of the sense of 'historicist' is obscure, one can surmise that Gramsci is thinking of the general conditions of existence of a historical bloc. The laws of history are in some sense emergent upon the activity of real empirical men and women and, above all, they depend on, among other things, the social relations that structure society. Such laws, then, are not independent of what human beings do, though they at the same time determine their activity, or at least, the general conditions under which they act. The constitution of a new historical bloc, which is equivalent to the constitution of new social relations, and hence of the emergence of new laws, is a process of transformation which begins in the old historical bloc, and one whose outcome depends on the structure of the old bloc and on the political organization of groups and classes determined by the old social relations.

Historicist laws, one can conclude, are neither 'metaphysical laws of determinism' nor 'general laws of causality'; they are the result of the historical process in which social relations constitute 'relatively "permanent" forces ... which act with a certain regularity and automatism'.[123] Long-term structures, rather than mere unstructured conjunctions of events, produce the automatism, or the 'generative mechanism', as Bhaskar calls it, which is said to be a tendential law. At one stroke, Gramsci rejected both the positivist conception of law and the speculative one, the former for its empiricism, the latter for its failure to oppose empiricism with a realist and truly immanent notion of history.

Let us now look at the more detailed notes which Gramsci devoted to the concept of historical laws. The sources of his reflections are Ricardo's conception of tendential laws on the one hand, and Marx's theory of the tendency of the rate of profit to fall on the other. Gramsci argues that the ground for a Marxist concept of tendential law is to be found in Ricardo's concept of the 'determined market' or 'determined relations of social forces in a determined structure of the productive apparatus'. The existence of a determined market reveals that 'certain decisive and perm-anent forces have emerged historically, forces whose operation presents itself with a certain "automatism" which allows a measure of "predictability"'. Once constituted, the relatively permanent forces are automatic because of 'their relative independence from individual will and arbitrary government intervention'.[124]

The concept of automatism, or structural determination of tendential laws, is founded on the conception of the long-term historical processes described earlier. However, the long duration is not in itself sufficient to distinguish the core of the historical process, for there are other processes, as we have seen, that can last centuries. Gramsci speaks of relations of production and permanent forces as the basis for the emergence of tendential laws, their long duration being but a sign of their vitality and importance. Obviously, natural processes exhibit the longest rhythm; apart from them, however, Gramsci notes that the least variable element in historical development is the ensemble of forces of production, which permits accurate measurement and allows the possibility of an 'experimental science of history'.[125] This is, Gramsci believes, the starting point for a Marxist theory of historical laws, a theory that must be carefully distinguished from statistical generalizations, which may be very useful for some practical purposes but hardly deserve to be taken as laws of historical facts.[126]

To distinguish generalizations of the kind he called statistical laws, and historical laws proper, Gramsci refers to the concept of 'determined abstraction'. A determined abstraction is not one that compares a manifold of individuals, but one that generalizes on the basis of 'determined historical categories'. For example, a Marxist conception of the *homo oeconomicus* is a determined abstraction because it does not take as a basis for comparison and generalization the biological or natural human being; instead, it takes human nature as historically concrete, or dated, not abstractly universal. Gramsci has little else to say about abstraction, but he seems to be struggling towards a theory of concepts not dissimilar in some respects from Marx's own exposition in the Introduction to the *Grundrisse*. The determined abstraction is Marx's concrete concept in that it is 'the unity of the diverse'[127] rather than a mere abstraction of similarities among a group of individual facts. The diversity of individual characters is, from the point of view of relevant historical concepts, or from the point of view of their function in the social system, a similarity. Hence, determined abstractions must be based on structural conceptions of the social whole, that is, on the complex of relations that confer a specific character on the individual elements or facts.

It is in this context that we must interpret Gramsci's assertion that 'the theory of history and politics is possible for although the facts are always individual and changeable in the flux of historical movement, the concepts can be theorized'.[128] The theoretical concepts of history, such as class, hegemony, etc., are the product of 'determined abstractions', they are what Marx called concrete concepts, concrete because they are 'the concentration of many determinations: and are the result of a "process of concentration"'.[129] German historicists, as we saw, emphasize the uniqueness of historical events, which entails the impossibility of applying the conception of scientific laws to historical research. Gramsci, in distinguishing different temporal dimensions and the different processes that underlie the occurrence of events, is able to avert the theoretical impoverishment that threatens narrative history, thus he is able to provide a more rigorous approach to the study of society. This approach would in fact be what is now called social history, or what Gramsci called integral history.[130] According to Kosellek, one of the basic characteristics of modern social history is precisely the concept that events and structures 'seem to have within the historical movement different temporal dimensions which should be studied separately by historical science'.[131] Although 'events and structures are interlocked with one another', they cannot be reduced to one another. Events in themselves are unique, and therefore difficult to forecast, while structures offer the possibility of predicting the general 'condition of possible events'.[132]

Tendential laws are obtained by isolating a 'certain number of elements, and hence neglecting counteracting forces'. Gramsci offers the law of the fall of the rate of profit as an example. The term 'tendential', he notes, has a historical, and not merely methodological, meaning; it indicates that the social process is a dialectical one, that is, a process characterized by fundamental contradictions.[133] Because of this, events are not uniquely determined by any given causal law, but rather by the conjunction of different and often opposed tendencies.

Absent from Gramsci's thought, at least in any formalized fashion, is a conception of the overall pattern of historical development from its beginnings to his own present. There are two reasons why this is so. First, any such overall pattern, if presented as an inevitable law of progress, could not have been accepted by Gramsci; he would have deemed it too speculative. In this regard, he indicates in a causal remark, that one ought not to think of slavery as a mechanically inevitable stage of historical progress.[134] Second, Gramsci sought to understand the case of the development of Italy since the middle of the seventeenth century. He was concerned with the conditions that led Italy to a fascist solution, hence with the weakness of the state forged by the

Risorgimento. And, above all, he was concerned with the political solution to Italy's problems or with the possibility of a fully democratic, socialist state. This means that, although from a methodological standpoint he posed questions of universal interest, with regard to substantive research, he was not focusing on the whole of history. As a consequence, he did not theorize any over-reaching laws of history, laws that, either as teleological tendencies necessitating a number of necessary stages, or tendencies that result from some property of society, inevitably impel history through a series of epochs. He did, as outlined above, suggest that the laws of one epoch are tied to those of the next, but no general hypothesis about history as a whole is advanced in the *Prison Notebooks*. It is perhaps no great exaggeration to assert, as Gallino does, that Gramsci held 'a completely modern concept of law',[135] although, as with most of his reflections, he only provided some general remarks about this concept.

Razeto and Misuraca have argued that there are two types of practical situations in history: (a) a situation where the masses are passive, and (b) one in which the masses emerge from passivity through political action. Thus, whereas in the first situation history appears as the fortuitous encounter of individual free acts, in the second situation human self-consciousness replaces the natural spontaneity of the first. Consequently, tendential laws govern the first type of situation, while self-awareness governs the second one.[136] This is, in general outline, the same argument advanced by Salamini. According to this theory, history would be regulated by the rhythm of the succession of passivity and self-awareness, for, as Razeto and Misuraca admit, one form of automatism gives rise to a new one.[137] The moments of self-awareness would thus punctuate the long-term cadences of passivity.

Gramsci, however, writes of the dichotomy between self-awareness and passivity only in relation to statistical generalizations, not with regard to historical laws. In fact, he argues that historical laws are not in opposition to group liberty, although they are in contrast with individual free will.[138] This suggests that, with respect to macro-determinism, that is, with the general operation of historical laws, Gramsci is a compatibilist, but with regard to macro-determinism, or with individual choice and action, he espouses incompatibilism. It must be emphasized that Gramsci's arguments on determinism concern history, not individual action, hence they offer little evidence on his view on freedom and determinism. This is a problem that does not seem to concern him at all. The laws of history, in so far as they apply to what he calls the 'common part' of individual men and women, determine the general social process, but not all the actions of individuals participating in this process. The will and the initiative of individuals, Gramsci maintains, must not be discarded.[139] However, he does not offer any theories as to whether this will and this initiative are, or are not, themselves determined by other factors or laws.

Furthermore, Gramsci's critique of economism, which he suggests is the theory that the economy uniquely determines all the other social processes, is mainly a rejection of mono-causal theories of history. This, however, does not entail indeterminism at the macro-level, for it would not be inconsistent for Gramsci to argue that the choices of individuals are determined by the conjunction of historical laws and other laws, such a psychological and biological ones. Since Gramsci does not discuss this issue, it is difficult to advance any hypothesis about his beliefs in the matter. What is clear, however, is that for Gramsci social groups are most free when they act according to the laws of history. If his language often suggests incompatibilism, it is because he is concerned with what he calls metaphysical or fatalist accounts of determinism. These, in effect, affirm that nothing one does can make any difference. Both libertarian indeterminists and compatibilists would agree on rejecting this claim.

Gramsci is primarily interested in clarifying an empirical connection, rather than a conceptual one, between metaphysical theories of determinism and dogmatism. He is concerned with situations in which a leader '"enlightened by reason" who has found the natural and infallible laws of historical evolution' disregards the actual possibilities inherent in reality. In this case, the belief in metaphysical determinism or fatalism becomes 'the only and dazzling intellectual motor' which may stimulate the emergence of autocratic rule.[140] As an example of this phenomenon, Gramsci refers to the thought of intellectuals such as Spirito and Volpicelli. They believe, he argues, that they are the guardians of a veritable truth 'while others . . . understand nothing'. Why they, and not others, possess the truth is never explained by them, Gramsci continues, but there is a 'hint of the means by which these two believe that the truth will have to be disseminated and become self-consciousness: it is the police (remember Gentile's speech at Palermo in '24)'.[141]

Historical laws are manifested through what Gramsci calls the 'homogeneous part' of individual wills. This homogeneous part is the automatism of the ensemble of social relations which, Gramsci seems to suggest, acts as a rule of behaviour, so that whatever the individual actors may do, the limits of their choices are governed by the rule.[142] The automatism is proposed by the structure of a society, and hence it is independent of the will of individuals. Its operation must be manifested in countless acts, repeated many times over, such as selling labour-power, or buying commodities in the market, etc. It must be noted that this manifestation or appearance of the structures and their tendential laws as rules of behaviour, established norms, etc., constitutes the basis for Gramsci's theory of the identity of politics and economics, and it highlights the importance of hegemonic institutions. We have, then, at the level of individual behaviour, rules which are more or less known and which have the character of conformism; they are the repetitive nature of the 'homogeneous part' of individual initiative. Sociological generalizations of these events, acts, etc., are found to be inadequate because they are mere descriptions which do not disclose the 'inner aspect', that is, the structures, such as social relations, and the resultant tendencies, such as the law of the fall of the rate of profit, which account for their existence.

The actors are more or less aware of the rules, even if it is only at the low level of recognizing their existence in their own practice. Becoming conscious of their origin, of their historicity and hence of the possibility of changing the underlying structures, is the process of the formation of organized social groups, a process analysed by Gramsci in terms of the concepts of situation and the relations of forces within each situation.

Given this, one can conclude that consciousness of the structures and of their automatism does not descend upon the masses from time to time; it is rather a process that is coterminous with the historical process itself, so that as the structural elements develop so does the consciousness of the masses. Gramsci's theory of hegemony, of popular culture, and of intellectuals. is the attempt to understand this complex, contradictory process. Historical necessity does not act behind, or beside, the actors themselves. True, structures are relatively independent of their will; but it is also true that, as Gramsci writes, 'historical necessity exists when there is an efficient and effective *premiss*, consciousness of which in men's minds has become operative, proposing concrete goals to the collective consciousness'.[143] This does not preclude the possibility of error, nor does it entail that society is transparent, so that full knowledge of it is readily acquired. As we saw, objectivity is a struggle, a process of deepening one's knowledge of reality, not an immediately given clear and distinct image of the world.

Linked to the problem of historical laws is the issue of prediction in history. On the one hand, Gramsci writes that if prediction in history is not possible, then 'irrationality cannot but dominate and any organization of men is anti-history'.[144] On the other hand, Gramsci rejects a theory of history based on a superficial imitation of the natural sciences which seek to predict by means of law-like regularities.[145] As Bhaskar has pointed out, prediction in history is not possible because of the very complexity of social processes which are open (that is, one cannot isolate a number of variables as is the case in controlled experiments).[146] The tendential laws of which Gramsci writes are obtained by means of what he calls determined abstractions. In reality the various contradictory forces that constitute social reality allow for little predictability of events. Furthermore, simple, discrete events, or individual acts, are in a sense unique, which makes them unpredictable in general. Structures, on the other hand, due to their duration and inherent tendencies, offer some possibility of prediction. Gramsci writes that to predict is to see the past and the present as movement, that is, it is 'to identify accurately the fundamental and permanent elements of the process'.[147] The permanent elements, in Gramsci's terms, are the structures; and since the structures form a contradictory whole, what can be predicted is 'the struggle, but not its concrete moments, which cannot but be the result of contrasting forces in continuous movement, not reducible to fixed quantities for in them quantity becomes quality'.[148]

Prediction, however, is not simply a 'scientific act of knowledge'; it is in reality 'the abstract expression of the effort made, the practical mode of creating a collective will'. These statements are sufficiently ambiguous and obscure to permit differing interpretations; the one advanced here does claim to exclude other possibilities. It does claim, however, that, given Gramsci's historicism, it makes sense. Economic forecasts, such as those elaborated by bank economists, government departments, industries, etc., are based on a general assumption which can be said to be eminently practical or to involve a definite socio-political practice. They are based on the assumption that the general structure of society will not change, however much consumer preferences, investment patterns, etc., may change. The practical character of this assumption lies in the fact that the institutions within which such forecasts are made, such as banks, government offices, and the like, are actively engaged in preserving the structure of society, so that the truth of their forecast is guaranteed, in part, by their involvement in securing the continuance of the present social system. Thus, although individual economists may think that they are engaged in a pure 'scientific act of knowing', the basic assumption they make is not only theoretical; it is a practical stance.

Similarly, one could say that forecasting a future with a different socio-economic structure, when it is not done idly or as a pastime, involves a practical stance, namely, that of guaranteeing or preparing the ground for the new socio-economic structure.

As Gramsci writes, in this case one '"foresees" to the extent that one acts, to the extent that one applies a voluntary effort and hence contributes concretely to create the result "foreseen"'.[149] It is important to notice that Gramsci does not claim that one creates the result out of one's prediction by means of a pure act of the will; he writes of contributing towards an end, which must be understood as the process of becoming conscious of the possibilities inherent in the structure and acting so as to bring them to realization. This suggests, as Texier has observed, that historical necessity and creativity or liberty are not in opposition; they form a unity. The failure to understand this unity leads to the opposition between empty, arbitrary, and individual freedom, on the one hand, and mechanical determinism, on the other.[150]

It might be objected that not all predictions made by those who want to change the social system contain, as an assumption, this practical stance. For instance, in order to overthrow the present state of society at some future date, it is necessary to anticipate, that is, to predict as far as possible its state at that date; this would not imply that those who make such predictions are determined to preserve the present *status quo*. Nevertheless, theirs is a practical stance. Gramsci's theory may not be clear enough, or it may not be satisfactory in many respects; there is no need, however, to interpret it as a voluntarist conception of history, a conception according to which willing is a sufficient condition for the realization of desired goals.

Gramsci's conception of historical laws, causality, and prediction set him apart from both Croce and the German historicists, who in general argued against the notions of historical laws, causality, and prediction, and for whom the inner aspect of history was spiritual, generally identified with freedom and not historical necessity as it is for Gramsci. The issue that still remains to be solved is that of the unity of scientific method. As we have seen, Gramsci suggests that each science has its own method,[151] which would indicate that rather than two general methods, one for the sciences of nature and one for the social sciences, there would be as many different methods as scientific disciplines. If this is true, Gramsci's historicism could easily lead to epistemological anarchism with no general rules for seeking and ascertaining truth. A close reading of the *Prison Notebooks*, however, produces a more satisfactory approach to this problem, although it does not resolve it completely.

To begin with, when Gramsci writes of method he has far more in mind than the logic of explanation which Hempel and others offer as the only scientific method. There are in the *Prison Notebooks* a number of principles or criteria said to be methodological, which leave little doubt that, for Gramsci, method is more than logic or a procedure, as it involves concepts and principles that can be considered constitutive of the subject matter itself, that is, ontological principles. A few examples will suffice to clarify this issue.

The distinction between domination and intellectual and moral leadership is presented by Gramsci as a 'methodological criterion on which our study must be based'.[152] He also refers to the principles that 'an independent intellectual class does not exist, but any social group has its own order of intellectuals', as a 'criterion of historico-political research' which appears to be methodologically consistent.[153] Finally, he puts forth as a methodological criterion the principle that 'the historical unity of the

111

leading classes takes place in the state, and their history is essentially the history of states and of groups of states'.[154] From these instances it can be concluded that at least some methodological principles are suggestions for classifying documentary evidence as well as for relating different types of phenomena. In other words, some methodological principles suggest appropriate concepts about what exists as well as explanatory schemas about the causal or other links between the objects thus conceptualized. By calling these principles methodological, Gramsci seems to suggest that they are to be regarded as tentative, always liable to be found inappropriate, and hence that they must never be uncritically superimposed on reality.

Given the broad meaning of 'methodological', it is not so odd that Gramsci should call for a distinct method for each discipline. For if we were to take a concept from physics, for instance gravitation, and attempt to apply it to sociology, it would be difficult to see what it could actually mean in the case of societies. At most, it would be a metaphor for the processes that keep societies unified; but it would not be of great service in describing and explaining that process. On the other hand, concepts such as mode of production or hegemony seem to be of far greater service and are methodologically far more appropriate for explaining social reality. This is not to deny completely that a scientific theory can suggest hypotheses for fields of research other than its own. In this regard Gramsci points out that Cuvier's principle 'of correlation among single organic parts of a body' seems to be useful in the study of society, but it must be understood, he adds, that 'for past history, the principle of correlation (or that of analogy) cannot take the place of the document'.[155]

It has already been noted that Gramsci thinks that the economic structure of society can be the object of an experimental science in so far as it is the more permanent, as well as exactly measurable, element in a social whole.[156] There is no clarification, however, of what 'experimental science' might concretely mean when applied to history. It is clear, however, that, as Marx pointed out, it cannot really mean experimental, for no experiments are possible in social science; instead 'the force of abstraction' must replace experiments,[157] that is, the method cannot be really experimental, it must rely on what Gramsci called 'determined abstraction'.

It is with these considerations in mind that one must read Gramsci's statements that 'there is not a science *par excellence*, there is not a method *par excellence*, a "method in itself"',[158] or that it is an error to think that a method that has been successful in one type of research will be useful in another field; or that each science develops its own method. There is nothing very strange in these statements, for they do not imply that there is a rationality for physics and another rationality for biology, and so on. For, in reality, Gramsci claims that, despite the differences among the sciences, differences that stem from the distinct characteristics of their subject matter, 'there are general criteria which can be said to constitute the critical consciousness of any scientist'.[159] One such general principle that Gramsci thinks is part of any distinct method, 'consists in its being "adequate to the end"'. To which he adds that 'the most generic and universal methodology is none other than formal or mathematical logic'.[160] Since social phenomena are dialectical, the conclusion we can reach is that for Gramsci formal logic and dialectics are not incompatible. The main point is, however, that there are universal methodological criteria.

We have already seen that the concepts of causality, law, and necessity is not rejected by Gramsci, provided these basic scientific concepts are properly applied to the complexities of social processes. These general concepts are elements of the most general scientific methodology, which, together with formal logic, belong to the 'collection of abstract instruments of thought that have been discovered, purified, and refined through the history of philosophy and culture'.[161] What Gramsci objects to is the uncritical application of these general methodological concepts to any subject matter without due regard to the actual constitution of that subject matter.

Some implications of Gramsci's position need to be stressed. Clearly, he argues for a historiography that explains phenomena in terms of the 'causal nexus'. Since this expression arises in the context of explaining why a hegemonic principle in opposition to another is capable of overcoming this opposition, Gramsci implies that the relations between the various levels in a social whole are causal, not merely isomorphic. This sets him apart from Kantian models of society. A transcendental Kantian social science would be one in which a set of transcendental categories would structure all social phenomena, as they would be manifestations of the human mind. An empirical variation of this conception would substitute the structure of the brain, or some such concept, for the transcendental categories. In both cases, the same set of structures would be manifested in myths, economic relations, etc. As Runciman has pointed out, both Lévi-Strauss and Dilthey can be said to be Kantian despite some differences in some areas of their thought.[162] The conclusion that can be drawn from this is that, despite Gramsci's use of the terms structure and function, he cannot be said to be a structuralist. For him, isomorphic relations, like statistical generalizations, are facts that need explanation. The 'meaning' that originates in the relationship between the parts and whole in Dilthey, and to a certain extent in discourse theory, involves, for Gramsci, as it does for Marx, the underlying causal nexus. In order to study them, Gramsci proposed the concept of situation, which is a concept of the causal interrelationship between temporal processes of different durations.

The Kantian approach to the study of society assumes the existence of a fixed human nature, either as a set of transcendental categories of thought and action, or as a set of characteristics of the brain. This means that the ultimate explanation for society and for history remains outside history. Gramsci, rightly or wrongly, insists on producing historical explanations. Their foundation is his conception of human nature as the ensemble of social relations, and his conception of history in general as an interchange between nature, socialized as forces of production, and human beings. In this interchange nothing is fixed: nature is never taken as a whole in itself, but as a means to reproduce life, hence as socialized or historicized nature. Human beings are also socio-historical products. Although the biological determinants of human nature cannot be dismissed, they merely provide the general problem of survival, or general constraints to action. The solution, the real intercourse of humanity and nature, is a historical process. For this reason, a combination of transcendental or biological structures can never completely account for history and for society.

We must then conclude that Gramsci's historicism is not a denial of the concepts of historical causality and laws, but merely an attempt to produce a conception of them that is suited to the complexities of the historical process and that takes account of the open character of that process. Furthermore, he seeks to give explanations for social phenomena that avoid reference to ahistorical entities, be they metaphysical laws, transcendental categories, or empirical constructions about the nature of the brain. Ultimately, historicism means precisely this: that all explanations of social phenomena should be based on strictly historical, or what he sometimes calls immanent, causes.

Realism

A few brief comments will suffice to complement previous arguments regarding Gramsci's realism. Again, Gramsci's critique of sociology will be the starting point for an elucidation of the kind of realism that seems to be most consistent with his theories.

In a few instances, Gramsci's objections to what he called sociology can be seen to stem from his realism, and thus they furnish further evidence for my interpretation of his historicism. He writes that Michels' classification of political parties is based on generic and external characters. He adds, significantly, that the sociological types developed by Michels 'do not correspond to the concrete fact'.[163] Taking into consideration what I have suggested above about Gramsci's use of the distinction interior/exterior in history, it can be concluded that not only must sociological concepts correspond to concrete facts, but they cannot remain descriptive of superficial characteristics. Concepts, of course, are not true or false; nevertheless, their meaning must be related to the facts, it must be an adequate 'reproduction of the concrete by way of thought', to use Marx's expression in the *Grundrisse.*[164]

It is fashionable to espouse theories of meaning that disregard, or even call into question the external reference of language. For these theories, meaning is constituted within a system of intra-linguistic references, in what can be thought to be variants of Wittgenstein's language games. Apart from the undeniable merits of such theories, especially with respect to the interpretation of literary texts, the fact that for them language tends to be a myth or a metaphor with nothing beyond itself makes them inadequate for scientific theories that claim to appropriate the real in thought. For some of these theories of language, one system of signs may be as appropriate as another with respect to the object, because the object is linguistically constituted. In Gramsci's terms, however, scientific concepts must ultimately be defensible in terms of an extra-discursive reality. This entails a rejection of what S. James has called '*holism of form*', which is 'the view that each term owes its meaning to its relations with the others, so that they are all more or less closely interdefined, and a change in the meaning of one will have repercussions for the rest'.[165]

That the internal relations of a language are important is not denied; nor does Gramsci reject the view that language is often laden with metaphors, myths, images that together constitute part of common sense, the mentality of a society which often fogs the reference-relation of scientific as well as everyday concepts. These images can be very powerful; Gramsci was certainly aware of the philosophy, or general conception of the world, contained in language itself.[166] There are, furthermore, conditions of knowledge that also diminish the adequacy of scientific concepts. Nevertheless, such concepts are discovered, refined, and purified through the history of culture; they are the object of the 'struggle for objectivity', which means that they must not only be made internally consistent, or intra-linguistically adequate and meaningful, but also adequate for describing what is not discursive. Gramsci's historicism, as we saw in Chapter One, emphasized the social process of scientific discovery and the social function of science, without denying either the independent existence of reality or the correspondence theory of truth. The same theory can be applied to language. Hence, to assert that meaning, that language, is a historical production, does not entail a denial of the external reference of language.

Although Gramsci devotes notebook No. 29 to the study of grammar, he does not discuss the question of meaning. There is today a vast literature on meaning and reference which would challenge Gramsci's scant remarks on the issue. Nevertheless, his theory of meaning, simple as it may be, is in keeping with his realist historicism. This interpretation of Gramsci's historicism avoids the danger of relativism; for, to use Bhaskar's elaboration of the problem, in respecting 'a distinction between the sense and the reference of propositions, while insisting that all speech acts are made in historical time', we accept the 'correct thesis of the *epistemic relativity*', while denying 'the incorrect thesis of *judgemental relativism*'.[167] And this is precisely the sense of Gramsci's historicism: it calls for the referential adequacy of concepts, for a correspondence theory of truth, while he admits that language and knowledge are historical products. It must be stressed that Gramsci's historicism, despite his assertion to the contrary, is not an absolute historicism, but an open one.

This open character of Gramsci's historicism has already been observed by Melchiorre who, interested in the possibility of a dialogue between Marxism and Christianity, argues that absolute or pure historicism cannot guarantee adequate understanding of history, and that Gramsci's historicism finds its 'dynamism precisely where it ceases to be absolute'.[168] For Melchiorre, however, the understanding of history ultimately comes from a transcendent 'idea-limit', which is absolute and superior to temporal multiplicity. The idea which illuminates the historical process is an ethical principle, socialism. In Melchiorre's model, then, history is explained by a limit which may never be completely obtained, but which draws the historical process forward.[169] Moral, as well as teleological transcendence marks, for Melchiorre, the limits of Gramsci's historicism. It does not appear plausible that Gramsci would accept this interpretation. Nevertheless, its merit rests on the question it poses regarding the intelligibility or, more precisely, the value of knowledge in a pure historicist conception. This question runs deep in the *Prison Notebooks*; it hardly ever comes to the surface but it seems to guide Gramsci's thought at crucial junctures.

Closely connected to realism and meaning is the question of values. As we saw in Chapter One, both the German historical school and Croce placed values at the core of the historical process. Their conception of values, however, raises the questions both about the origins and objectivity of value. German historians thought that they could avoid relativism by positing an extra-historical world of values, a transcendent sphere of reality which Gramsci rejects. We must face the possibility, then, that even if Gramsci does not maintain general judgmental relativism, he may still espouse moral relativism. In fact, it is plausible that his rejection of transcendent moral values may lead to a conventionalist view of ethical systems and with it to the view that all ethical systems are equally valid. For our purposes it will suffice to outline the main lines of argument that can be drawn from the *Prison Notebooks*.

The first point that Gramsci makes in defence of historicism is that relativism affects other moral theories as well. As an example, Gramsci points out that Kant's categorical imperative is not free from relativism. For, while the principle may be formally universal, it will differ in its application from culture to culture, depending on what is believed to be natural or universal. Kant's principle thus 'does not surpass a given climate, with all its moral superstitions and its barbaric customs'. It seems, then, Gramsci adds, that the right question to ask is not about the changeability of moral beliefs, but about their capacity to last, that is, their character as organic or long-term phenomena.[170] Although he does not explicitly make the connection at this point, it is evident that the rationality or justification of a moral system is to be conceived in terms of its links to the structural elements of a society. The point Gramsci is trying to make is that in real terms, that is, in terms of the historical record, ethical systems change, that they change with ideas about the nature of human beings, which in turn are an expression of the ensemble of social relations. Morality, in short, changes with the changes in social relations and, as a consequence, any principle, such as Kant's categorical imperative, that claims to be universal will always be limited in practice by the existing moral climate. Because of this, Gramsci adds, Kant's formula 'can be regarded as a truism, since it is difficult to find any one who does not act in the belief that, in the conditions in which he finds himself, everyone else would act in the same way'.[171]

This, although perhaps not completely satisfactory as a critique of Kant, points to a conception of ethics that underlies Gramsci's thought. It seems that in the same way that the use of electrical energy must be preceded by the discovery and the understanding of this form of energy as well as by the infrastructure necessary for its exploitation, an ethical principle must first emerge in the consciousness of men and women before it can be effective in any manner. The difference is that whereas electricity is independent of history, ethics is not, for it contains the basic rules for communal life,[172] and as these rules depend on the existence of such life, their type depends on the kind of community that has evolved in the course of history. This, of course, is first of all a rejection of the view that there are absolute moral values in the sense that there is a moral substance or a God that dictates rules of behaviour. It does not rule out, however, that there may be ethical principles whose long duration is coterminous with the existence of communities, and which can be thought to be necessary conditions for the existence of communities. Whether these rules can be apprehended *a priori*, as Kant argues, or historically is another question, one that Gramsci does not approach; nevertheless, Gramsci's preference for the historical approach would clearly indicate that such rules are known through historical experience.

Could one argue, however, that strict equality and democracy are good moral norms of universal value? It would seem that if these principles are good today they should be equally good at any time, anywhere. In an abstract sense, this may be so. But in an abstract sense also, electrical energy is good anywhere, anytime, assuming of course that it is good. However, without the technical knowledge and the socio-economic structure that the production and use of electricity requires, it would be of no use to a feudal society. In fact, it is inconceivable to think of a feudal society, just as it existed historically, with an electrical plant. Similarly, strict equality and democracy would have been useless principles in a type of society where the ensemble of social relations had not opened up, so to speak, the real possibility of equality and democracy.

I think that these considerations help to understand Gramsci's thinking on ethics, as well as his insistence that a sound base for a Marxist theory of ethics is to be found in Marx's principle that no society sets itself problems for whose solutions the conditions do not yet exist. The emergence of ethical principles is thus linked to the existence of problems whose solutions require new forms of communal life. With the existence of the conditions, the solution '*becomes* "duty", and the "will" *becomes* free'.[173]

The origin of ethical principles lies, according to this theory, in the ensemble of social relations. The long-term process that accounts for the development of contradictions, as well as for consciousness of these contradictions, constitutes the causal ground for the emergence of new ethical principles, consciousness of which first develops within a group whose expansion tends to universalize the new ethical principles. As we saw earlier, historical necessity becomes effective when there is consciousness of the material conditions that are, so to speak, the backbone of such necessity. Similarly, the consciousness of the existence of the conditions for the solution of social problems imposes a new duty. From this point on, a historical process takes place which can be defined as a struggle of hegemonies, or, as we saw earlier, the struggle between different forms of conformism. It is at this level that consciousness and ethical principles become effective historical forces for change. A full analysis of this process is not necessary at this juncture. The point we are pursuing concerns the historical character of Gramsci's ethical theory. Without communal life, values would not exist. The existence of moral values is a feature of societies; they are not embedded in the fabric of nature. They are not, however, dependent on the will of individuals. It is social relations which produce principles of right action. For Gramsci, morals originate in material life. In this respect, his theory of ethics is consistent with his theory of the origin of philosophical problems, according to which it is history, not philosophy itself, which produces philosophical problems.[174]

With this theory the question of the relative value of different ethical systems becomes meaningless. Aside from the difficulty of comparing value-systems without assuming a standard set of values, which of course casts doubt on the validity of the comparison, value systems can be adequate only to the social system of which they are a part. Comparing values is thus transformed into the task of comparing social systems, for rules of conduct are dependent upon the development of the material forces of production. At this level of complexity, however, there is an element that permits a more or less exact measure and comparison, and that is the development of material forces of production and the well-being of individuals. The explanation of the existence of societies with different moral values is hence the problem of elucidating their 'historical necessity', or the objectivity of their rules of communal behaviour.[175] Although Gramsci does not explicitly assert it, it is nevertheless suggested that moral rules are adequate or right to the extent that they further the well-being of all human beings. This would indicate that Gramsci espouses a consequentialist theory of ethics which would be most consistent with the denial of the existence of any spiritual, divine, or metaphysical moral order.

Finally, on the question of the objectivity of moral values, Gramsci maintains that values are objective to the extent that they 'correspond to historical necessity'; consciousness of moral principles, however, is not universal or objective to the extent that a contradictory ensemble of social relations results in contradictory forms of consciousness.[176] The unification of humanity is a necessary condition for the universal acceptance of objective moral principles.

A presupposition of Gramsci's consequentialism is that moral principles must apply universally. Put in other terms, Gramsci accepts some unspecified principle of the equality of all men and women. However, his thought is directed to the 'empirical origin' of the principle of equality. He argues that, at the level of common sense, the saying 'we are all born naked', expresses what biology maintains about the '"natural", that is, psycho-physical equality of all the individual elements of the human race'. Similarly, the philosophical principle that we are all endowed with the faculty of reason, expresses the basic principle of equality.[177] This 'empirical origin', however, does not provide a sufficient explanation, the kind that Gramsci would consider a historical one, of the origin of this principle, nor does it provide a justification for it, for, as Gramsci concedes, 'the environment does not justify but only "explains" the behaviour of individuals'.[178] Gramsci does not advance any hypothesis either as historical explanation or as justification of equality. In the end, and as a complement to his consequentialism, Gramsci seems to espouse some form of deontological theory about the dignity of all human beings, and hence their moral equality. This is perhaps the sense of his apparent approval of the democratic character of both materialist and idealist philosophies; the former because they emphasize biological equality, the latter because they refer to reason as a common faculty of all individuals.[179]

Gramsci's theory of ethics, as well as his remarks on consciousness generally, strongly suggest that he did not hold any theory of a transcendent sphere of being. All that exists, he maintains, is either natural or historical. Furthermore, in spite of his slips into forms of idealism in which nature would exist as part of human history and not independently of it, Gramsci's realism in general asserts the existence of the object of knowledge independent of the knowing subject, as well as the existence of nature independent of human history. This is, at any rate, the sense of his assertions that 'the various physical properties (chemical, mechanical, etc.) of matter' constitute matter itself and that 'as an abstract natural force, electricity existed even before it was reduced to a productive force',[180] as well as other statements

121

already cited. It is true that he claims that the subject matter of historical materialism is not nature, or ideas, in the abstract, but as they exert an influence on the historical process. This is a historical judgement, not an epistemological one.

Benton has defined as 'materialist' a theory of knowledge that fulfils the following conditions:

1. it recognises the reality of the object of knowledge, independent of the 'knowing subject', the process of production of the knowledge, and the knowledge itself;
2. adequacy to the object of knowledge is the ultimate standard by which the cognitive status of thought is to be assessed;
3. it recognises the existence of 'thought', 'ideas', 'knowledge' as realities in their own right;
4. it theorises those realities as not *sui generis* but as the result of underlying causal mechanisms.[181]

If this is supplemented with the condition that nothing exists except nature and society, so that, as with Gramsci, no transcendent sphere of being, such as spirit, Providence, etc., is admitted, we can conclude that Gramsci's theory is a materialist one. For the distinction between ontological objectivity and epistemological objectivity allows Gramsci to avoid judgemental relativism while maintaining epistemic relativity. This enables him to apprehend the historicity of knowledge, the social process of the production of consciousness in general, including ethics, while accepting the independent reality of the object of knowledge. This satisfies criterion number one.

In his theory of scientific concepts, as well as his acceptance of the correspondence theory of truth, Gramsci's theory meets criterion number two.

The recognition of the effectiveness of consciousness of historical necessity, his effort to understand the function of superstructures, as well as his theory of the different durations of structures, mentalities, etc., entail the fulfilment of criterion number three.

Finally, inasmuch as the ensemble of social relations, or history itself, poses the problems philosophy must solve, and, furthermore, because ethical principles originate in material life, it can be concluded that Gramsci's theory of consciousness in general, and of knowledge in particular, meets criterion number four.

It is important to stress that Gramsci's historicism is not only realist, for Hegel's philosophy is also realist, but also materialist, for he disowns any theory of consciousness or reason as an uncaused entity. It is in communal life, in the attempt to solve social problems, that consciousness is born. This does not signify that consciousness is a mere epiphenomenon, or that it is nothing but material life. It has its function and its effectiveness within the limits of historical necessity.

The conclusion that we must reach is that Gramsci's philosophy is a historicist realism. What remains to be done now is to explain the qualification 'historicist'. We have already seen, in the previous discussion of transience, the importance of the passage of time for a correct understanding of social phenomena; the reason, simply put, is that the character of social phenomena is revealed by their consequences as well as their antecedents or their intrinsic features. The problem for a realist conception of scientific concepts and theories is to determine the relations and objects to which they will refer and which they will explain. Gramsci's historicist realism is the first step towards a solution to these problems. Put succinctly, the object to which a concept refers, such as 'class', is not to be taken as an unchangeable object existing in itself at any point in time; rather, that object is a history, and the concept is an attempt to capture the underlying reality of a cluster of phenomena, forms of behaviour, etc., over a period of time. In short, historiographical concepts denote processes rather than things. To paraphrase E. P. Thompson's *The Making of the English Working Class*, historiographical concepts refer to entities in the making rather than to fully constituted things. Historicism is, then, not a denial of the external reference of concepts, nor a rejection of the correspondence theory of truth; it is, rather, an adaptation of these theories to historical objects, that is, objects whose full identity is revealed not through their intrinsic characteristics at any point in time, but through their development in a temporal process. Gramsci's conception of historical time can now be seen as serving two purposes: first, it draws our attention to the different temporal scopes to which concepts and theories will apply, and hence it suggests a theory about the nature of historical concepts and of historical explanation; second, it seeks to establish a general theory of historical causality, that is, of the generative mechanisms of different duration whose coincidence produces historical effects. These are the main conceptual tools advanced by Gramsci for a concrete analysis of concrete situations.

Humanism

The foregoing account of Gramsci's historicism may appear to call in question his definition of historicism as humanism. In particular, the emphasis on the long-term approach to the study of society, of structures, functions, etc., may be thought to deny any humanist thesis about the nature and dynamic force of history; for it seems to give more importance to the conditions under which decisions and actions take place than to the elements of freedom and human creation that are central to a humanist approach. On the other hand, Gramsci's conception of historical necessity requires both the existence of a set of objective conditions and consciousness of them, as well as of the existing possibilities for action. In other words, Gramsci does not deny either the determining effect of structural conditions nor the decisive role of politics, that is, organized action.

Gramsci is neither a structuralist nor a humanist; for he does not write of individuals as carriers of structures or of history as a process without a subject; nor does he, on the other hand, think of history as a process of individual wills forging the emergence of greater happiness, or less alienation, or more freedom. The importance of organized will, as Gramsci refers to political organizations, stems not merely from the obvious fact that human will has a function in history, but from the view that history is the result of a confrontation of organized wills, or conformisms, rather than the result of a unified general will. It seems, then, that the problem with the sociology Gramsci refers to is that it lacks a dialectical approach to society, that is, it lacks any understanding of the complex process of struggle of hegemonic forces.

Gramsci's humanism, then, can best be described as the view that 'history is a continuous struggle of individuals and of groups to change society'.[182] It is this basic principle that seems to guarantee the earthliness and worldliness that characterize his humanism,[183] for it understands history as an earthly process, not merely a moral one. Gramsci's humanism is little more than the recognition that it is not Providence, nor a cosmic or metaphysical law of evolution that can produce, and explain, history.[184] Historical necessity emerges from given structures, but these would not exist unless human beings were practically engaged in transforming the world. Little else can be said, except that Gramsci does not affirm anywhere that the struggle to transform society is without conditions. For the very word used, namely struggle, as well as the contradictions in the struggles, groups or forces, but also individuals, suppose an array of objective conditions which Gramsci sometimes refers to as 'the situation'. Among those contradictions, there are those responsible for the definition of the forces, which is itself the result of the historical process.

One can thus conclude that Gramsci's humanism is a warning against two kinds of excess. First, it is a warning against speculative thought which seeks to explain history by appealing to some deity, or Providence, or otherwise unearthly entity. The ethical and cultural values associated with these entities are not *sui generis*, they do not originate or exist on their own; they are predicates of human existence, that is, they describe real men and women, their actions, organizations, and institutions. In this context we should remember that Gramsci's Anti-Croce is the denial that the predicate, be it liberty, equality, or whatever, is the subject of history.

Second, it is a warning against the abuse of theoretical categories, for in dealing with history ultimately we are dealing with human material, and that means that we are not only dealing with the ways in which real men and women are conditioned to act according to structural determinants, but also how they react upon such conditions, and how they experience the process. Whether history is a process with or without a subject is the wrong question to ask for it is hardly conducive to a deeper understanding of history. The danger that the abuse of theory poses is that of taking theoretical categories as speculative philosophers tend to take their concepts; in both cases real empirical women and men play their assigned roles in a drama that happens to them. This, Gramsci suggests, forgets that the social sciences are political, that is, they are engaged in predicting the future because they have a practical stake in that future. Prediction in history, as we saw, is a practical act, for it requires the active participation of the social scientist in bringing about the predicted outcome. It is here that the basis for the unity of theory and practice is to be found. As Badaloni has observed, absolute historicism signifies 'a total reappropriation by the masses of science separated from politics' which ceases to be a technique of domination, as sociology is thought to be by Gramsci.[185] Science and politics, theory and practice, reappropriated by the masses in the struggle to change society, in the attempt, that is, to organize an effective collective will which will materialize the possibilities inherent in the present.

Ultimately, then, Gramsci's historicism does not cease to conceive historiography as basically political. As we saw earlier, the idols of politics, individuals, and narrative dominated earlier historicist thinking. With the new historiography, in particular the *Annales* school, politics ceased to hold a prominent place in historiography. However, while attempting to develop a deep understanding of history as a whole, Gramsci did not dethrone politics. For him, the focus of historical investigation is politics in a broad sense, because it is concerned with unearthing the long-term process that explains the present as well as the possibilities of the future. But whereas for the old historicism, politics meant the actions of kings, politicians, etc., for Gramsci politics becomes synonymous with the organized attempt to change society. We witness, then, a change from the emphasis on politics in the traditional sense, stressing the subject matter of history, to politics, in the broad sense, as the interest that guides the committed intellectual. In this attempt, the future will provide the best basis for understanding the present; but it is a future whose reality depends on the historicity, on the realism and the rationality, of our actions in the present.

A word of caution is, however, necessary especially because Gramsci is not very clear on the role of intentionality in history. As Sánchez Vázquez has pointed out, substituting the teleology of human intentionality for that of Providence does not provide an adequate foundation for understanding history. For the outcome of history must either be thought to coincide with the intentions of human beings, which the historical record shows mostly not to be the case, or there must be an *a priori* goal that underlies all their actions,[186] which would contradict Gramsci's emphasis on the historicity of human nature, and hence, the historicity of intentions as well as his denial of any transcendent mind or will.

Although Gramsci's humanism at its worst seems to imply that historical phenomena occur as intended, one must not forget that his conception of history as struggle among opposing forces implies that the result of the clash of wills may not coincide with the intentions or desires of any individual or group. Furthermore, the rationality of action does not depend on a presumed content of reason or a dialectic of consciousness, for Gramsci precisely stresses the dependence of consciousness on material conditions and defines rationality as historical necessity.

In conclusion, Gramsci's definition of historicism as humanism is designed to accomplish two tasks: first, it emphasizes the subjective element in historical necessity, understood as organized politics; second, it underscores the practical significance of knowledge about society. Thus, while emphasizing an integral historiography, Gramsci does not allow us to neglect the importance of politics. The primacy of politics means in effect that the study of society has a practical significance, for the correct identification of the trends of the present is a necessary condition for changing the world. Politics is not the sole subject of historiography; it is the light that illuminates the historian's work.

CONCLUSION

We can now draw some general conclusions about the nature of Gramsci's historicism. First, Gramsci's historicism is not a theory about the relative, because historical, character of all truths or values. In so far as it is a theory of knowledge, it seeks to understand the origin as well as the function of ideas in the historical process. This is done by considering all human activity as forming a single process, so that the distinctions between ideal activities and material ones, or between subjective and objective processes, superstructures and structures, is an analytic one, not an organic one.[187] In other words, although we can separate these various activities in thought, and furthermore, we can discover inherent properties and tendencies in each, they not only coexist but cannot exist separately.

The consequence of this conception of historical reality and of the origin and function of ideas is that, as Rodríguez-Aguilera has pointed out, 'history has a totalizing character'.[188] This character of Gramsci's historicism can be, and has been, interpreted to mean that all truth is exclusively dependent on the historical conditions of its production. Furthermore, in so far as for Gramsci the historical process is centred on the class struggle, truth can be seen as a function of historically progressive classes. This has been interpreted in a Husserlian fashion by Nemeth, for whom reality is a class-centred construction; Salamini has deduced the subjective idealist proposition that nothing exists outside history. In short, Gramsci's statement that Marxism is an absolute historicism has been immediately thought to mean some form of Crocean historicism, only that the hegemony of a class takes the place of the concept of liberty or the great intellectuals.

Our analysis of Gramsci's notes points to a different interpretation. On this interpretation, we avoid equating absolute historicism with Croce's philosophy, as it is demanded by Gramsci's own statement that Marxism is an absolute historicism, that is, one of a kind, not necessarily Croce's. As we have seen, Gramsci uses 'historicism' in four senses, which have been identified with reference to transience, historical necessity, realism, and humanism. These form the basis of several interrelated theses, central to which is Gramsci's conception of transience.

The central thesis of Gramsci's historicism is that social phenomena are processes whose identification and appropriate description is adequate only when their consequences are known. Hence, the scientific study of social phenomena requires the long-term view or historical method. Different types of phenomena tend to develop at different rhythms, and in constructing a complex situation, that is, the convergence of various temporal processes, care must be taken to assign to each of them its proper causal significance.

The types of relations or structures that have a long-term life or relative permanence provide the basis for historical laws. However, these laws cannot be reduced to regularities that hold between types of events; such regularities are in reality the effect of causal mechanisms, which Gramsci generally, but not exclusively, identifies with social relations of production. In short, for Gramsci historical laws are not descriptions of regularities; rather, they identify the generative mechanisms of different durations that together account for the historical process. Historical necessity is the concurrence of both objective and subjective premises that result in a given event or phenomenon. Furthermore, historical laws are tendencies that can be identified by isolating certain aspects of the social process. In reality, history is an open process where a number of contradictory tendencies produce events that are not always predictable, though the general conditions of the process are rational, that is, predictable.

Perhaps the most controversial aspect of Gramsci's historicism is his realism. One must admit that there are many passages in the *Prison Notebooks* which can be clearly characterized as subjective idealist. Nevertheless, other passages point to philosophical realism and, on balance, they seem to predominate in Gramsci's thought. Also, the tone of his historical and political writings and his conception of reason are more consistent with realism than with idealism. On this basis it is clear that Gramsci is a realist; after all, he uses the term 'historicist' as synonymous with 'realist' in a number of passages. Given this conclusion, it is evident that those commentators who propose a phenomenological or an idealist subjectivist interpretation of the *Prison Notebooks* must have misinterpreted some aspect of Gramsci's work.

In the view of some of his interpreters, Gramsci's absolute historicism cannot but mean that all truth is a function of its historical origin and function; hence, historicism and the correspondence theory of truth are incompatible. This apparent difficulty can be solved by drawing a distinction between ontological objectivity and epistemological objectivity, a distinction, I admit, not explicitly formulated by Gramsci but certainly necessitated by the historicism he seeks to develop. Gramsci's historicism thus claims that all knowledge is a historical production and fulfils a social function; furthermore, there are limits to our capacity to discover truth, some of them due to the historicity of knowledge. Thus, full epistemological objectivity may never be achieved; in this sense, knowledge is relative to the conditions of its production. However, this limitation of epistemological objectivity and its consequent epistemic relativism do not entail the denial of ontological objectivity, or judgmental relativism. There is, then, the need for a standard of truth that is independent of the historicity of knowledge, and this is provided by the correspondence theory of truth, as well as by the referential meaning of concepts in what concerns the theory of language.

The theory of the transience of social objects has, however, an important effect on the application of the correspondence theory of truth. Because the objects that social science studies are only completely known when their consequences are exhausted, the reference of a theory or a concept cannot always be given in a slice of time. At least some social concepts and theories have as a reference a temporal process. For this reason Gramsci often refers to fundamental historiographical concepts and theories as methodological principles. Thus, they have a double function: on the one hand they serve as guides to the historian in collecting and ordering data, and framing explanations and revealing patterns; on the other hand, they are intended as referring to already existing phenomena. It must be reiterated that their reference ranges over a temporal manifold of events.

It seems obvious then that Gramsci's absolute historicism is not so absolute or, at least, it is not absolute in the Crocean sense, for the very intelligibility and value of knowledge depend on the possibility of a standard of truth which is not subject to historicity. Gramsci's historicism is absolute not in the sense of holding that all truth is relative to its historical conditions and function, but in the sense of holding that to explain history no extra-historical entities, other than geographical conditions, are necessary. In this sense, Gramsci's absolute historicism is a critique of Croce as well as of the German historical school, for they had to refer to an eternal ideal history, an ever-present metaphysical reality, in order to explain the historical process. Gramsci's criticism is simply that their historicism was not absolute in that it appealed to extra-historical forces and entities. Also, Gramsci's absolute historicism is a rejection of certain forms of naturalism, prevalent among some Italian positivist sociologists, for whom such phenomena as the backwardness of the Italian south were accounted for by appealing to the natural inferiority of southern people. Hence, Gramsci rejects not only metaphysical entities but also psychologism and any form of biological or physical reductionism as a basis for explaining historical development. The explanation of history, as of social phenomena in general, must have recourse only to historical phenomena, as presented in the available evidence: this is the sense of 'absolute' in Gramsci's historicism, as well as the sense of 'immanentism' found in the *Prison Notebooks*.

It is this sense of 'absolute' that gives us a clue to the meaning of 'humanism' in Gramsci's thought. In the few passages where

Gramsci characterizes Marxism as absolute historicism or absolute humanism, it is clear that the intended sense is related to the earthliness and worldliness of thought. If 'humanism' means anything, then, it must mean the view that social phenomena exist because human beings engage in certain activities which result in the establishment of definite relations with nature and among themselves. To explain history one must not have recourse to anything other than those activities, those relations, and their consequences. These consequences do assume a character of their own, such as long-term structures, forms of oppression, etc., which condition the activities of human beings. This does not deny Gramsci's position, for he is simply stating that these developments are not due to divine disposition, world spirit, the kingdom of ends, or any other non-human agency.

There is a second aspect to Gramsci's humanism which is linked to the unity of theory and practice, and this is the position that all human activity has a political significance, that is, it is related to efforts to organize communal life. In this sense of 'humanism', Gramsci advances the thesis that politics is primary inasmuch as the production and reproduction of life, culture, etc., affects the well-being of communities and individuals. He expresses this view by affirming that all of life is politics. Whereas the previous theories define the basic epistemological, ontological, and methodological character of historicism, the last one defines the focus of the interest in the knowledge of history. This interest, stated simply, lies in the fact that knowing the development of a society is an important condition for changing it. And this points to Gramsci's theory of politics, which will be discussed next.

To summarize, central to Gramsci's historicism is the thesis that the long-term view is the only appropriate one for the study of society. Since social phenomena are characterized as processes, that is, as undergoing systemic change, an accurate description of any element in the system depends upon its consequences. Hence, the concepts and theories of the social scientist must refer not to single events or synchronic structural elements, but to definitive temporal processes. From this follows the importance of distinguishing the various kinds of temporality and of giving to each of them an adequate causal weight. Furthermore, the explana of historical phenomena must not refer to extra-historical en' laws and entities are constituted in the intercourse o'

131

beings with their environment and with themselves. Finally, achieving knowledge of the development of society is not simply an exercise in achieving pure knowledge for its own sake; it is an exercise directed at changing society for the better according to its inherent possibilities. Knowledge has a political significance.

CHAPTER THREE

HISTORY AND POLITICS

INTRODUCTION

Gramsci's historicism provides a most useful foundation for historical research and political action. In contrast with the historicism of the German school or that of Croce, Gramsci's theory of history does not restrict the sense of the social process to an inner meaning of the actions of men and women which translates into the understanding of history as an ethical drama. Gramsci recognizes the importance of each facet of historical development at the same time as he seeks to provide a general understanding of the relative weight of each one. In so doing, he does not generally impose a given schema on historical data; he seeks to understand the process from a materialist standpoint, without denying the complexity of social processes or the intricacy of the causal nexus that explains historical change.

It is within this framework of historical explanation that we must seek to understand the role of politics in human existence. In what follows, an attempt will be made to elucidate the essential features of Gramsci's conception of society and his general theory of politics. Although they do not follow deductively from his historicism, they are nevertheless connected with it, at least to the extent that his historicism disallows certain interpretations. We shall not develop in any great detail Gramsci's thought on these topics, which has in any case received a great deal of attention. It will suffice to outline, as if it were a matter of developing a research programme, the main lines of argument that are suggested by, or are more compatible with, Gramsci's historicism.

In attempting to define the most general aspects of Gramsci's theory of history and politics, a number of basic problems must be dealt with. We must first consider the nature of the relationship between structure and superstructure; second, the nature of civil society and the role of hegemony; third, the state as both the coercive apparatus of a class and, in its larger sense, as an educational institution. As we shall see, Gramsci maintains a dual conception of politics, one that can be said to be Aristotelian, the other classical Marxist. This dual conception is clearly evidenced in his conception of hegemony and the state. It is not clear, however, from reading the *Prison Notebooks* whether these two conceptions are compatible.

THE RELATION BETWEEN STRUCTURE AND SUPERSTRUCTURE

Some conflicting interpretations

Gramsci's theory of the relation between structure and super-structure has been the subject of some controversy, notably between Bobbio and Texier. It is certainly a crucial issue for those who seek to link Gramsci to Marx and Lenin or to show that, in some sense he is an incipient post-Marxist. The various inter-pretations given to his thought fall into two main classes; those who establish a topographical model and therefore a synchronic relation between structure and superstructure, and those who propose a temporal model and hence a diachronic analysis of that relation. Furthermore, some commentators stress the primacy of the structure, whereas others that of the superstructure, and yet others place the greatest importance on the unifying link.

In an essay first published in 1968, Norberto Bobbio argues that in Gramsci, as in Marx 'civil society . . . represents the active and positive moment of historical movement'.[1] However, because Gramsci's use of the term 'civil society' differs in crucial respects from Marx's, Bobbio concludes that for Gramsci the superstructure is the primary moment in the 'reciprocal relation' between structure and superstructure.[2] Furthermore, in the distinction between hegemony and domination, or between civil society and state, which is a distinction within the superstructure, the moment of hegemony, or the private institutions of civil society, 'is always the positive moment', whereas the state is the negative or subordinate one.[3] In short, according to Bobbio, Gramsci asserts that a reciprocal relation exists between two contemporary factors, structure and superstructure, and that the second one in general, and its ethico-political aspect in particular, is the primary and dominant element in a social system.

Bobbio's interpretation has been challenged by Jacques Texier, who cites many passages from the *Prison Notebooks* which suggest a classical Marxist theory of the relation between structure and superstructure. Texier points out that Bobbio's account would mean that Gramsci's historicism 'would go no further than the historicism of Croce'.[4] Texier, in agreement with Bobbio, notes that 'in Gramsci civil society is not the infrastructure',[5] as it is for Marx. The difference, however, consists merely in the use of a term, it does not have any theoretical significance. For if we look at the concepts of civil society and hegemony as elements in a historical bloc and if, furthermore, we conceive of the relation between structure and superstructure as a process,[6] then we must reach the conclusion that the content of civil society is economic, as 'all superstructural activities have a class character'. Civil society, Texier argues, represents 'the complex of practical and ideological social relations . . . which is established and grows up on the base of determined relations of production'.[7] In short, Texier affirms that a determining relation exists between two parallel kinds of phenomena, structural and superstructural ones, which undergo a process of change and in which the structural ones, understood as the social relations of production, are primary or dominant.

A distinct third position is that taken by Portelli in a pertinent book titled *Gramsci et le Bloc Historique.* He asserts that 'the study of the relation between structure and superstructure is the essential aspect in the notion of historical bloc'. But, he continues, 'Gramsci never conceived this study in the form of the primacy of one element of the bloc over the other'. It is futile, then, to attempt to argue for the primacy of any one of the elements; what is essential in 'the relations structure/superstructure is the link that realizes their unity'. And he notes that the organic link between the social structure or classes, which depend on the relations of production, and the ideological and political superstructures, is provided by intellectuals.[8] Thus, 'to pose the question of intellectuals is to pose the question of the historical bloc'.[9]

There is an aspect of Portelli's account which is attractive, namely, the emphasis on the unifying link in a historical bloc. However, Portelli's position is not quite clear, for in his analysis, classes and ideological superstructures appear to be reduced to two separate realms which are brought together by the efforts of a mass of intellectuals. His position is ambiguous because he clearly recognizes the class determination of the superstructures, while at the same time he affirms that the intellectuals are the unifying link in a historical bloc. However, the most serious weakness in Portelli's reconstruction of the concept of historical bloc is that despite his recognition that the 'static study must be completed by a dynamic one',[10] he does not provide a full analysis of the dialectic of the integration and disintegration of historical blocs. It is precisely this dialectic that helps us understand the process of unity which explains the structure as well as causal relations between structures and superstructures.

A salient feature of both Texier and Portelli is their emphasis on the study of the relations between structure and superstructure as a process. This implies that the relation of reflection between structure and superstructure is not an immediate one, but one that develops and that as a consequence has a temporal aspect. The diachronic view of the relation between structure and super-structure has been defended by Nardone, Misuraca, and Salamini. In general, they argue that structure and superstructure constitute two poles of a temporal process, so that the structure represents the past, while the superstructure signifies the future.

In his book *Il Pensiero di Gramsci*, Nardone argues that a schema of temporal development of the relation structure/superstructure provides a more adequate explanation[11] and that it is in fact coherent with Gramsci's thought as a whole.[12] In Nardone's account, 'the social group is the principal subject of political becoming'.[13] Its function as the subject of history exhibits two forms, first as the 'historical agent insofar as it is identical with the economic base' and second as a political group whose full development is materialized in the party. The temporal process of the relation between structure and superstructure is precisely the 'passage from the economy to politics', or from an economic past to the foundation of a state.[14] In its final stage as a state, a social group unifies and leads all the social forces of a bloc and hence realizes its hegemony.[15] The temporal perspective of the relation between structure and superstructure does not imply that 'the two terms have the same value'. Nardone understands the dialectic structure/superstructure as that between quantity and quality, where the moment of quality, the superstructure, is the 'condition for the appearance of the structure at the same time that it indicates its final destination'.[16]

Salamini, greatly influenced by Nardone's book, has developed a similar interpretation. For him, the relation between structure and superstructure is that between necessity and freedom and the nature of this relation is that of a passage from the first to the second, a passage that corresponds to the 'general direction of history'.[17] He argues that 'Gramsci ascribed to superstructural activities a primary role',[18] which is not a deviation from classical Marxism but rather the return 'to its idealist beginnings'.[19] Like Nardone, he claims that the superstructure is 'the condition for the appearance of the structure',[20] that is, freedom is the condition for the emergence of necessity as well as the overcoming of necessity.

Both Nardone's and Salamini's interpretations of Gramsci are in fact a modified version of Croce's dialectic of church and state, the ideal and the practical. The dialectic of history is thus removed from the clash of classes to the confrontation between necessity, as exhibited by the objective economic order, and liberty as incarnated in the organized will of the party. Since the passage from necessity, or structure, to freedom, or superstructure, is a temporal process, it is difficult to make sense of the assertion that the superstructure is the condition for the emergence of the structure. Unless, of course, one assumes the view that the ideal–eternal history of liberty spawns, as so many steps towards its full realization, negative moments of structural constraint; or unless one is prepared to accept teleological causation. Both these views, however, are contrary to Gramsci's historicism; specifically, they violate the absolute historicism according to which we are not to seek extra-historical or transcendent explanations for what is an earthly process.

A somewhat different interpretation of the diachronic view of the relation between structure and superstructure is that presented by Misuraca in a short paper on the Gramscian reconstruction of the concepts of 'structure' and 'superstructure'. Misuraca adduces textual evidence from the *Prison Notebooks* to the effect that by structure Gramsci means 'the ensemble of real historical conditions insofar as they are factually active'. In this sense, structure is the past, and it comprises both the material conditions and the ideological and cultural conditions. However, not all conditions, that is, not all the past without distinction forms part of the structure; the ideological and cultural conditions are considered structure to the extent that they 'are effectively operational in a given situation'.[21] The superstructure, in turn, consists in 'the initiatives which concretely realize this new history, this new structure'.[22]

This interpretation of Gramsci's thought seeks to displace the problem of the relation between socio-economic structure and political and cultural institutions to the problem of the emergence of a new historical bloc out of the disintegration of the old one. However, Misuraca's interpretation must still deal with the problem of the specific link that unites the economic moment and the political and cultural moment within the present historical bloc. This brings the debate back to its beginning. There is, however, some textual justification for Misuraca's position on the use of 'structure' in Gramsci. As we have seen, it is not altogether unjustifiable to take this term in Braudel's sense of long-term processes which include both economic and intellectual elements. Nevertheless, this is merely a linguistic question, one that does not touch on the fundamental problem of the relation between economic structure and political and cultural phenomena.

The diactronic model neglects the simple fact that, regardless of how the terms are defined, there is at any time some sort of relation between two co-existing types of phenomena, what classical Marxism defines as 'structure' and 'superstructure'. In contrast, the synchronic model tends to disregard the character of becoming of a social system and the manner in which this character affects the relations among various kinds of phenomena. It would seem that the difficulties involved in interpreting Gramsci's thought on this issue stem from the fact that he attempts to explain different sorts of phenomena that involve the relation between structural and superstructural elements. On the one hand, Gramsci defines the concept of historical bloc in terms of the general relation between structure and superstructure; on the other hand, he is concerned with the study of the development of a class from its beginning as an economic class to its final hegemonic moment, as a state.

In the analysis of the relation of political forces from the level of the structural determination of classes to the development of a new state, Sassoon has argued, the various levels described by Gramsci 'are separate only in a methodological sense since they are aspects of a single phenomenon at a single moment of time'.[23] And in a footnote she adds that Gramsci's use of the expression 'a subsequent moment' must be taken in a 'schematic sense', not in a temporal one.[24] However, it seems that it is precisely the development of political forces which is most amenable to some form of diachronic analysis, albeit one that takes place in a historical bloc, that is, within a given set of structural and superstructural conditions. It seems that, despite Sassoon's belief that diachronic and synchronic analysis are incompatible,[25] they are both necessary for a full understanding of a historical bloc, for we need to know both the relation that exists between any elements at any point in time as well as their process of transformation during a historical period. Gramsci's analysis of situations is precisely this, namely, the investigation of how temporal processes of different durations intertwine at any given moment in time, so that their long-term causal process and their contemporary relations can be clearly understood. Although Gramsci is primarily concerned with the function of political intervention in social change he does not reject the thesis of the primacy of the structure in the last instance.

Gramsci's analysis

The concept of 'historical bloc'
There are two kinds of texts which offer the solution to the relation between structure and superstructure: first, texts specific to this relation itself, generally contained within Gramsci's discussion of the concept of 'historical bloc'; second, the very important text on the moments of a political situation already mentioned above.

Gramsci gives different formulations of the concept of 'historical bloc', which are not necessarily different in content. In one of his first attempts he argues that 'if men take cognizance of their task in the terrain of the superstructures, this means that between structure and superstructure there is a necessary and vital link, such as is the case in the human body between the skin and the skeleton'.[26] And later, returning to the theme of the role of popular beliefs, he adds that 'the material forces are the content and the ideology the form', a distinction that is 'merely didactic because material forces without form would not be historically conceivable and without material forces ideologies would be individual whims'.[27] The first conclusion that we can draw is that Gramsci conceived of ideas on the one hand and the material forces on the other as two inseparable aspects of one single reality. Moreover, their unity is not just a mere coexistence but it is a function of a necessary link: the 'complex and discordant ensemble of the superstructures are the reflection of the ensemble of the relations of production'.[28] There is, furthermore, a 'necessary reciprocity between structure and superstructure (a reciprocity which is precisely the real dialectical process)'.[29]

The theme of the unity of structure and superstructure as that of the form and content of the historical process appears elsewhere in the *Prison Notebooks*. It forms the basis for Gramsci's critique of Croce's conception of ethico-political history, which he regards to be too speculative. Ethico-political history, Gramsci writes, cannot discard the concept of historical bloc for the social organism 'cannot be conceived without its "material" or practical content'. To write ethico-political history without taking into account the material forces is equivalent to classifying animal species by the colour of their feathers or their skin and not on the basis of their anatomy. Finally, he makes the point that 'it is necessary to demonstrate that form and content are identical, but it is necessary to do so every time in the concrete, individually, otherwise one engages in philosophical speculation, and not history'.[30] The identity of structure and superstructure, or form and content, is thus taken as a methodological principle, that is, as a general hypothesis for gathering and controlling evidence and for generating particular theories about the link between structure and superstructure in given societies. The general methodological character is not a denial of the reality of the link; it is, rather, the denial that a single formula can take the place of research, or that philosophical speculation from general concepts can produce sound knowledge of empirical reality. These are concerns that, as we have seen in Chapter Two, were clearly in Gramsci's mind, as they were in Engels' thought.

So far little has been said about the content of the terms 'structure' and 'superstructure'. Gramsci uses them in the general sense that they have acquired in historical materialism. One peculiarity of most of Gramsci's texts, however, is that he uses the plural 'superstructures', but the singular 'structure', as if a single structure were reflected in several superstructures. The reason for this is to be found in his partial acceptance of Croce's concept of the distinctions in the circle of the spirit. Gramsci argues that Croce produced a 'merely verbal solution' to what is a real methodological problem, for 'it is true that not only oppositions exist, but also distinct moments'. The solution to this problem can only be a historical one based on the concept of historical bloc,[31] which is defined as the 'unity between nature and spirit (structure and superstructure), unity of contraries and of distinct moments'.[32] The superstructure is thus conceived as a unity of distincts, of several levels such as civil society and political society. It is precisely the unity of these levels that constitutes the main field of research in the *Prison Notebooks*.

The structure, however, is also said to be a unity of distinct elements in so far as one can distinguish various elements in it, such as technology, labour, and classes.[33] This is an area of social theory to which Gramsci devotes few pages. A probable reason for this is that he believed that political economy had already been substantially developed, whereas political theory had not received as much attention. The need to develop this theory had clearly been felt by Lenin and now by Gramsci because they were both engaged in the task of establishing political organizations to contest the existing form of the state.

In short, Gramsci proposes the concept of a historical bloc as the necessary unity of several levels. The structure is conceived first as the terrain of the interchange between humanity and nature, an interchange that constitutes the process of production. In this process we can distinguish the technological elements, the labour process, and the classes that result from the organization of this process. For Gramsci, the element of class is the link between the structure and the superstructure, in so far as the latter contains the forms of organization that guarantee the development of the structure in its present form. It is because of this fundamental link that the concept of class plays a fundamental role in Gramsci's theory of history. The superstructure, too, is divided into several levels, notably the private institutions of civil society and the state. There are, moreover, processes of long duration, such as is the case with the cosmopolitan character of Italian intellectuals, which are not directly linked to the structure of the present historical bloc, though they continue to play an important role in the determination of its character.

Historical examples

A brief look at Gramsci's notes on Americanism and Fordism will provide further evidence for this account. We cannot expect, however, a full analysis of political economy; his notes take much for granted, but regardless of the empirical accuracy of his particular thesis, they show the intended use, relevance, and importance of the structure in Gramsci's thought. These notes can be construed as the attempt to understand the restructuring of the state that took place in the USA after the First World War. At the same time, they are a reflection on the Italian situation in which the fascist regime was faced with a similar task. For these reasons, these notes are important for the analysis of the modern state, hegemony, and passive revolution. Most interpretations of these notes are concerned with Gramsci's specific analysis of the emergence of the new form of the state, as well as with the historical accuracy of that analysis. Nevertheless, as Sassoon suggests, in the notes on Americanism and Fordism Gramsci 'indicates the extremely complex nature of the relationship between structure and superstructure, at the same time insisting on the multitude of essential features of any political phenomenon'.[34] In a similar vein, Buci-Glucksmann argues that 'the American model poses new questions for the concept of hegemony, both as a topical political theme and as an occasion for deeper theoretical reflection on the relation of base and superstructure'.[35]

In an unfinished note written in 1934, Gramsci provided a list of the problems he thought were important to discuss under the 'general and somewhat conventional heading of "Americanism and Fordism"'. However one must first consider the 'fundamental fact' that their solution is 'necessarily formulated and attempted within the contradictory conditions of modern society'.[36] From the start, then, we must consider the contradictory nature of a social bloc; in other words, the starting point is never the unity and homogeneity of a social system, rather its heterogeneity. The problem to consider then is the functioning unity of such a system and how it is achieved. In general terms, Gramsci defines Americanism and Fordism as the result 'of the immanent necessity to achieve the organization of a planned economy'. The various problems associated with this necessary change signal the passage 'from the old economic individualism to a planned economy'. The problems emerge because of the resistance to this change, resistance that comes not only from the subaltern classes but also from the allies of the dominant ones.[37]

The list of some of the most important problems associated with Americanism includes the following issues:

1) substitution of a new mechanism of accumulation and distribution of finance capital immediately founded on industrial production for the present plutocratic class; 2) the sexual question; 3) the question of whether Americanism can constitute a historical 'epoch'. . .; 4) the question of the 'rationalization' of European demographic composition; 5) the question of whether this development must have its starting point within the industrial and productive world or whether it can come from the outside. . .; 6) the question of the so-called 'high wages' paid by the Fordized and rationalized industry; 7) Fordism as the extreme point of the process of successive attempts by industry to overcome the tendential law of the fall of the rate of profit; 8) psychoanalysis. . . as expression of the increased moral coercion exercised by the state and social apparatus on single individuals and the morbid crisis that such coercion determines; 9) Rotary Club and Free Masonry. . . .[38]

The note is left unfinished, but it provides a good deal of evidence both of the scope of problems that Gramsci includes under a single phenomenon, as well as the care he takes to relate structural and superstructural phenomena.

Part of Gramsci's analysis deals with the differences between the American and the European and, more specifically, the Italian case. These differences stem from the different demographic conditions found in the two continents. It is important to note that they are differences in the class structure of the countries he contrasts. He argues that in Europe, and specifically in Italy, there is a large parasitic class of individuals without an essential function in the productive world, whereas this stratum of 'producers of savings', does not exist in the USA. The existence of that parasitic class depends on a number of conditions, some of which are related to forms of land-ownership; in particular to the existence of absentee owners who draw their wealth from sharecroppers, rents, etc. Others derive their income from the state, through pensions of various types. What is common to all of them is that they consume and save, but they are not active in economic production.[39] The existence of this class is linked to European culture, and to the strong resistance offered to the modernization of production in Italy.[40] The suggestion is that modernization in Italy must be different from the American case, and that the fascist state may constitute the attempt to accomplish the same end.

At the structural level, then, Gramsci makes some distinctions. First, there is an economic fact, the tendency of the rate of profit to fall, which prompts the capitalist class to introduce changes. This is done at the individual level, as he notes, with the view to obtain and 'maintain a position of superiority over the competition'. Ford's initiatives in developing more efficient work methods, in organizing transportation and distribution of the commodities produced in his enterprises is an instance of such an effort.[41] The element of technique, in this case, work methods, is a second distinction within the structure. Furthermore, beyond the attempt of individual industries to overcome the fall of the rate of profit, the economic power of the class, which is the third element, must be restructured, so that a more effective accumulation and distribution of finance capital may be achieved. To a certain extent, the restructuring of the state, whether through the New Deal policies in the USA or through fascism in Italy, was the result of immanent needs of the economy. There are, therefore, two sets of problems which must be solved, namely, those that will increase productivity and those that will secure a universal solution to the problem of the fall of the rate of profit. The individual solution is that which is attempted from the point of view of the self-interest of individual capitalists. The universal solution to the problem is a hegemonic one, one that must ultimately involve the state. These

144

two solutions are not in contradiction even if a true hegemonic solution will necessitate that concessions be made in order to attract the consent of possible allies. Gramsci's analysis of Americanism and Fordism is in fact an analysis of the emerging hegemony in the USA.

Gramsci notes that the rationalization of production was accomplished in two ways: by means of force, such as the destruction of trade unions, and by means of consent, such as social benefits, high wages, and ideological and political propaganda.[42] High wages were necessary to select and keep well-trained workers. The new methods of work required a stable working force, which meant that traditional puritanism had to be articulated in a new social ethics that emphasized monogamy, and, of course, prohibition.[43] Also, the workers had to be educated so that the 'trained gorilla' in the assembly line, bored with meaningless work, could resist the temptation to entertain 'non-conformist thoughts'.[44] This process is, in short, the attempt to create a new type of worker who will be well adapted, both physically and psychologically, to the new conditions of production. The reason, then, for the ideology of high wages, and, one must add, the puritanism that was expected to produce well-adjusted individuals, 'is a phenomenon derived from an objective necessity of modern industry. . . and not a primary one'. Nevertheless, Gramsci argues, this does not diminish the importance of the influence that ideology in itself had on the development of the new state.[45]

The foregoing analysis, while shedding light on important aspects of American society, does not provide an exhaustive view of that society. Among the items in the list of problems that Gramsci thinks are of some importance, the sexual question cannot be fully explained within the framework of analysis presented above. Gramsci in fact provides some interesting suggestions on how this question should be treated, hints that, while scant and little developed, provide evidence for his originality; furthermore, they show that, while he regarded the economic structure as the motor of history, he did not reduce all problems to economic ones.

Gramsci affirms that 'the "economic" function of reproduction is not only tied to the productive economic world, but it is also an internal one'.[46] In the second draft of this note, he writes that the economic function of reproduction 'is not only a general fact that

145

is of interest to the entire society . . . but it is also a "molecular" fact, internal to the smaller economic aggregates such as the family'.[47] The exact meaning of these two passages is not clear, though it is reasonably safe to assert that Gramsci thinks of the sexual question as being simultaneously part of the economic structure at the same time that it is independent of it. It is a general economic question to the extent that the reproduction of the population, and hence of the labour force, depends on it; furthermore, sexual morality inherited from the past, such as is linked with puritanism in the American case, can be adapted to new emerging conditions with the end of forging a new attitude towards work. It is independent of the economic structure to the extent that it is an 'ethico-civil' question.[48]

Gramsci considers the issue of the 'formation of a new feminine personality' to be 'the most important ethico-civil question tied to the sexual question'.[49] This question, however, cannot be solved by the party or by any group of legislators. It can only be solved, he writes, 'when women have attained independence *vis-à-vis* men' and have developed 'a new conception of themselves and of their role in sexual relations'. Any attempt to legislate on sexual questions before this new feminine self-image is achieved, he warns, must proceed with great caution, for 'the sexual question will be rich with morbid characteristics'.[50]

One can conclude that any social reform is faced with problems that, although they are set within a specific class framework, both in their long history and in their scope, transcend socio-economic relations. It is in the attempt to include these problems in his study of historical blocs that Gramsci develops the concept of hegemony. The hegemony of a group depends not only on its ability to organize consensus on problems related to the economic structure, but also on those problems of an extra-economic nature, or of mixed nature as Gramsci regards the sexual question, that, whether they emerge under new circumstances or whether their origin is in the very distant past, are faced by society. As Gramsci writes, 'any innovative historical movement is mature to the extent that the elderly, the young and women can participate in it'.[51] It would seem, then, that those who have lately sought to develop a socialist theory of democracy have been on the right track in examining Gramsci's conception of hegemony as a fundamental concept upon which to ground such a theory.[52]

The various texts discussed above indicate that Gramsci quite clearly thought of 'the objective necessity of modern industry' as being primary. This objective necessity originates in the need to overcome the tendency of the rate of profit to fall, and it requires structural changes as well as superstructural ones. Hence the economic thrust, the necessity of the structure, must be supplemented by superstructural elements, such as education, legislation, etc. However, some of the characteristics and the concomitant problems of these superstructural questions, notably patriarchy, are not caused by the economic structure, though they must be made to conform to it or at least not to impede its automatism. It seems, then, that one cannot affirm the unqualified primacy of the economic element without begging some questions. In the study of any given situation, one may conclude, it is always difficult to ascertain that the economy is dominant or primary in any absolute sense, though it certainly sets the general conditions of existence of any society. In Gramsci's analysis of Americanism, the economy poses problems whose solutions are structural and superstructural at once. The problems themselves often depend on the relations of forces, that is, on the relative strength and organization of the fundamental classes. To provide a solution to this question we must turn to Gramsci's analysis of the relations of forces. Before that, however, a brief look at his analysis of the Italian Risorgimento will provide further evidence for his theory.

Pizzorno has argued that Gramsci's thesis on the Risorgimento, in particular that of the effect of the failure on the part of the Moderates to carry out an agrarian reform, 'cannot be considered a historiographical thesis' because a 'historiographical problem is always the problem of the *identification* of historical subjects and the *attribution* of historical actions to one or another subject'.[53] In short, because Gramsci is concerned with the types of effects that follow from types of actions, his is a theoretical analysis, not a historical one. It is true that, just as his analysis of Americanism and Fordism is an attempt to deepen his understanding of the modern state and of fascism, his analysis of the Risorgimento is an attempt to understand the origins of the bourgeois state in Italy; in both cases, a crucial aspect of the analysis is the contrast that he draws between two different situations, and the conditions he identifies as responsible for the different solutions to similar problems. In the case of the Risorgimento, he contrasts the Italian case with the French Revolution so as to understand the reason for the weakness of the Italian State.

In Gramsci, history and theory are not two separate disciplines; they are not conceived as a discipline of precise empirical research and a theory of society, a narrative of facts and sociology which formulates some general laws. Gramsci's historicism, to the extent that it is a theory of historiography, is the demand for a history with depth, and hence, a history that understands any situation in terms of the confluence of structures of different durations. Furthermore, it is premissed on the possibility of identifying general tendencies, or historical laws, and networks of necessity which allows him to compare different social processes. Comparative history, it was argued earlier, is premissed on the conception that history is not simply the narration of unique events.

For these reasons, Gramsci's argument on the lack of an agrarian reform is not mere speculation on what might have been, but rather experimental historiography to the extent that this is possible in history. It is the stability of the structure that permits such experiments even if only in the form of abstractions, as Marx argued in *Capital*. This is, after all, what Gramsci probably means when he writes that Ricardo's hypothetical method has a philosophical importance for Marxism.[54] The importance of this is that, in his historical reflections, especially in his analysis of the Risorgimento, Gramsci had to start from the secure foundation of the structure, for he thinks that it is the most adequate for an 'experimental science of history'.[55] The existence of social groups with a productive function, or the existence of groups without such functions who consumed surplus-value but did not produce any, is, for him, of crucial importance. There are, of course, other elements of importance; but the structural ones are the cornerstone of his *experiments*, of his application of theoretical considerations about the generative mechanism of historical processes and about the degree of 'automatism' or necessity of these processes.

The first note fully devoted to the Risorgimento is titled 'Political direction of a class before and after its journey to power'.[56] He later rewrote this note, giving it a new title: 'The problem of political leadership in the formation and development of the nation and the modern state in Italy'.[57] In both cases, however, the problem is set out in the following way:

The whole problem of the connection among the various political currents of the Risorgimento, that is, of their reciprocal relations and their relations with homogeneous or subordinate social groups that exist in the various historical sections (or sectors) of the national territory, can be reduced to this fundamental factual datum: the moderates represented a relatively homogeneous social group. . . whereas the so called Party of Action was not specifically based on any historical class.[58]

In the first draft of this note, Gramsci employs the expression 'relatively homogeneous class' instead of 'relatively homogeneous social group'.[59]

The terms in which Gramsci seeks to analyse the problems of the Risorgimento are clear. For although the problem is conceived in terms of political connections, the fundamental fact is the relationship of representation between political parties and classes. There is, furthermore, the regional problem, which cannot be defined merely in terms of geographical location, but rather as the emergence of different social blocs within the geographical boundaries of the emerging Italian state. These social blocs are defined in terms of class structure, as well as culture. The general theoretical position that Gramsci seeks to develop is that the relationship between north and south is similar in some respects to that of urban centre and countryside. There is, however, an important difference; this relation is not a normal organic one, but one 'between two vast territories of very different civil and cultural traditions' which give rise to conflict of nationalities.[60] This conflict has a very precise significance for, as Buci-Glucksmann argues, the backwardness of the south is considered by Gramsci as 'the condition for the capitalist development of the north'.[61]

As the analysis proceeds, Gramsci's conceptual framework becomes more complex. Nevertheless, both the structural and the regional elements continue to provide the backbone of his analysis. Posing the problem in terms of the unification of a class in the state, he seeks to analyse the political process by means of which the Italian northern-bourgeoisie managed to accomplish the integration of a heterogeneous population as well as that of the various regions. We see then, in Gramsci's thinking, the progress from the problem of relations among political groups to the

149

problem of the integration of a new historical bloc. The task that the Moderate party faced was that of unifying the five main forces so as to build a forward moving train. These forces were: (1) the northern urban force, which was the locomotive, (2) the northern-central rural force, (3) rural/south, (4) rural Sicily, (5) rural Sardinia.[62]

It seems clear, then, that whatever the historical accuracy of his specific theses may be, Gramsci sought to study the Risorgimento as a problem similar to that of the French Revolution, a problem that was essentially a political process. The elements of this process, which were social forces, would eventually determine the outcome of the process, i.e., the specific type of the new Italian state. Again, the analysis is complex, and there is no suggestion that either the structure or the superstructure are primary in any immediate sense. Furthermore, the unification of Italy, which is seen as the unification of the bourgeoisie in a new state, is presented as a task, a task which, he writes, presented problems that the Moderates were able to solve with great skill.[63] Nevertheless, the basic historical subjects were social forces; it is to this concept of the relations of forces that we must now turn.

Analysis of the relations of forces

It is in a note on the relationship between structure and superstructure that Gramsci broaches as 'another aspect of this same problem', the question of the relations of forces.[64] In the relations of forces three moments or degrees are to be distinguished. First, 'a relation of social forces closely connected to the structure', this is said to be an objective relation, or 'naturalist datum' that 'can be measured with the system of mathematical or exact sciences'. Second, the relation of political forces, which is the 'degree of homogeneity and of self-consciousness attained by the various social groupings'.[65] Third, there is the relation of military forces, which is often the decisive one.[66] The second moment, or that of political relations, is itself divided into three moments, 'which correspond to the different degrees of political consciousness, such as have hitherto been manifested in history'.[67] These moments are, in brief, the economic-corporative, where there is consciousness of the unity of the professional group, but not of the class; the moment where 'consciousness of the solidarity of interests among all the members of the social grouping is attained' but this is still limited to the economic sphere; and lastly, there is the moment where consciousness of the narrow corporative interest is transcended. This last phase, Gramsci writes 'marks the clear passage from the pure structure to the complex superstructures'.[68]

These three moments of political forces represent the process from the origins of the individual consciousness of narrow economic interests to the hegemonic moment, where a universal solution is possible. The solution, however, is limited by the form of the state which is still the organ to 'create favorable conditions for the maximum expansion' of a group, though this expansion and development 'are conceived and presented as the motor force of a universal expansion of a development of all "national" energies'.[69] This is the hegemonic moment, the moment where concessions can be made in order to obtain the consent of allied groups, where moral and intellectual reform organize that consent. In real history, Gramsci contends, these three moments of the relations of political forces 'imply each other reciprocally, horizontally and vertically so to speak; that is, according to socio-economic activity (horizontally) and according to territory (vertically), combining and dispersing in different ways'.[70]

This analysis presents several problems. First, as we noted earlier, it is possible to interpret these various moments as existing at the same time, thus forming a complex set of relations whose morphology would constitute the object of the science of politics; or, they could be conceived as a temporal process. Second, the idea that the three moments imply each other, but that they can form diverse combinations or even split up, is intriguing, but not very clear. We must now attempt to clarify these issues.

To begin with, it seems to make perfect sense to interpret Gramsci's analysis as a temporal process. He himself speaks of 'reaching' degrees of consciousness, and he refers to the second moment as a 'successive moment'. It would seem that Gramsci is writing on the process in which a class is formed in the economic world and becomes conscious of its position and of the possibility to found a new state. In real history, this process is often a long one; one fraught with problems, setbacks, etc. This genetic approach is fully consistent with Gramsci's general principle that social problems should be studied historically. Furthermore, this analysis offers a conception of the theory of reflection as well as an interpretation of Engels' view that the economy is determining in the last instance. For in the genetic conception of the development of forces, the existence of classes as structured in the world of production is the temporally prior and necessary condition for the development of the second moment, that is, for the development of political forces, and the hegemonic solution of the problems that confront them.

These tasks are those of securing the expansion of the dominant class or of securing an acceptable rate of profit. The solutions to this problem, however, are not and cannot be simply economic. The lack of homogeneity, the very existence of conflicts of various kinds, and of class struggle, necessitate solutions at the political level, at the level of hegemony and the state. In this case, the reflection of the structure in the superstructure is a process, essentially a political process, in which the activity of the various historical subjects, classes, determine the specific structure of the state. This means that the political institutions and the moral and intellectual elements that predominate in a social system are not immediately or mechanically determined by the economy. In other words, there is no iron law of history that produces concrete political and ideological forms out of the changes in the structure. Rather, the political and ideological forms are responses to the historical problems within the limits of the class structure, and thus ultimately, of the economy. In this interpretation politics and culture are characterized by a certain degree of autonomy which allows for significant intervention in these fields. Most importantly, however, the specific solutions to historical problems depend upon a great variety of factors. In the case of the crisis of the 1920s and 1930s, demographic conditions, cultural traditions, etc., determine the final solution to similar problems, solutions that are in themselves as different as the New Deal or the fascist Italian state.

This view is consistent with Gramsci's conception of historical necessity. Since laws are tendencies abstracted from empirical reality, their effects on an open system cannot have a unilineal and inevitable character. It is because of this that, as Femia points out, 'although men are rooted in an economic reality that circumscribes their free initiative, this objective world of fact is not passively registered, human intervention is decisive'.[71] Such intervention is necessary because the existing structural tendencies may not be realized.[72] For, as Gramsci points out, 'at certain moments the automatic thrust due to the economic factor is slowed down, obstructed, or even momentarily broken down by traditional ideological elements', in which case 'appropriate political initiative is always necessary to free the economic thrust from the shackles of established politics'.[73] Historical necessity, as we concluded earlier, is not solely a function of the structure or of an objective premiss, but also a function of the degree of consciousness and organization of the existing forces.

Since the development of class consciousness, or of an alternative hegemony, is not an automatic development or immediate reflection of the structure, the mechanisms by which this development can take place are of foremost importance. Hence, Gramsci's analysis of the development of parties, of intellectuals, and the role of culture in general is of crucial importance. In this respect, Gramsci can be said to develop Lenin's political theory, in so far as the latter clearly saw the importance of political intervention, and implicitly the falseness of any mechanistic theory of the relation between the structure and the superstructure.

The genetic approach is also consistent with Gramsci's theory of historical time, for it allows one to trace the lines of development of the forces whose relations constitute the fundamental problem in a situation. It is important to stress that the note in which Gramsci presented his analysis of situations and relations of forces begins with his distinction between structures and conjunctures. This approach, then, when fully developed, would lead the historian to uncover the 'molecular'[74] processes which repeated *ad infinitum*, become the 'homogeneous part'[75] in the activity of individuals. That is, they become structures, but also rules of behaviour; customs as well as ethical norms.

In short, the genetic interpretation of Gramsci's analysis of situations is consistent with his historicism. It provides a general sketch for the theory of the reflection of the structure in the superstructure, and affirms the temporal primacy of the structure, so that a given type of structure becomes an empirically necessary prior condition for the foundation of a historical bloc. The theory of reflection and the determination of the economy in the last instance are interpreted as methodological principles in the sense

153

elucidated in Chapter Two. As such, they are taken as controlling hypotheses, but also as real historical processes whose specific character must be confirmed by documented evidence.

If this is so, then it is possible to interpret Gramsci's assertion that the three moments of political forces imply each other, in the sense that the lower level, that is, the level of economic-corporate interests, is an empirically necessary temporal pre-condition for the others, inasmuch as it is closely linked to the structure. The existence of the other two levels are sufficient evidence for the existence of the structural ones, for they would not exist unless adequate structures did. In this manner, the appearance, for instance, of a working class party is sufficient evidence of the existence of the working class, and the latter must exist before its corresponding cultural and political elements emerge. At any point in time, however, a class may exist but not its corresponding superstructural elements. The various combinations and dispersions of the various elements constitute the process of the development of a class from its subaltern position to its hegemonic one.

However adequate the above view may be, there are good reasons for construing the relation between the three moments of political forces as a synchronic one. Two main reasons can be given in its support. First, a situation has been defined as the conjunction of several processes, and hence it is but a slice of time in the historical process. Second, the emphasis on the relations of forces suggests that Gramsci is attempting to unravel the general structuring of a social whole at a given time in order to assess the possibilities inherent in it as well as the appropriate form of political intervention most conducive to their realization.

Given this approach, it is clear that the various social forces are not necessarily whole classes, for there can be sectors of classes that are more developed than others, that is, sectors that have reached a higher level of consciousness and organization. The analysis of a specific situation, in this case, must first identify the various social groups, as well as their objective class base, their degree of development and, of course, the possibilities of political intervention. The analysis in this case is not simply founded on the existence of classes, but rather on the existence of groups, which are defined mainly in terms of both their class belonging and their degree of consciousness and organization. In this sense, Sassoon

154

would be right in that the three levels coexist. Furthermore, since the problem now is to assess the relative strength of the various forces, as well as their interrelationships, and since, furthermore, the structural determinants, as we have seen, may either be actualized or obstructed by superstructural elements, there is no good reason for asserting that any of the levels is necessarily primary or dominant. This would be fully consistent with Portelli's view that the essential problem for Gramsci is the relation between structure and superstructure and not the primacy of any one of these elements.

This approach is appealing in so far as it recognizes the complexity and uneven development of situations and it stresses the discordant combinations and dispersions of political and ideological forms. Its primary interest can be said to be political, in that it seeks to gain a firm understanding of the present so as to develop the appropriate strategy for political action. Two weaknesses, however, seem to be present in this approach. First, there is Gramsci's insistence on solving theoretical problems historically, and this can only mean genetically. Second, and this is perhaps only an aspect of the first problem, Gramsci's theory of transience indicates that the consequences of a phenomenon may only come to full fruition in a rather long period of time. As a consequence, it is always necessary to look at the past for a better understanding not only of the present situation but also of future possibilities, for, in general, the consequences of past phenomena, of past situations, may not yet have been fully realized. Hence, even if the interest of our knowledge is political intervention in the present, we cannot neglect the general tendencies that have been formed in the past.

But the most important point that can be made in order to appreciate fully Gramsci's theory is that there is no need for presenting the two approaches as exclusive alternatives, for Gramsci did not think in these terms. In fact, both approaches are but abstractions which are untenable in isolation. For the problem in understanding history, and hence, the problem of the knowledge that is necessary for political action, entails that we must unravel the origin and development of classes, that is, the long-term structural process, as well as the various processes of 'combination and dispersion' that form, at any given time, the structuring of a situation. These are not two problems in reality;

155

they become so only by theoretical fiat. The point that Gramsci seems to be attempting to make is that the concept of class only makes sense in the long term, that is, the reference of 'class' is to a long-term process. This view of class is close to that espoused by E. P. Thompson, who defines it as 'a *historical* category: that is, it is derived from the observation of the social process over time'.[76] At the more empirical or immediate level, we can distinguish social groups with different degrees of homogeneity, consciousness, and organization. Today, these would include social movements such as those devoted to specific causes like the ecology, peace, women, etc.

As I stated earlier, the structure of society, understood as the class structure, is temporally primary. This means that the economic formation of classes, that is, of groups within the production function, is temporally prior to their various forms of development. Also, the concept of class is theoretically primary in that it is designed to make sense of long-term historical processes. However, given any situation, the empirical groups may or may not act in class ways; they may have reached different degrees of consciousness and thus constitute different levels in the structuring of the relations of forces. If the concept of class has any validity, a class can only be fully evaluated by taking into consideration the behaviour of its members, and of the various groups it may give rise to, over a complete historical period. This full validation of the concept, however, does not imply that before the end of the historical period, we cannot use the concept with a high degree of accuracy. There is, after all, considerable historical evidence, as we find in the work of E. P. Thompson, Vilar, and others, to validate the use of this concept. Gramsci's historicism constitutes an important effort to specify the concept of class, to justify it historically, and to indicate both its uses and its limits.

In this synthesis of the diachronic and the synchronic approach, Gramsci's assertion that the various moments of the relation of political forces imply each other contains, in a nutshell, his theory of historical necessity discussed earlier. The structure is not only the empirically necessary prior condition for the existence of the corresponding superstructure in the development of a class, but, in the larger context of a historical bloc, structures and superstructures affect each other. This is the sense of the dual analysis of causality implied by some of Gramsci's reflections, that is, linear causality and structural causality, which underlies the concept of historical necessity as the concurrence of objective and subjective processes of different duration.

Gramsci's analysis, in all its complexity, seems to be a viable alternative to economistic theories in which class consciousness is said to be immediately determined by the structure. The distinction between the long-term class conditions of historical development, on the one hand, and the various relations of forces at any given time, on the other, is translated in political action as the distinction between stragetic goals and conjunctural or tactical political intervention as it is possible at any given time.

The analysis of situations, Gramsci believes, can be understood as 'an elementary exposition of political science and art, understood as a set of practical canons of research and of observations particularly useful to arouse an interest in effectual reality and elicit more vigorous and rigorous political insti- tutions'.[77] And he adds that empirical observations must be centred on the relations of forces, including international forces. Along with this, he states that the correct meaning of strategy and tactics must be developed.[78] In the same vein, Gramsci distinguishes 'great politics' which is the activity directed to found new states, the 'struggle to destroy, defend, preserve determined social-economic organic structures', from 'minor politics' or the partial or daily questions that arise within an established structure.[79]

In these Gramscian texts the intention of the author is clear, even if their formulation is not always well developed. Taken together with the analysis of situations, they stress the need to distinguish the long-term processes, the making of classes to use E. P. Thompson's expression, from the various combinations of social forces which, in their daily encounters, present the problems of minor politics. The latter offer the field for immediate empirical observations; the former suggest the generative mechanisms that produce a general direction to history; that is, they provide the meaning of historical events. The dominant classes, Gramsci observes, often attempt to exclude the issues of great politics from the internal life of the state; this is, however, great politics: it is their attempt to defend and preserve the existing socio-economic structure.[80]

Having made the distinction between the long-term class process and the various social forces that result in different combinations, that is, a distinction between the structural generative mechanism on the one hand, and the various structurings of immediate and empirically observable political formations on the other, we can arrive at some formulation of the general problem of the primacy of the structure. In fact, Gramsci himself provides a succinct formulation:

> A class is formed on the base of its function in the productive world: the development and the struggle for power and for the preservation of power create the superstructures which determine the formation of a 'special material structure' for their own diffusion, etc.. . . .Logically and even chronologically there is: social structure – superstructure – material structure of the superstructure.[81]

By the 'material structure of the superstructure', Gramsci means the necessary means for the existence of superstructures, such as the printing press. Nevertheless, the character of those superstructures which depend on material structure for their existence and propagation, is not determined by these material conditions but by the social structure.[82] The importance of this fact is crucial, for instance, in the study of the media. It does not deny the importance of the type of technology used, but it certainly denies that the medium is the message.

The important point that Gramsci makes in the text quoted above is that both logically and chronologically the social structure precedes the other elements. And this is precisely the position we have developed so far. As we have seen, the structure has a temporal primacy, in so far as it is a prior necessary condition for the development of the superstructure; and it also has theoretical primacy in so far as it is thought of as a generative mechanism that, as Femia asserts with respect to the productive forces, explains '*the basic trajectory of human history*' although it does not explain the '*specific course of any given society*' in so far as that may 'vary in accordance with the dynamics of its own individual situation'.[83] The dynamics of any individual situation, that is, the relations of forces in that situation depend, as we have seen, on a number of factors, such as geographical, demographic, and cultural

158

conditions and, in particular, on the existence of strata of intellectuals and the development of alternative hegemonies which contribute to the unification of social groups and classes.

In the general process of history, however, the distinction between structure and superstructure, or between material forces and ideology, is merely a didactic one, for one cannot exist without the other.[84] The logical and chronological primacy of the structure must then be seen in terms of the development of a class from its origin in the world of production to the founding of a new hegemony and a new state. This is what some commentators, as we have seen, refer to as the passage from necessity to liberty, and hence, they see the relation between the structure and the superstructure as holding between tradition and the future. Nevertheless, this is not the social process as a whole; there are other classes with their own superstructures which undergo transformations of their own and whose political initiatives react upon those of the emerging class. In the analysis of situations, Gramsci sketches the most general elements for the study of both the development of a new state and the relations that exist between the given structure, the various classes, and the superstructures. For this, both the diachronic and the synchronic approaches are necessary.

Finally, Gramsci feels that the crucial problem in historical materialism is that of the manner in which the historical movement emerges from the structures.[85] As I suggested earlier, this must not be taken to signify a distinction between two different objects, such as logic and history. Rather, given Gramsci's historicism, it implies two temporal orders; the relatively permanent order of structural phenomena, and the faster tempo, hence the expression 'historical movement', of the group formations of social forces. Historical necessity is constructed as the superimposition, or rather, the concurrence of the various orders, rather than the single effect of the logical or structural order. As Fontana has noted, Gramsci's theory is far from a linear theory, limited to a schematic analysis of global facts; he does not assume that social classes are homogeneous by definition. Indeed, he is aware of the uneven development of classes, of the contradictory evolution of classes and of class consciousness.[86] It is the recognition of this fact that led Gramsci to forge a theory of the historical bloc as the conjunction of different processes, of partial and often contradictory superstructures, of groups that have a common origin in the social structure but which have developed in different ways.

Although Gramsci focuses most of his analysis on the development of intellectuals, popular culture and, in general, hegemonic systems, his reflections on historical situations point to a global conception of historical investigation, what he called integral history. Fontana points out that 'a global study should begin with the examination of structural transformations ... proceed then to the examination of the ways in which these changes in the structure of production... affect the various classes ... to examine ... how the relations of production already analysed bring about a configuration of ideologies and political programmes'.[87] Above all, however, Gramsci's theory should not be taken as a fully structured schema that can be readily applied to any society or any situation. For, as he writes, 'reality is rich in the most strange combinations and it is the theoretician who must find confirmation for his theories in this oddity. He must translate the elements of historical life into theoretical language; and it is not, vice versa, reality that must present itself according to abstract schemas'.[88]

GRAMSCI'S DUAL CONCEPTION OF POLITICS

Roger Simon argues that in Lenin politics was primary only in revolutionary periods[89] whereas for Gramsci, politics is always primary. Furthermore, he argues that Gramsci avoids economism and class reductionism inasmuch as his concept of hegemony is 'based on the recognition that popular democratic struggles, and the parliamentary institutions which they have helped to shape, do not have a necessary class character'. As we have seen above, the formation of social forces which are not directly linked to class-structure is the terrain of political intervention, but, as Simon also recognizes, it is also the 'terrain for political struggle between the two major classes – the working class and the capitalist class'. The problem for the socialist movement, he suggests, is 'to find the way to link these popular democratic struggles with its socialist objectives', a problem which consists in forging an alternative hegemony.[90]

There is in this interpretation of Gramsci the suggestion that he holds two views of politics: (a) a classical Marxist view, in which the state is an instrument of the dominant class; and (b) an Aristotelian view of politics as the science of the good life. The emphasis on hegemony as moral and intellectual leadership implies, Simon argues, that politics embraces 'a much wider field of human activity than the struggle for state power'.[91] This double conception of politics renders the expression 'primacy of politics' somewhat ambiguous; for it may indeed be primary in the Aristotelian version, but not primary in the Marxist sense. This ambiguity permeates much of Gramsci's writings and gives rise to radically different interpretations of his thought, ranging from those that emphasize the Leninist and orthodox views of politics as class politics, to those who believe Gramsci is a post-Marxist who has no use for the concept of class, or who, like Laclau and Mouffe, think that Gramsci was unable to realize fully and develop the implications of his concept of hegemony.[92]

From our general interpretation of Gramsci's historicism and of his theory of the relationship between structure and super-structure, it would seem that the ambiguity exists only if one does not realize that the two meanings of politics function within different theoretical orders, orders that are specified in Gramsci's theory of historical time. However, this is a general solution which follows from Gramsci's historicist position. In order to understand the role of this dual conception of politics we shall now turn to the concepts of civil society, hegemony, and the state.

Civil society and hegemony

It is in the attempt to understand the process of unification of the Italian state that Gramsci first defines the concept of hegemony. He writes that 'the historico-political criterion on which one's research must be founded is the following: that a class is dominant in two ways, that is, it is "leading" and "dominant". It leads the allied classes and dominates the oppressed ones'.[93] Later, he defines this 'methodological criterion' and substitutes 'supremacy of a class', for 'a class is dominant',[94] so as to distinguish more precisely between domination and consent. Two aspects of this concept must be immediately clarified, one with respect to the context in which the concept appears; the other pertains to the double function it plays in Gramsci's theory.

161

First the concept of hegemony is presented in the context of the analysis of the politics of the Risorgimento. The suggestion is that hegemony is a permanent element in society, that is, that no society exists without a certain degree of hegemony, however slight that degree may be. That Gramsci thought so can be confirmed by reference to his statement that public opinion, which 'is closely connected with political hegemony inasmuch as it is 'the point of contact between "civil society" and "political society"', has always existed.[95] Furthermore, to the rhetorical question whether there has ever been a state without hegemony, he answers that 'there is a struggle between two hegemonies, always'.[96] Later, returning to the same idea, he writes that there has always been 'struggle between two hegemonic principles'.[97]

Although it is true that, as Sassoon points out, 'Gramsci develops the concept of hegemony in his attempt to analyse the state in a specific historical period',[98] it is not valid to infer, as she seems to do in her book on *Gramsci's Politics*, that it 'arises from the development of modern society'.[99] Furthermore, in the text on public opinion cited above, Gramsci seems to suggest that civil society is also a permanent feature of society. This being so, one must conclude that the difference between modern capitalist societies and other societies is not the existence of civil society and hegemony in the former, and their absence in the latter; rather, the difference is in the degree of development of the institutions of civil society and hegemony. Gramsci often thinks of dialectics as, among other things, the passage from quantity to quality. Perhaps this is applicable to the development of the modern state; the proliferation of the private institutions of civil society, and the corresponding growth of the dependence of hegemony on these private organizations, results in a qualitative change. This qualitative change, in turn, demands new strategies for political activity.

The text that is probably most often quoted from the *Prison Notebooks* is the one in which Gramsci identifies the main difference between Eastern and Western European states. He writes that, in contrast to the West, in the East 'the state was everything, civil society was primordial and gelatinous'.[100] In fact, he does not affirm that either hegemony or civil society were non-existent in the East; he argued, and in that the leadership of the Russian Social Democratic Party agreed, that the private institutions of civil society were as yet inchoate. In a note on Italian politics after 1870, Gramsci argues that, in Italy, there was a clear separation between state and civil society, and that because '*civil society* was something amorphous and chaotic' it was possible for the state to dominate it.[101] At the same time, however, Gramsci contends that one of the functions of the modern state is to adapt civil society to the economic structure.[102] Thus, whereas private institutions can be formed independently of the power of the state, their potential for real opposition, whether it is progressive or regressive, must be continually checked by the state. In so far as the institutions of civil society are not well developed, they are easily controlled and dominated by the state. As Gramsci writes of post-1870 Italy, the state could easily 'overcome the conflicts that, from time to time, would emerge sporadically, in a localized fashion, without national nexus or simultaneity'.[103]

Once civil society has developed, that is, once there is some national unity and hence simultaneous action at the national level is possible, then the state must change its relation to private institutions, for it can no longer dominate them and overcome conflicts in an easy way. The potential for conflict must be transformed into organized consensus; conflict must be contained within the limits of permissible opposition. That is, the role of the state as force diminishes, while the importance of its ethico-political character of hegemony grows. It is in terms of the relation between civil society and state, and the various degrees of the relation force/consent, that the development of the modern state is analysed. Crucial in this analysis is the degree of development of civil society, and hence, the approach that the state must take to secure its continued hold on possible conflicts.

The second point that must be made with regard to the concept of hegemony is that, as has been well noted by commentators, it serves a double purpose: it is a concept for historical interpretation and also a concept for the art of politics. Gramsci introduces this principle as a 'politico-historical criterion for research'[104] and, in the second draft of the same note, he refers to it as a 'methodological criterion'.[105] Furthermore, Gramsci states that 'the most important observation' with respect to the analysis of situations is that they 'cannot and must not be ends in themselves (unless one is simply writing a chapter on past history), but they acquire significance only if they serve to justify a practical activity, an initiative of the will'.[106] It is this double function of theoretical concepts that sets the foundation for the unity of theory and praxis. If the assertion that politics is primary has any concrete sense, it must be sought in Gramsci's statement that the significance of historical analysis is given by its justification of political action. Political intervention, then, is the goal of Gramsci the historian. This is, of course, based on the belief that knowledge of the past, if expressed in the right conceptual framework, can help make the decisions of the present, for there are patterns or tendencies in history. This has already been discussed earlier; the point, however, bears repetition: the theory of the unity of theory and praxis is firmly founded on the belief in the regularity of some historical processes, as well as on the belief that the potentialities inherent in the past may only be fully developed in the future. This is one of the senses that Gramsci draws from the two principles from Marx that he often cites.

This double function of concepts is not limited to the concept of hegemony. Other concepts, such as that of 'passive revolution', are also used in this dual form. It is the analysis of this last concept that leads Davis to the conclusion that Gramsci's political and historical methods are inseparable.[107] Apart from the significance of this for the philosophy of praxis, it must be stressed that politics is, for Gramsci, a historical science. This means that it is not a purely normative theory of power, state, etc., which seeks merely to justify a given form of society on some moral or practical grounds, but one that seeks to intervene so as to realize some inherent possibilities. Pure normative theories, Gramsci would argue, are already forms of intervention.

The concept of hegemony is the item in the *Prison Notebooks* that has received by far the most attention. It is, in a way, central to Gramsci's theory, for it unifies his various studies on the intellectuals, popular culture, folklore, and the state. Hegemony, Gramsci writes, 'signifies a determined system of moral life'.[108] It is also defined as 'government with permanently organized consent'.[109] In a more general sense, Gramsci also speaks of 'intellectual and moral leadership'.[110] And in a letter to Tania Schucht he defines it as the moment of 'consensus, of cultural leadership' and contrasts it to 'the moment of force, of constraint, of legislative and state or police intervention'.[111]

Gramsci is not the first political thinker to analyse politics in terms of the dichotomy between coercion and consensus. In the *Prince*, Machiavelli wonders whether it is better to be loved or feared and his response is that a ruler should be both loved and feared but 'because it is difficult to reconcile them, it is much more secure to be feared than loved, when one cannot have both'.[112] Modern liberal political theory is also concerned with such alternatives to coercion so as to minimize conflict. Thinkers such as Dahl argue that in a situation of conflict, such as is wont to arise in human society, there are only three solutions: coercion, deadlock and peaceful adjustment.[113] The latter, of course is favoured, but is conceived in terms of a multi-party, liberal democracy in which the electorate is to have the ultimate power of political decision. Gramsci often cites Machiavelli's double perspective and the image of the centaur with two heads. However, the concept of consensus in Gramsci, as Buci-Glucksmann suggests, is more complex than it is for those who emphasize the acceptability of a social system as a condition for its reproduction.[114]

It is perhaps important to stress that the dichotomy between hegemony and dominion, or consensus and coercion, is not simply meant to describe some of the conditions under which the actions of individuals take place. The meaning of consensus in Gramsci's theory of hegemony must be found not in the apparent willingness of an individual to engage in certain activities, but rather in the conditions for that willingness to be present. For, as Gramsci puts it, hegemony is not the result of the sum of individual acts of consent, but rather, the organization of a collective will. To create a new hegemony means to organize the will of individuals so that in their free actions they nevertheless choose within permissible limits, limits that are set by the interests of a ruling class. Femia has emphasized the 'psychological state, involving some kind of acceptance . . . of the socio-political order or of certain vital aspects of that order' as the core of the meaning of consensus. In his view, Gramsci's concept is thus purely descriptive, excluding 'the moral and prescriptive connotations' which are often attached to it.[115] This view, helpful as it is in understanding the individual's response to the socio-political order, must be complemented by the analysis of the structural basis of consent. Gramsci's analysis of the moments of the relation of forces is relevant and highly signif- icant to this issue, because it is the basic interests that originate at the lowest level of the development of the relations of forces that provide the foundation for spontaneous consensus. Further development of that consensus is coterminous with the development of a political consciousness, a process which does not occur spontaneously, but which is subject to ever higher degrees of organization and control. It is this aspect of the organization of a universal consensus that is the core of Gramsci's concept of hegemony.

As we saw earlier, Gramsci analyses the activity of individuals into two elements: a common element, which is related to the structural basis of society; and an element of differentiation between individuals, which of course is undetermined by historical laws. The reproduction of a social system is contingent on the character of habit, and of 'norm' or 'nature', that the constant element acquires. This constant element, such as is expressed in theories of human nature or on the assumption of the naturalness of *homo oeconomicus*, originates in the actions of individuals in a given economic system and is defended, justified, and made acceptable by the work of intellectuals. Hegemony, then, is not spontaneous, but 'organized consensus'. But that, one must immediately point out, is not to be taken as simply a theory of false consciousness which is somehow made to prevail with the uninformed masses. For Gramsci, the emergence of a new hegemony is a genuine act of historical creation in which a class, showing that it is capable of solving all the problems of the moment, can forge a higher moral and intellectual system. As Buci-Glucksmann argues 'Hegemony is not force . . . it is not imposed: it is conquered through a specific and intellectual and moral dimension'.[116]

The analysis of hegemony requires the concept of the historical bloc, that is, the unity of structure and superstructure, for it is only in terms of the development of the relations of forces within a historical bloc that a given hegemonic system can be understood and assessed. The development of a hegemony is contingent on the development of a political group which is able to go beyond its class's immediate economic-corporative interests. In order to do this, the class or most progressive section of the class, as for instance the Jacobins during the French Revolution, must be able to make concessions to other groups, so that they will become allies rather than enemies.[117] In his notes on 'Americanism and Fordism', Gramsci speaks of high salaries as an attempt to win the consent of the workers;[118] but as we have seen above, other questions must also be solved, questions that transcend the narrow economic interest of classes, or ethico-civil questions. In his analysis of the Risorgimento, Gramsci points out the failure to carry out an agrarian reform which would have created a wider consensual basis for the emerging Italian state.[119]

Of course, solving some of the problems of potential allies is but one step in the development of a hegemonic system. As important, if not more so, is intellectual and moral reform, the creation of a new conception of the world with its consequent ethics which must show itself to be both viable and superior to the prevailing one. Nevertheless, the possibility of the triumph of one hegemony over another does not derive from its logical character, namely its superior intellectual qualities. Gramsci points out that the reasons for the triumph of a hegemony over another is to be sought in the 'causal and necessary nexus'. In other words, the reasons for the triumph of one hegemony are to be found in the specific relations of forces that characterize a given situation, and this requires a careful study of the various temporal processes, the different causal elements and their scope, that result in any given event.[120] Gramsci also contends that when a social group is progressive, the other groups are spontaneously attracted by it.[121] The 'spontaneous consensus given by the great masses of the population to the direction impressed in social life by the fundamental dominant group' is said to 'originate "historically" from the prestige . . . derived by the dominant group from its position and from its function in the world of production'.[122]

Gramsci's insistence on the historicity of hegemony and on the historical, rather than intellectual, reasons for the triumph of one hegemonic system over another are of the utmost importance for a clear understanding of this crucial concept. As we have seen, Gramsci's historicism is, among other things, the rejection of all transcendentalism, as well as a rejection of the view that reason contains in itself a set of ideas, or ethical norms, whose development provides the basis for the dialectic of history. For Gramsci, thought derives from being, philosophical problems are presented by history.[123] The conclusion we must reach is that hegemonic principles, or hegemonic systems, are not ethical-cultural ideologies which pre-exist historical development and one-sidedly determine the movement of history. On the contrary, hegemonic principles originate in the social and economic organization of life. What presents itself as spontaneous consensus to efforts of a group to organize society is not related to the discovery of some principle of reason that finally makes itself noticeable, but rather to the discovery that the new organization of socio-economic life offers the possibilities of greater individual as well as group development and satisfaction. The prestige that a group derives from its position and its function in the world of production is the result of the perception that the group can solve the problems facing a society. The problems facing a society are both economic and ethico-political. For this reason, Gramsci contends that hegemony 'cannot but be also economic, cannot but have its foundation in the decisive function that the leading group exercises in the decisive nucleus of economic activity'.[124.]

Hegemony, then, is not merely an ethico-political phenomenon. It is, rather, the ethico-political aspect of the historical bloc. Admittedly the problems that a social group faces are not merely economic problems. They are also problems of the development of culture, of education. Above all, in our times, they are the problems of the various social movements whose connection to the economic base is not direct, if there is one at all. In general, the problem faced by the ruling class *vis-à-vis* these groups is one of leading society in general towards genuine equality in the areas of gender, race, etc., as well as the problems of peace and ecological rationality. The significance of this is that some social groupings with no necessary class identity have entered into political activity; these groups may be formed by members who objectively belong to different classes. This, it has been argued, is a serious problem which traditional Marxist class-reductionism cannot solve.

Hegemony and Gramsci's essentialism

The attempt to extract a non-economistic and non-class-reductionist theory of politics has been undertaken by several recent interpreters of Gramsci, among whom Laclau and Mouffe, under the influence of Derrida, have presented the most elaborate theory. In her several essays on Gramsci's concept of hegemony, Mouffe has argued that for Gramsci 'the struggle for hegemony is a struggle *within* ideology and not, as with Althusser, a struggle *between* ideologies'.[125] The significance of this point is that ideological elements in themselves do not have a class identity, so that 'the class character of an element will be the result of its articulation to a determined hegemonic principle'. The aim of cultural struggle, according to this interpretation, is that of appropriating ideological elements and organizing them according to a new hegemonic principle. The class that succeeds in this task will become hegemonic; success does not result from its imposing a 'class ideology on other social groups', but rather from its ability 'to articulate to its hegemonic principle the majority of the important ideological elements of a given society'.[126]

Evidence for this reading of Gramsci's concept of hegemony is found in two notes. First, Gramsci argues that:

> What matters is the criticism to which such an ideological complex is subjected by the first representatives of the new historical phase. This criticism makes possible a process of differentiation and change in the relative weight that the elements of the old ideologies used to possess. What was previously secondary and subordinate, or even incidental, is now taken to be primary – becomes the nucleus of a new ideological and theoretical complex. The old collective will dissolves into its contradictory elements since the subordinate ones develop socially'.[127]

Second, as ideology is the 'terrain of an incessant struggle between two hegemonic principles',[128] the question of the disarticulation of the old ideological elements and their articulation by a new hegemonic principle is proposed by Gramsci in the following way:

> How then must this determinate historical consciousness be formed autonomously? How must the elements be chosen and combined for such an autonomous consciousness? Will each 'imposed' element be rejected a priori? It will be rejected a priori, but not itself; that is, it will be necessary to give it a new form which is appropriate to the given group.[129]

Mouffe then concludes that

> for Gramsci it is not a question of making a clean sweep of

169

bourgeois ideology with all the elements which constitute it, but that there are within it some elements which must be appropriated by the working class provided they are transformed and given a new form.[130]

Given that Gramsci never defines the term 'hegemonic principle' with any precision, Mouffe suggests that 'it involves a system of values the realization of which depends on the central role played by the fundamental class at the level of the relations of production'. It is through this basic system of values that the 'ideological elements acquire their class character which is not intrinsic to them'.[131]

This is a valuable attempt to develop a radical theory of politics able to deal both with those political movements which bear no connection to classes and those which do. In her interpretation, Mouffe still accepts the class identity of the articulating hegemonic principle. However, lately she has become more critical of this remnant of essentialism in Gramsci's thought. Laclau and Mouffe in their book *Hegemony and Socialist Strategy* argue that, for Gramsci, 'an organic ideology . . . is formed . . . through the articulation of elements which, considered in themselves, do not have any necessary class belonging'.[132] They reject the 'naturalist fallacy' because of its consequence 'that hegemony must always correspond to a fundamental economic class'.[133] Moreover, Laclau, in another essay, argues that the limitations of Gramsci's approach lie precisely in his view that 'only the fundamental classes of society can be hegemonic subjects'.[134] It would seem that Laclau and Mouffe argue that Gramsci's theories can be formulated in a non-essentialist discourse, but that his thought is still based on, and limited by, essentialist assumptions. In short, they point to what they regard as a deep contradiction in the *Prison Notebooks* between what is in effect the old Marxist essentialist discourse, on the one hand, and the new non-essentialist discourse they approve and seek to develop.

There are, however, some other fundamental differences between Gramsci's historicism and discourse theory (these are already quite visible in the two essays by Mouffe discussed earlier) whose full consequences only begin to appear in Laclau's and Mouffe's latest book. These fundamental differences arise out of radically different philosophical positions. The fundamental

170

philosophical thesis that characterizes discourse theory is the rejection of what Althusser refers to as the Hegelian conception of expressive totality.[135] This is, in effect, a form of essentialism in which a single historical element produces, or is reflected, in all the others. The first consequence of this is class-reductionism, in so far as classes are thought to be the subjects of history. To replace this conception of history, the advocates of discourse theory propose a conception of the intrinsic neutrality of all social elements. This, of course, is based on a theory according to which the meaning of a term is a function of its place in the discourse, not of a possible reference to something non-discursive. This emphasis on the intra-discursive constitution of all meaning is, in effect, equivalent to a kind of reduction, in the sense of Husserl's *epoche.*

As we saw, Gramsci denies that all meaning is relational: a function of the relations between terms in a discourse. Although Laclau and Mouffe do not deny that there are, in some sense, real objects in the world, independent of consciousness, they nevertheless affirm that they are constituted as objects only within a discursive practice. Hence, they sever the reference relation as if the object itself were devoid of importance. Perhaps this is a modified version of the conception of historical experience that was held by Croce as well as by Collingwood and some of the German historicists; in the present case it is a discursive practice, rather than the re-enactment of the past or the contemporaneity of history, which confers identity on social phenomena.

The significance of this lies in the attempt to provide a model for an adequate analysis of modern social movements. In their theory, discourse theorists such as Laclau and Mouffe espouse a concept of politics that is based on the non-fixedness of all elements and of human nature, so that any particular social configuration is to be explained in terms of whatever hegemonic principle succeeds at the time. Because all identity is conceived as relational and since the principle of articulation, that is, the principle that links to some unity the various elements of a social system, is hegemony, the meaning or identity of social elements depends on a practice of articulation.[136] This is defined as a 'practice establishing a relation among elements such that their identity is modified as a result of the articulatory practice'.[137] The identity of social elements depends on the hegemonic principle that brings them together as a more or less, but never completely, unified or closed system.

Needless to say, Gramsci does not draw an analogy between society and language, an analogy that presents some difficulty inasmuch as it is not clear at all that non-referential meaning relations are similar to social relations. However, the point is not whether Gramsci was consciously thinking along these lines, but whether his concept of hegemony necessitates this form of discourse to develop its meaning fully. We have already seen Gramsci's conception of the meaning or identity of social phenomena. He rejects both the idealist historicist version of the inner meaning of historical events, and the positivist theory of mere external description of types of events. Instead, he proposes a conception of historical events in terms of the causal nexus, or the network of temporal processes which together become historical necessity. The meaning of a social phenomenon is not merely a function of its own intrinsic characteristics, nor simply a matter of the hegemonic practice that articulates it. It is, rather, its position in a system of generative mechanisms, some of which are dependent on hegemonic articulation, some of which are not. That is why Gramsci insists that to understand the victory of a hegemonic principle one must look beyond the character of that hegemony, for not to do so would be to engage in mere external description.[138] The meaning, or the content of identity of hegemony, is to be found in the causal nexus. And this seems to be a far more complex and richer analysis of hegemony than the one proposed by discourse theorists.

Whatever their merits, however, their discourse is radically different from Gramsci's. The contradiction they claim undermines Gramsci's thought is in reality not an inconsistency. Gramsci's theory is a form of essentialism, for it does not deny the primacy of classes as the long-term causal mechanism of the historical process. His essentialism, however, is not the one rejected by Laclau and Mouffe, for it does not deny either the relative autonomy of politics and culture, or the importance of distinct groupings that emerge in civil society. Whereas discourse theory stresses the importance of the empirically evident groupings that exist and seeks to provide a model to understand their dynamics, Gramsci attempts to understand both the 'combinations and dispersions' of social elements as well as the deeper, long-term causal process determined by class-structures.

The groups that are formed in the terrain of civil society advance claims on the state, or even attempt to change the state according to the problems that emerge from their position in the social system or from some other area of concern. Gramsci's theory, however, is not an ethical one. Despite his stress on the concept of hegemony, it is an explanatory one, a historical one; the main question is not about the moral worth of any kind of action or hegemonic principle, but about the generative mechanisms of history. On this question, Gramsci's position is clear. The full specification of a historical bloc demands that both economic and extra-economic factors be taken into consideration and that their causal weight be assessed carefully. As a matter of historical hypothesis, Gramsci claims that the class structure of a social bloc is the strongest causal determinant in the long run.

Perhaps it is true that in the present, the working class has not been as politically active as it was after the Russian Revolution, and that, in general, its practice is reformist. And so the banner of political intervention is carried by other groups which have no class identity. The question, however, is whether this is sufficient reason to change the philosophical basis of socialist theory. A positive answer to this question reveals the most relativist form of historicism, a form to which Gramsci certainly did not adhere. Of course, there may be good reasons for altering specific empirical hypotheses. The question that must be asked is rather whether the present theoretical crisis, if one exists, is a conjunctural one or a permanent one. Gramsci's historicism suggests that the answer to this question must be sought in the long-term development of the socio-economic structure.

As we saw earlier, the growing complexity of civil society represents a problem for the dominant groups. For conflict can arise out of the various institutions of civil society, conflict that, admittedly, may not have a necessary class character. It is under these circumstances that hegemony becomes a decisive force, for it is the means by which the supremacy of the dominant class is preserved. Hegemony serves the function of unifying civil society so that it remains adequate for the existing socio-economic structure. The decisive function of hegemony is, then, that of unifying the heterogeneous and dispersed wills of individuals, of transforming them into a homogeneous, coherent whole. It is because of this decisive function of hegemony which stems from the growing complexity of civil society, that hegemony has acquired its vital strategic role. And this means that socialist forces must be able to show both their willingness and their ability to solve the problems facing society today.

Hegemony, power and the state

The view of hegemony as both the universal solution to the problems of a society, which includes all the liberation movements, and as the class-based foundation of a new state, points to Gramsci's dual conception of politics. When Gramsci affirms that all of life is politics, he endorses a view that politics is the activity of organizing a society so that the best possible life for everyone is secured. In this sense, the concern for equality and democracy is paramount. This is mainly an ethical concern, one whose central value is perhaps a deontological emphasis on the equal dignity of all human beings. It is, perhaps, no different from Marx's desire to construct a society where each receives according to his or her needs and each gives according to his or her abilities. However, the ethical universality of this conception of politics is limited in various ways. First, ethical principles must be discovered; this depends on the growth and development of societies. Second, class-structure limits the scope of politics; accordingly the rules of the good life are not intended to secure universal equality but, rather, to promote a certain inequality. Hence, politics is linked to coercion, to power understood as the supremacy of one class over the other, or of one group over another.

In this sense of coercion, politics is concerned, as Gramsci writes of the state, with adapting 'civil society to the economic structure'. And this is not possible simply by persuasion and propaganda. To expect that civil society adapt to a new structure, that is, 'that the old *homo oeconomicus* disappear without being buried with all the honors it deserves is a form of economic rhetoric, a new form of vacuous and inconclusive economic moralism'.[139] In short, ethico-political or hegemonic methods are not sufficient for effecting structural changes. The possibility for developing a social organization truly conducive to the good life does not depend on the higher moral and intellectual features of

174

a counter-hegemony alone; it cannot be materialized by moral means alone. Gramsci is far from espousing a liberal theory of politics. The ethical, or Aristotelian, conception of politics is concerned with the possibilities of a truly human organization of society. In reality, however, the obstacles to the realization of human dignity make us think about the real historical processes which give rise to possibilities within power structures or class structures which, in the long run, set the limits of any conscious intervention designed to change society.

It is in this realist conception of politics that Gramsci espouses a theory of the identity of politics and economics. The origin of this identity is found in Marx's *Capital*, where he argues that the exploitation of the working-class by capital, defined in economic terms as the appropriation of surplus-value, develops 'into a coercive relation'.[140] Whereas surplus value is an economic category, coercion is a political one; it is in effect a relation of power between two classes. In its restricted sense, Gramsci's conception of politics is based on this identity of politics and economics, an identity that, it is suggested, imprints a form of behaviour, a homogeneous element in the otherwise differentiated mode of behaviour of individuals. In short, the permanent structures of a society become 'spontaneous' or 'natural' forms of behaviour, feelings, etc. for great masses of people. The role of hegemony in this situation is that of making homogeneous the dispersed will of individuals, of creating the conditions under which the structural coercion is freely accepted as a mode of living.

In this case, hegemony finds its source, its original principle, in coercion, or more precisely, in the exploitation first of labour but also of other identifiable groups. This social relation of production is transformed into a political one. However, politics, for Gramsci, is not reduced to this power relation. Although it constitutes the essential aspect of any hegemonic system, an aspect that cannot change without transforming society as a whole, it is possible and necessary to make concessions, as Gramsci puts it, to 'the groups over which hegemony is exercised', that is, the ruling group can make 'sacrifices of an economic-corporate order; but there also is no doubt that such sacrifices and such a compromise cannot touch that which is essential, for though hegemony is ethico-political, it cannot but also be economic, it cannot but have its foundation on the decisive function exercised by the leading groups in the

175

decisive nucleus of economic activity'.[141] As we saw earlier, the high salaries paid by Ford industries was an attempt to win the consent of workers to the new work methods. Perhaps a better example is to be found in recent attempts to introduce equal pay legislation in Ontario. Apart from the narrow scope of this law, its meaning lies in the fact that it can make economic–corporate concessions to a group, without giving up any of the essential conditions of capitalism. In this sense, the Liberal government is exercising the hegemony of the dominant classes, making concessions which will be costly in economic terms, but which will control the conflicts that emerge in the private institutions of civil society.

In hegemonic struggles, then, the two conceptions of politics are synthesized. For civil society, as we saw earlier, gives rise to conflicts which are not linked to class-structure, and whose solution is, from an ethical point of view, as important as class conflicts. However, the solution to these problems can only be a partial one, as it must take place within the limits of the existing class-structure. For a fuller solution to be possible, it must be articulated to a new hegemonic class, as Mouffe suggests, a class that can present itself as being able to solve all the problems facing a society, that is, it is mature enough to include in its programme the interests and concerns of non-class groups, such as women, children, the elderly, etc.

The growing complexity of civil society, with the need for the dominant class to control any conflicts that may arise in the sphere of private organizations, has resulted in a new relationship between state and civil society. Under these circumstances, the function of the state has been expanded, involving, as Buci-Glucksmann points out, 'an incorporation of hegemony and its apparatus into the state'.[142] This is what Gramsci calls the integral concept of the state, which is defined as the unity of dictatorship and hegemony,[143] as 'political society and civil society, that is, hegemony armoured with coercion'.[144]

There are two kinds of circumstances that lie at the source of the expansion of state functions. First, as has been mentioned, there is the growth of civil society. Gramsci points out that with the colonial expansion of European countries and the increasing complexity of the internal and external relations of the state the 'formula of civil hegemony' replaces that of permanent revolution. Among the changes he thinks are significant, he lists the emergence of political parties and trade unions, as well as other associations; and he suggests that proliferation of important urban centres also contributed to this development.[145]

Second, there are economic reasons for the expansion of the state. As we have seen, the reorganization of the state in the 1930s, in the contrasting variations of the New Deal in the USA and the corporate state in Italy, were prompted by economic factors. But, as de Giovanni has observed, 'a central knot in the morphological transformations of politics' lies in 'the shift of great human masses to a *direct* relationship with the state'.[146] This shift, Gramsci argues, originates in the desire of 'the mass of savers to break off any direct connection with the *ensemble* of private capitalism'. The mass of savers, however, do 'not refuse their confidence to the state: they want to take part in economic activity, but through the state, which can guarantee a modest but sure return on investment'.[147]

In its extended role, then, the state includes civil society, but it does not cease to be political society, that is, the expression of class power. This conception of the expansion of the state seems to obliterate what may be a useful distinction between the ethical or consensual aspects of social life and the coercive aspects that are part of the state power as it controls the judicial system, the bureaucracy, and the army. However, the intervention of the state in education and other social services, as well as its interest in containing the growing demands from the voluntary associations of civil society, force the state to be more interventionist, to participate more directly not only in preserving law and order, but in organizing civil society. What Gramsci suggests is that the ruling group, through the agency of the state, must take a direct interest in civil society in order to control it and to steer its possible conflict along permissible channels. Because the state represents the 'historical unity of the ruling classes',[148] it must intervene both by means of force and by hegemonic means wherever this unity might be compromised.

The distinction between civil society and political society is thus somewhat blurred because 'in actual reality civil society and state become identified'.[149] There is, however, a deeper reason why the state's function expands as much as it does; this is that the state in its historical meaning is not identical with the government or with any institutional framework.[150] For, as Simon rightly points out, in Gramsci's theory 'power is conceived as a relation',[151] a relation that permeates all social activity. What Gramsci suggests, in Simon's words, 'is that the social relationships of civil society are relations of power just as much (though in a different way) as are the coercive relations of the state'.[152] The expansion of the state is then to be conceived as the historical process in which the fundamental relation that structures the relations of production penetrates more and more aspects of social life, so that, as Gramsci points out, the modern state, as opposed to the medieval state, 'substitutes for the mechanical bloc of social groups their subordination to the active hegemony of the leading and dominant group; hence it abolishes some autonomies, which, however, re-emerge in other forms, as parties, unions, cultural associations'.[153]

The historical meaning of the state, then, lies in the social relations, or power relations that exist between classes, although not all the problems that arise out of civil society are related to class-struggle. Nevertheless, the power relations must be made to prevail in all areas of social life. The state, in short, must educate;[154] it must adapt 'civil society to the economic structures'.[155] In the words of Bonomi, the optimum condition for the members of the ruling class is one in which they 'govern with the "spontaneous consent" of the adverse classes, and can give a "universal character" to their goods and their interests'.[156] The more they can do so without resorting to force, making concessions within the necessary limits, the more viable, secure, and strong the state will remain.

It is in this expanded conception of the state that Gramsci's analysis of the superstructures is synthesized. Although one can distinguish several levels of the superstructures, and hence distinguish civil from political society, their unity is guaranteed by the fundamental social relations that originate in the world of production. Civil society is often the source of problems, some of which have no class identity. The continued power and prestige of the leading groups depends on their response to these problems. The hegemony of a class depends on its ability to present the solutions to social problems as universal, coherent, and viable. It is in this theory of the superstructures, and in particular, of the role of the state in preserving and expanding the unity of the ruling classes, that Gramsci's thought differs from that of Marx. Luporini has argued that Marx maintained that the working of the internal mechanism of the mode of production was sufficient for the reproduction of class domination. The question that arises is, 'why does the political state not only exist but gets improved?'[157] Though Marx did not completely disregard the importance of politics, as Luporini thinks he did, he did not, and could not, anticipate the expansion of the state's functions, its changing relationship to what Gramsci calls civil society. Gramsci's theory attempts to adapt Marx's thought to the new situation. In so doing, he kept the foundational role of social relations of production, and attempted to provide a conceptual framework for the analysis of both class and non-class conflicts that threaten the hegemony of the ruling group. In his analysis of the state and politics in general, Gramsci did not, as Marx seems to do, emphasize the logic of capital or derive, as some have attempted to do, the forms of the state from the necessary forms of development of capital. It is in this respect that Gramsci's historicism most differs from Marx's thought, for Gramsci's historicism is not the attempt to derive politics from the socio-economic structure, though it does not disregard the fundamental determining role of the economy in the last instance. In the attempt to understand the complexity of the historical bloc, to fathom both its long-term phenomena and its conjunctural ones, its economic determinates as well as its ethico-civil ones, Gramsci is much more sensitive to the open character of the historical process, much more capable of understanding the role of both class and non-class politics in history. This being said, however, it is also true that, for Gramsci, no historical explanation and no political movement can dispense with the stable and long-term, though often invisible, determination of the socio-economic structure.

Finally, whatever concrete strategies may be drawn from Gramsci's *Prison Notebooks*, they must take account of the complex analysis of politics that Gramsci proposed. It is not only in the changing relations between civil society and state, but also in the relation between structure and superstructure, that the basic strategic principles must be sought.

CONCLUSION

The foregoing discussion is no more than an attempt to provide a general framework for the analysis of Gramsci's theory of history and politics. It is not, then, a full interpretation of his thought; the main purpose is to point to the kind of interpretation that seems to be the most consistent with his historicism.

Gramsci's historicism, it must be stressed, does not commit him to a theory of the ethical meaning of the inner aspects of history. This means that it does not commit him to a theory of the causal or generative primacy of politics. In so far as Gramsci makes the distinction between the exterior and interior of history, it is primarily a distinction between description and explanation. Gramsci's concern with the interior of history is to find the causal nexus, the generative mechanisms whose concurrence produces social phenomena. The explanation of social phenomena must take into consideration two levels of explanation; on the one hand, the processes of development that result in the phenomena, their history, must be carefully analysed; on the other hand, the structure of the social systems at any given point in time must also be known. Needless to say, a correct appreciation of the relative temporality of each aspect of a social system is necessary for an accurate analysis of the causal nexus.

This model of explanation is advanced as a probable solution to the problem of the relationship between structure and super-structure, that is, the problem of the reflection of the structure in the superstructure. Given the existence of non-class groups which have entered the political arena, it is not possible to claim that all political activity and all ideas are reflections of the structure. Yet, in some sense, Marxism claims that, in the last instance, the structure determines historical movement. It is the relationship between structure and historical movement, as Gramsci contended, that constitutes the most important problem of historical materialism.

According to Gramsci, society is structured in three main levels. First, the class-structure of society; second, the voluntary associations of civil society; third, the state or political society. Whereas the objective existence of classes as well as the relations between them is determined by the structure, their development as political agents is subject to mechanisms that do not bear a

180

direct relationship to the structure. Furthermore, other non-class groups and movements make this political development far more complex. In the conditions of modern capitalism, then, the state is related not only to the world of economic production, but also to civil society. Indeed, the relationship between civil society and state has become so complex and important that it often masks the other relation between state and structure. Those who claim that Gramsci holds a theory of the primacy of politics are not too far from ignoring, or even dismissing, the state-structure relation. But this is based on a mere external description of Gramsci's *Prison Notebooks*.

The empirical or descriptive reading of Gramsci's prison work, will certainly conclude that Gramsci gave primacy to the superstructures, and in particular to hegemony, for this is the problem that occupied most of Gramsci's attention. This reading, however, fails to give an account of Gramsci's theoretical assumptions. In part, as I have tried to illustrate, this is due to the scant attention given to Gramsci's uses of 'historicism', which has led to an unwarranted Crocean interpretation of his thought.

It is undeniable that, for Gramsci, the class structure of society plays a fundamental role in the determination of history. But the concept of class is a historical one, which means that its reference ranges over a whole period of history. In empirical terms, the groups that emerge in civil society and the individual who objectively belongs to the class, may or may not behave in class ways. The long-term process, however, is mainly determined by the class structure of the historical bloc. This does not deny that interests other than class interests arise in any society. But in the terrain of political activity, these interests are satisfied in ways and by means that are designed to preserve the power of the ruling classes, to add to their prestige by convincing the masses that they are capable of solving the problems of the day. The struggle for hegemony, then, is presented as taking place on two fronts: on the economic front, as the struggle to eliminate classes; on the ethico-political front, as the struggle to create a truly democratic world. A truly progressive force is one that can offer solutions to both kinds of problems, solutions that are not merely dreamt up as necessary concessions, but that are evolved on the basis of equal participation by those directly affected by them.

181

Gramsci's claim is that the modern state has been expanded to allow the ruling classes to intervene effectively in civil society. This means that the historical meaning of the state as a power relation between classes, expands to allow for the state's exercising its supremacy by other than coercive means, that is, by presenting its *Weltanschauung* and its ethics as universally valid. In so doing, the state fulfils the role of educator.

Gramsci's theory, one must conclude, is a form of essentialism, but not the one so often criticized by structuralists and discourse theorists. For according to the latter, essentialism is a form of historical determinism in which the essence, the economic structure, determines all other social phenomena. In their language, the essence determines the meaning or identity of all social elements. In Gramsci's theory, the essence, class-structure, determines the general direction of historical movement; but the causal-nexus that determines every event, every change, every social element, consists in the concurrence of processes which are characterized by their own particular dynamism. In this regard, his analysis of situations and of the relations of forces offers a theoretical model for understanding how historical movement emerges out of the structure. Historical necessity, then, is not merely constituted by the structure, but by the structure plus the organized actions of groups that emerge on the basis of their position in the social world.

It has been noted that Gramsci holds two conceptions of politics. The most general one, which I have called Aristotelian, is best exemplified by his identification of life with politics; it is the theory of the good life. The other one is a classical Marxist one; it is the theory of class power as exerted by the state. What Gramsci seems to suggest is that the hegemony of a class is composed of two kinds of elements. There is, first of all, a set of basic principles that is closely related to its class interests, and which is expressed under capitalism in theories of the *homo oeconomicus*, i.e. economic individualism, property, etc. Second, there are elements that, in so far as they can be accommodated within the scope of the first ones, allow for a higher form of civilization. For instance, as long as the claims of the women's movement can be accommodated within economic individualism, property and contract laws, etc., they may be satisfiable. In a class state, then, the ethical conception of the good life is second to the principles of class power.

To transcend class structures, then, is to establish the possibility of the good life. And this is, Gramsci writes, 'the end of the state and of law as they become useless, as they exhaust their task and are absorbed by civil society'.[158] And it is here that Gramsci's conception of democracy finds its deeper meaning; democracy is not conceived, as is the liberal model, in terms of the relations of power and in terms of elections, but in terms of the collective decision-making of all parts of society, in a society without classes, without any power relations.

CONCLUSION

In his reconstruction of historical materialism, Gramsci often used terms that had important theoretical functions in the philosophy of Benedetto Croce. 'Absolute historicism', 'transcendence', 'immanence', are all terms that played important roles in Croce's thought. Furthermore, Gramsci also espoused a theory of the identity of philosophy and history, a theory that, in Croce's system, acquires a fundamental meaning: history is the history of universal or pure concepts, in particular, it is the story of liberty. Thus, when Gramsci argues that 'split from the theory of history and politics, philosophy cannot be but metaphysics' and that the 'great conquest of modern thought . . . is the historicization of philosophy and its identification with history',[1] he seems to be arguing for a position that is very close to that of Croce. The similarity in the language used by both thinkers, however, should not lead us to believe that there is a similarity of content as well.

Croce's conception of the unity of history and philosophy is a re-translation of historical materialism into speculative language, of the 'progressive acquisitions of the philosophy of praxis', such as is developed in the 'Theses on Feuerbach' and in Engels' *Feuerbach and the End of Classical German Philosophy*.[2] What is then, for Gramsci, the unity of history and philosophy? The historicity of philosophy in its largest sense, he writes, consists in its having 'become the conception of reality of a social mass (with a corresponding ethics)'.[3] It is in this sense of a conception of the world with practical implications, that the philosophy of our epoch forms a bloc with the history of the same epoch.[4] The reasons for the diffusion of a philosophy, however, are not to be found merely in the intellectual and logical character of the philosophy itself. As

184

he argues in the case of hegemonic principles, this expansive character must be justified historically: its 'necessary and causal nexus' must be explained.[5] Whereas for Croce the problems of philosophy emerge out of the dialectic of ethical ideals and practical requirements, for Gramsci they emerge out of the depths of material life, they arise in the terrain of social relations.

It is obvious that by 'philosophy' Gramsci does not mean the thought of professional philosophers. Philosophy, for him, is synonymous with the ideas of an epoch: 'The philosophy of an epoch is not the philosophy of one or other philosophers', it is a combination of the thought of intellectuals, groups, and popular masses which 'become the norm of collective action'.[6] In short, philosophy and politics form a unity.[7] This implies that, as Cloutier has argued, one must 'envisage philosophical work in terms of philosophical hegemony, or, more precisely, within the Gramscian programme of a "cultural and moral revolution"'.[8] Whereas for Croce the work of the philosopher is concerned with contemplating the eternal life of spirit,[9] and the philosopher, as Gramsci suggests with respect to Croce himself, becomes a lay Pope,[10] for Gramsci the task of the philosopher is that of disseminating hegemonic principles or participating in the political process of social transformation.

Gramsci does not deny the truth value of philosophical theories or of knowledge in general. He is concerned, however, with the analysis of the social function of knowledge. He investigates the role of science, philosophy, etc., as ideologies, that is, as superstructural elements that shape the way men and women view natural and social reality and respond to social change. The point Gramsci develops is that the social function of knowledge need not coincide with its truth-value. A thoroughgoing study of a social system must bring to light the complex interrelationships that exist between all its elements; the study of the relation between science and society is but an aspect of that study.

This conception of historicized philosophy does not deny the other philosophy, that is, the basic logical, ontological, and epistemological conceptual frameworks with which professional philosophers deal most of the time. This type of philosophy, as we have seen in the preceding pages, is not totally foreign to Gramsci, nor is he silent on some of its fundamental problems. The attempt to define Gramsci's concept of historicism has brought out the general outline of Gramsci's philosophy, a concept that he himself often defined with reference to philosophical concepts, in particular, with reference to the concept of 'realism'. We can now establish the fundamental theses that together define Gramsci's 'absolute historicism'. Some of these theses pertain to philosophical realism, others to an ontology of social systems, still others to the general methodological principles for a science of society. Together, they amount to a general approach to the study of society.

The basic epistemological thesis espoused by Gramsci is philosophical realism. He asserts that reality exists independently of its being known or perceived. He also asserts that reality can be known, although its vastness and complexity make it impossible as a matter of fact to know it completely. Although this knowledge may have a social function that does not coincide with its truth, it can nevertheless be objectively true. In addition, Gramsci espouses the correspondence theory of truth. Furthermore, he maintains (a) that ideas reflect reality, or that being is prior to consciousness, and (b) that there are no transcendent beings, such as Providence, Spirit, Reason, etc., so that only nature, and men and women in social systems exist. The first thesis of Gramsci's historicism, then, constitutes a materialist theory of knowledge.

Gramsci's ontology of social systems is contained in six basic theses. First, social relations, rather than the decisions of great men, or single events, are the basic facts to be established, basic because they provide the real causal mechanism for social transformation. Second, social systems are not static; they are involved in transformational processes, so that even the laws of social systems are subject to change. Third, social systems are composed of several sub-processes of different temporal rhythms; their conjunction at any given time constitutes a situation. Fourth, historical events are not uniquely determined by any single law, but by the coincidence of several law-like processes of different duration. Fifth, social systems are determined by diachronic laws of the succession of various situations, and by synchronic laws determining the connections among the several component parts of the system. Although Gramsci does not develop this thesis enough for us to be able to assess it, he suggests that the two types of causality that rule succession and contemporaneity respectively are not independent of each other. In general, the theory of the reflection of the structure in the super-structure is construed as a complex process of development. Sixth, although society and the state do not exist otherwise than as the activities of, and relations between, individuals, the laws that rule their social existence are emergent upon those activities and relations, that is, they cannot be reduced without remainder to the dispositions of the individuals of the system. Gramsci defines this emergence as the dialectical transformation of quantity into quality.

A salient point of Gramsci's social ontology is his rejection of any form of reductionism to psychological, biological, or physical laws. He maintains that the explanation of social phenomena must rely on appropriate concepts obtained by means of a complex procedure of abstraction, what he calls 'determined abstraction'. In this procedure, the long-term transformations of a system yield the best evidence for constructing the appropriate conceptual and theoretical frameworks. Thus, although Gramsci does not fully reject the conception of methodological criteria general to all disciplines, he nevertheless defends the substantive autonomy of history from psychology, biology, or physics.

From a methodological point of view, the basic thesis of Gramsci's historicism is that, because society is a transformational process, the long-term perspective, or diachronic approach, is the most adequate for studying social phenomena. This is not intended as rejecting all sociology, as he often appears to do. It is, rather, a denial of the scientific character of merely synchronic studies of society. His efforts at explaining social phenomena in terms of underlying causal mechanisms, his theory of tendential laws of history, and in general his conceptual framework are part of his effort to integrate history and social theory. In this respect, Marx, as well as the *Annales* school among others, have developed similar views of an integrated scientific history. The emphasis on the long-term view and the realist theory of scientific concepts and theories suggests a second methodological principle. Some historical concepts are complex abstractions from a multitude of events, forms of behaviour, etc., over long periods of time. The reference of the relevant concepts and theories is not to a thing in a slice of time; it is to a process whose visible features are due to underlying transformational processes, and explained by means of long-term concepts and theories.

187

The long-term view is crucial for the study of social systems. It alone makes it possible to understand the structure of a social whole. Full description of societies, Gramsci maintains, is only possible when all their inherent possibilities are exhausted. This implies that, without the benefit of knowledge of the future states of a social whole, one can only describe and know its present state imperfectly. The long-term view, then, is essential for both describing and explaining social phenomena. This view, which many historians accept, entails that, as more of the effects of an event come to light, our understanding of its meaning will change, and its history will have to be rewritten. However, this does not commit Gramsci to the Crocean view that all history is contemporary history, nor to a conception of historical experience such as that espoused by some historicist thinkers. In Gramsci's view, the present is the consequence of the past and as such it contains the vital aspects of the past; the structure of the present constitutes the best evidence of what was historically necessary in the past.

The specificity of Gramsci's historicism is contained in his theory of historical time. His conception of laws as relatively permanent structures, the suggested temporal scope of concepts and theories, his emphasis on the long-term perspective, all point to the crucial importance of the rhythms of change of social phenomena. The different tempos of the various social sub-processes are an indication of various underlying causal mechanisms, whose relative weight must be carefully assessed for an adequate understanding of historical facts. The coincidence of the various sub-processes, their mutual relations, and their potential development constitute what Gramsci calls the situation. It is the situation, and in particular, the array of social forces that are engaged in struggle for hegemony, that constitutes the unit of analysis of history.

The contrast between Gramsci's historicism and that of Croce or the German historical school is quite evident. First, Gramsci does not reject the conception of laws in history, though he rejects any simplistic application of the concepts of natural science to history. Second, the subject-matter of history is not, as it was for the various forms of idealist historicism, values or meanings, liberty, or the decisions of great men; for Gramsci, the subject-matter of history is the complex and contradictory relations and struggles that are formed on the basis of social relations of production. It is,

188

hence, the economic order, as well as politics, culture, and morality. Although Gramsci's own research focused mainly on cultural and political issues, on what he generally defined as hegemony, the inner aspect of history was not constituted simply by values or meaning, but rather by a set of historically specific causal mechanisms. Thus, whereas the historical experience to which historicists in general referred was the empathetic re-enactment of the past in the mind of the historian, Gramsci's concept of historical experience is a question of the knowledge of the past as it is carefully documented and as it informs the practice, above all the political practice, of the present. As a consequence, whereas for the idealist historicists in general the values and problems of the present gave a meaning to historical experience and, through it, the past; for Gramsci the social reality of the present is evidence for the elements of the past that corresponded to historical necessity at the same time that it contains the necessary conditions for the future. Knowledge of them is of great political significance.

Gramsci's *Prison Notebooks* are mostly concerned with political, cultural, and historical issues. His comments on philosophical issues are not negligible, but they are often inconsistent. They are also easily misunderstood, as he used a language that suggested Croce's influence, and because he often had recourse to the arguments of idealist philosophers in his critique of positivism and vulgar materialism. Although his philosophy offers some interesting suggestions for the study of social phenomena, his most important work, it is generally agreed, relates to political theory. Among the most important theoretical issues that he discussed is the relation between structure and superstructure as well as the role of politics in social change.

Gramsci's focus on cultural and political studies should not be taken as an assertion of the primacy of politics, or the primacy of the superstructures. His analysis of historical subjects, such as the Risorgimento, or Americanism and Fordism, points to an interpretation that is much closer to the classical Marxist theory of the determining role of the structure. Gramsci's conception of historical laws, and of the varying temporal dimensions of different structural and superstructural processes, allows him to assert that the structure is primary in the long run, while the superstructural elements undergo changes that are not immediately determined by the structure. Because Gramsci holds a multi-causal conception of historical necessity, he can argue that the effects of the structure manifest themselves over the life of social systems, but do not uniquely determine the superstructures. There are, furthermore, long-term phenomena that do not originate directly in the socio-economic structure but which have considerable importance in the development of the historical bloc. Nevertheless, in terms of temporal succession, the various superstructural orders either originate in the social relations of production, without which no society would be conceivable, or they are inherited from the past and adapted to the class structure of the present. Gramsci engages in a dual analysis of the relation between the structure and the superstructure. First, he studies the passage from the structure to the superstructure as a temporal process, hence he focuses on the forms of political and cultural activity that originate from a given social structure. Second, he develops a conceptual framework for the study of the complex set of relations that exists among the various forces that vie for social control at any point in time, as well as between structural elements and superstructural ones. These forces are generally considered to be grounded on socio-economic classes, though they also include groups with other interests, such as women, children, and the elderly. Thus, the full specification of a historical situation must include these various elements and care must be taken to assess their respective causal weight in a realist manner.

The concept of hegemony can be studied from the point of view of class developing from a mere economic existence to its hegemonic function through the state. It can also be studied as an aspect of the domination of a class over other groups in a social system. Both kinds of analysis, diachronic and synchronic, are fundamental to Gramsci's approach to social theory. Whereas the first kind emphasizes the transformational character of the system, its process of integration and disintegration, the second attempts to show the systemic character of historical blocs. The two forms of analysis, however, cannot be taken as two mutually independent methods for the study of two different aspects of society, such as the methods of a history and a sociology. Gramsci's conception of integral history, his attempt to integrate history and a social theory, demand that the two methods be integrated. The basis for this integration is to be found in his theory of causality, and in particular his suggested, but never explicitly developed, theory of the mutual interdependence of diachronic and synchronic causality.

It has been noted that Gramsci's concept of hegemony points to a dual conception of politics. First, there is the classical Marxist conception, in which the state, hegemony, etc., are said to serve a function of domination of one class over others. Second, in its Aristotelian conception, Gramsci's expanded ideas of politics can be defined as the science of the good life. In this second conception, which is an ethical one, the problems facing a historical bloc are not merely, or not all of them, class-related problems. Nevertheless, the solutions to the problems are framed within the forms of domination prevalent in the system; that is, the long-term determination of the structure limits their possible solutions. A complete solution to all problems of this kind, Gramsci suggests, is possible only when all forms of domination disappear. The unification of humankind, as a necessary condition for objective knowledge, is seen as the process that can lead to a rational social order, an order in which the state, as coercion, has been absorbed by civil society, or by consensual decision-making.

There is a dual conception of the state in the *Prison Notebooks*. The state is conceived first as the relations of power, rather than the institutions that exercise such power, between dominant and subaltern classes. In its second, or integral, definition, the state is conceived as both hegemony and force. In this expanded role, the state must intervene in civil society, educating, making concessions, and in general controlling the conflicts that arise in the terrain of civil society. In this role, the state must ensure that civil society remains within the permissible bounds imposed by the economic structure of society. This dual conception of the state must not be construed as a Crocean liberal idea of the ethico-political state. In Gramsci's view, the supremacy of a class, and power in general, is manifested through both domination, or force, and hegemony, or ethico-political leadership. In this respect, Gramsci's analysis of culture represents the effort to understand the subtle ways in which power is manifested, or alternatively, the ways in which a new conception of the world begins to emerge in popular culture. For this reason, he paid more attention to the function of culture than to its actual content, though this is not to say that Gramsci disregarded the latter or that he thought one could be understood without the other.

Today, the proliferation of social movements seems to have cast some doubt on the validity of some of the central theses of historical materialism, in particular the thesis of the economic determination of historical change. Because of this, radical social theorists have attempted to develop Gramsci's insights on the hegemonic functions of the state from a non-class-reductionist perspective. In so doing, however, most of these interpreters of the *Prison Notebooks* have based their reading of Gramsci on assumptions about his historicism that a close reading of his work does not bear out. From Gramsci's perspective, the various groupings that originate in the terrain represent conflicts that the state must solve within the limits of the present social structure. The various forms that these groups take, the degree of consciousness that they reach, he suggests, must not be thought to challenge the Marxist concept of class structure. Whereas the former are the most empirically evident forms of struggle, the latter contains the mechanism of social transformation, a mechanism that, like Braudel's prisons, exerts its influence over long periods of time, in an often imperceptible fashion. To assert this, however, is not to deny the importance of the new social movements, or the urgency and well-foundedness of their demands.

Gramsci's theory of politics is not a denial of the primacy of economics. It is a denial that the structures are the only determining elements of a social system and that the super-structures are epiphenomena devoid of any causal import. This theory, hence, does not deny some form of essentialism, though it certainly rejects simplistic conceptions. The same reservations Gramsci had against economism, namely, that it neglects to evaluate the different causal weight of different social sub-processes, can also be addressed to those theories which deny any form of essentialism. The latter, in so far as they cannot point to any general causal mechanism of social wholes, must be limited to describing particular situations. Although in each case they may be capable of establishing the causal importance of the various elements, their findings cannot be generalized.

In conclusion, Gramsci's historicism is not an idealist, anti-scientific theory of society. Though he emphasizes the historical character of knowledge, he does so only in terms of its function in the organization and transformation of societies, not in terms of its truth value. Gramsci's political theory is his most important and lasting contribution to Marxist thought; his historicism, however, is an interesting attempt to reconstruct historical materialism that cannot be lightly dismissed.

NOTES

INTRODUCTION

1. G. Eley (1984) 'Reading Gramsci in English: observations on the reception of Antonio Gramsci in the English–speaking world 1957–82', *European History Quarterly*, 14 (October), 470.

2. L. Colletti (1976) *Il Marxismo e Hegel* vol. 1: *Su i 'Quaderni Filosofici' di Lenin* (Bari: Laterza & Figli), 121.

3. A. Gramsci (1975) *Quaderni del Carcere*, 4 vols. ed. V. Gerratana (Turin: Einaudi Editore), 2: 1438.

4. ibid., 2: 1427.

5. ibid., 2: 1438.

6. ibid., 2: 1438–9.

7. ibid., 2: 1480.

8. ibid., 2: 1316.

CHAPTER ONE

1. Gramsci, *Quaderni*, 2:1437; 3:1826.

2. A. Callinicos (1983) *Marxism and Philosophy* (Oxford: Oxford University Press), 77.

3. ibid., 78.

4. ibid., 73. See also p. 151.

5. Gramsci, *Quaderni*, 2:1437; 3:1826–7.

6. ibid., 2:1416.

7. ibid., 3:1599.

8. L. Althusser and E. Balibar (1970) *Reading Capital*, trans. B. Brewster (London: NLB) 119–40.

9. G. Vico (1976) *Principj di Scienza Nuova*, 3 vols, ed. F. Nicolini (Turin: Eindaudi Editori), 1:71.

10. ibid., 1:76.

11. ibid., 1:95.

12. ibid., 1:124.

13. ibid., 1:87.

14. ibid., 1:89.

15. ibid., 1:125.

16. ibid.

17. ibid., 1:127.

18. ibid., 1:15.

19. ibid., 1:4.

20. ibid., 1:125.

21. G. Vico (1972) *Opere*, vol. 1: *Della Antichissima Sapienza degli Italiani Rivelata delle Origine della Lingua Latina*, ed. R. Parenti (Naples: Casa Editrice Fulvio Rossi), 237.

22. ibid.

23. Vico, *Principj* 1:115.

24. I. Kant (1929) *Critique of Pure Reason*, trans. N. K. Smith (London: Macmillan), 467.

25. ibid., 471.

26. ibid., 470.

27. ibid., 471.

28. I. Kant (1963) *On History*, ed. L. W. Beck (Indianapolis: Bobbs–Merrill Co.), 11.

29. G. G. Iggers (1983) *The German Conception of History. The National Tradition of Historical Thought from Herder to the Present* (Middletown: Wesleyan University Press), 4–5.

30. W. Dilthey (1976) *Selected Writings*, trans. and ed. H. P. Rickman (Cambridge: Cambridge University Press), 94.

31. ibid., 159.

32. ibid., 248.

33. ibid., 191.

34. ibid., 203.

35. ibid., 208.

36. L. von Ranke (1973) *The Theory and Practice of History*, ed. G. G. Iggers and K. von Moltke (Indianapolis: Bobbs–Merrill Co.), 57.

37. ibid., 57–8.

38. Dilthey, *Selected Writings*, 166.

39. H. P. Rickman (1961) 'General Introduction' to *Meaning in History*, by W. Dilthey (London: G. Allen & Unwin), 37.

40. K. Popper (1961) *The Poverty of Historicism* (London: Routledge & Kegan Paul), 108–9.

41. Iggers, *The German Conception of History*, 5.

42. ibid., 8.

43. ibid., 127.

44. F. Meinecke, *Werke*, vol. 5: *Weltbürgertum und Nationalstaat*, 83, cited by Iggers, *The German Conception of History*, 9.

45. Iggers, *The German Conception of History*, 127.

46. Dilthey, *Selected Writings*, 255.

47. Iggers, *The German Conception of History*, 6.

48. ibid., 16.

49. ibid., 12.

50. M. Cruz (1981) *El Historicismo. Ciencia Social y Filosofía* (Barcelona:

Montesinos Editor), 59.

51. Iggers, *The German Conception of History*, 17.

52. J. Ortega y Gasset (1965) *Kant. Hegel. Dilthey*. (Madrid: Revista de Occidente), 149.

53. K. Marx (n.d., 1967, 1971) *Capital*, 3 vols, ed. F. Engels (Moscow: Progress Publishers), 1:29.

54. K. Marx (1976) *Grundrisse. Foundations of the Critique of Political Economy*, trans. M. Nicolaus (New York: Vintage Books), 605–6.

55. ibid., 606.

56. Marx, *Capital*, 1:85, n.1.

57. F. Engels (1946) *Ludwig Feuerbach and the End of Classical German Philosophy* (Moscow: Progress Publishers), 37.

58. K. Marx and F. Engels (1976) *The German Ideology* (Moscow: Progress Publishers), 37.

59. K. Marx (1973) *The Poverty of Philosophy* (Moscow: Progress Publishers), 95.

60. P. Rossi (1957) 'Benedetto Croce e lo storicismo assoluto', *Il Mulino* 6 (May), 327.

61. B. Croce (1909) *Logica come Scienza del Concetto Puro* (Bari: Laterza & Figli), 195.

62. B. Croce (1920) *Teoria e Storia della Storiografia* 2nd edn. (Bari: Laterza & Figli), 49–50.

63. K. Marx (1970) *Critique of Hegel's 'Philosophy of Right'*, trans. J. O'Malley (Cambridge: Cambridge University Press), 8.

64. ibid., 11.

65. Dilthey, *Selected Writings*, 235.

66. Rossi 'Croce e lo storicismo assoluto', 322–3.

67. Croce, *Logica*, 17.

68. ibid., 229.

69. ibid., 52.

70. B. Croce (1907) *Ciò che è Vivo e Ciò che è Morto della Filosofia di Hegel* (Bari: Laterza & Figli), 93.

71. ibid., 89–90.

72. Croce, *Logica*, 209.

73. ibid., 210.

74. ibid., 211.

75. Croce, *Ciò che è Vivo*, 91.

76. B. Croce (1930) 'Antistoricismo', *La Critica* 27, 407.

77. It must be noted that by 'religion' Croce meant 'a conception of reality and a corresponding ethics', B. Croce (1932) *Storia de Europa nel Secolo Decimonono* (Bari: Laterza & Figli), 23.

78. ibid., 13.

79. G. W. F. Hegel (1977) *Phenomenology of Spirit*, trans. A. V. Miller (Oxford: Oxford University Press), 478.

80. B. Croce (1967) *Etica e Politica* (Bari: Laterza & Figli), 284.

81. ibid., 285.

82. ibid., 288–9.

83. Croce, *Logica*, 215.

84. Rossi, 'Croce e lo Storicismo assoluto', 324.

85. B. Croce (1963) *Ultimi Saggi* (Bari: Laterza & Figli), 369–70.

86. Croce, *Teoria e Storia*, 118.

87. Rossi, 'Croce el o storicismo assoluto', 323.

88. Croce, *Teoria e Storia*, 87.

89. ibid., 12.

90. ibid., 4.

91. N. Badaloni (1975) *Marxismo come Storicismo* (Milan: Giangiacomo Feltrinelli), 135.

92. B. Croce (1928) *Storia d'Italia del 1871 al 1915*, 2nd edn. (Bari: Laterza & Figli), vii.

93. Badaloni, *Marxismo come Storicismo*, 135.

94. Croce, *Teoria e Storia*, 78.

95. Croce, *Ciò che è Vivo*, 91.

96. Rossi, 'Croce e lo storicismo assoluto', 351.

97. ibid., 353–4.

98. B. L. Kahn (1985) 'Antonio Gramsci's reformulation of Benedetto Croce's speculative idealism', *Idealistic Studies* 15 (January), 33.

99. Croce, *Etica e Politica*, 264.

100. ibid., 235.

101. B. Croce (1950) *Croce, the King, and the Allies. Extracts from a Diary by Benedetto Croce, July 1944–June 1945*, trans. S. Sprigge (London: George Allen & Unwin), 30.

102. Gramsci, *Quaderni*, 2:1088, 1225, 1477.

103. ibid., 2:1234.

104. ibid., 2:1433.

105. ibid., 2:826.

106. M. Finocchiaro (1979) 'Gramsci's Crocean Marxism', *Telos* 41, 32.

107. E. Laclau and C. Mouffe (1985) *Hegemony and Socialist Strategy*, trans. W. Moore (London: Verso), 90, n. 19.

108. ibid., 113.

109. Dilthey, *Selected Writings*, 235.

110. Laclau and Mouffe, *Hegemony*, 113.

111. Gramsci, *Quaderni*, 2:1018, 1478.

112. ibid., 2: 1079. In the same passage Gramsci adds a parenthetical note linking his analysis to Engels' interpretation of Hegel's statement to the effect that the real is rational.

113. ibid., 2:1487, 1489.

114. T. Nemeth (1981) *Gramsci's Philosophy*, (Brighton: Harvester Press; Atlantic City, N.J.: Humanities Press), 5.

115. *Quaderni*, 2: 1139.

116. ibid., 2: 838–9.

117. ibid., 2:1325–6. See also 2:958.

118. ibid., 2:1480.

119. ibid., 2:1393.

120. P. Vilar (1982) *Une Histoire en Construction. Approche Marxiste et Problematiques Conjoncturelles* (Paris: Editions du Seuil), 328.

121. Gramsci, *Quaderni*, 1:504; 2:1317.

122. ibid., 2:990, see also 3:1578.

123. G. McLennan (1981) *Marxism and the Methodologies of History* (London: Verson and NLB), 23.

124. Gramsci, *Quaderni*, 2:1048, 1454.

125. ibid., 2:1454.

126. ibid., 2:1290–1.

127. ibid., 2:1445.

128. R. Bhaskar (1979) *The Possibility of Naturalism. A Philosophical Critique of the Contemporary Human Sciences* (Atlantic Highlands: Humanities Press), 13.

129. Gramsci, *Quaderni*, 2:1415.

130. ibid., 2:1467.

131. ibid., 1:332.

132. ibid., 3:1855.

133. ibid., 2:1250.

134. ibid., 2:1412.

135. ibid., 2:1411–12.

136. ibid., 2:1397; see also 2:1456.

137. ibid., 1:435; 2:1434.

138. ibid.

139. ibid., 2:1456.

140. ibid., 3:1854–5.

141. ibid., 1:466–7.

142. ibid., 1:47; 3:2022.

143. ibid., 2:1033.

144. ibid., 2:1416.

145. ibid., 2:1415.

146. ibid., 2:1421.

147. ibid.

148. ibid., 2:1423.

149. ibid., 1:467, 2:1456.

150. ibid., 2:1456.

151. ibid., 2:1457.

152. ibid., 2:1421.

153. ibid., 2:977.

154. ibid., 2:1416.

155. ibid., 2:1452.

156. K. Marx (1970) *A Contribution to the Critique of Political Economy*, trans. M. Dobb (Moscow: Progress Publishers), 21.

157. Gramsci, *Quaderni*, 3:1583.

158. ibid., 2: 958, 1246, 1479.

159. ibid., 1:817, 3:1656, 1727, 1766, 2259.

160. ibid., 3:1724–5.

161. ibid., 2:1225.

162. G. Gentile (1974) *La Filosofia di Marx*, ed. V. A. Bellezza (Florence: Sansoni), 76–7.

163. Gramsci, *Quaderni*, 1:455, 2:1492.

164. A. Labriola (1973) *Scritti Filosofici e Politici*, vol. 2: *Discorrendo di*

Socialismo e di Filosofia, ed. F. Sbarberi (Turin: Einaudi Editore), 702.

165. Gramsci, *Quaderni*, 1:657.

166. ibid., 2:1493.

167. Nemeth, *Gramsci's Philosophy*, 78.

168. ibid., 7.

169. ibid., 140–1.

170. Gramsci, *Quaderni*, 2:1437.

171. ibid., 2:1478–9.

172. ibid., 2:1088, 1225, 1477; see also 1:657, and A. Gramsci (1965) *Lettere del Carcere*, 5th edn. ed. S. Caprioglio and E. Fubini (Turin: Einaudi Editore), 619.

173. Nemeth, *Gramsci's Philosophy*, 136.

174. Gramsci, *Quaderni*, 1:657.

175. ibid., 3:1826–7.

176. ibid., 2:1437.

177. ibid., 3:1864.

178. ibid., 2:1444–5; see also 1442.

179. ibid., 2:884–5.

180. Althusser and Balibar, *Reading Capital*, 127.

181. L. Salamini (1974) 'Gramsci and Marxist sociology of knowledge: an analysis of hegemony–ideology–knowledge', *Sociological Quarterly* 15 (Summer), 371.

182. Gramsci, *Quaderni*, 2:869, 1422.

183. N. Badolini (1975) *Il Marxismo di Gramsci* (Turin: Einaudi Editor), 156.

184. N. Badolini (1975) 'L'Historicisme de Gramsci face au Marxisme contemporain', *Les Temps Modernes* 30 (February), 1021.

185. ibid., 2:1022.

186. ibid., 1024.

187. N. Bobbio (1979) 'Gramsci and the conception of civil society', in *Gramsci and Marxist Theory*, ed. C. Mouffe (London: Routledge & Kegan Paul), 33, 35.

188. Badaloni, *Il Marxismo di Gramsci*, 143.

189. ibid., 142.

190. Gramsci, *Quaderni*, 2:869.

191. ibid., 2:1022.

192. ibid., 2:854, 1300.

193. ibid., 1:431; 2:1032, 1284: 3:1599, 1874–5.

194. ibid., 3:1599.

195. ibid., 2:1244.

196. J. Texier (1973) 'Gramsci: nécessité et créativité historique', *La Nouvelle Critique*, 69, 63.

197. Salamini, 'Gramsci and Marxist sociology of knowledge', 373.

198. L. Salamini (1981) *The Sociology of Political Praxis* (London: Routledge & Kegan Paul), 38; see also pp. 54, 160, and 162.

199. Salamini, 'Gramsci and Marxist sociology of knowledge', 373.

200. ibid.

201. Gramsci, *Quaderni*, 2:1397.

202. Salamini, *The Sociology of Political Praxis*, 12.
203. Marx, *Critique of Hegel's 'Philosophy of Right'*, 11.
204. ibid., 23.
205. ibid., 39.
206. See above, 25 and n. 62.
207. L. Colletti, *Il Marxismo e Hegel*, vol. 1: *Su i 'Quaderni Filosofici' di Lenin*, 115.
208. Bhaskar, *The Possibility of Naturalism*, 12.
209. Gramsci, *Quaderni*, 2:1236.
210. ibid., 2:1433.
211. ibid., 2:1246.
212. M. Bloch (1966;) *French Rural History. An Essay on its Basic Characteristics*, trans. J. Sondheimer (Berkeley and Los Angeles: University of California Press), 248.
213. Nemeth, *Gramsci's Philosophy*, 7.
214. Gramsci, *Quaderni* 2:1079.
215. ibid., 2:1443–4.
216. ibid., 2:1443.
217. Salamini, *The Sociology of Political Praxis*, 171. A similar view is expressed in: A. Pizzorno (1970) 'Sul metodo di Gramsci: dalla storiografia alla scienza politica', in *Gramsci e la Cultura Contemporanea. Atti del Convegno Internazionale tenuto a Cagliari il 23–27 Aprile 1967*, 2 vols, ed. P. Rossi (Roma: Editori Riuniti–Instituto Gramsci), 2:126.
218. Gramsci, *Quaderni* 2:1442.
219. ibid., 2:1457.

CHAPTER TWO

1. L. Gallino (1970) 'Gramsci e le scienze sociali', in *Gramsci e la Cultura Contemporanea. Atti del Convegno Internazionale tenuto a Cagliari il 23–27 Aprile 1967* 2 Vols, ed. P. Rossi (Rome: Editori Riuniti–Istituto Gramsci), 2:91–2.
2. Salamini, *The Sociology of Political Praxis*, 55–6.
3. L. Razeto Migliaro and P. Misuraca (1978) *Sociologia e Marxismo nella Critica di Gramsci* (Bari: De Donato Editore), 40.
4. ibid., 21.
5. ibid., 20.
6. ibid., 20–1.
7. ibid., 46.
8. ibid., 101.
9. Gramsci, *Quaderni*, 3:1765.
10. ibid., 2:886, 977; 3:1766.
11. Salamini, *The Sociology of Political Praxis*, 53.
12. Gramsci, *Quaderni*, 2:1388–89; 3:1612.
13. ibid., 2:1386–7.
14. ibid., 2:1387–8.

15. ibid., 2:1394.

16. ibid., 2:1388.

17. ibid., 1:434–35; 2:1432.

18. ibid., 2:738.

19. ibid., 3:1687.

20. ibid., 2:856, 142. Gramsci refers to Engel's letters to J. Block of 21–22 September 1890, and to H. Starkenburg of 25 January, 1894. See K. Marx and F. Engels (1965) *Selected Correspondence*, 2nd edn. ed. S. Ryazanskaya (Moscow: Progress Publishers), 417–19, 466–8.

21. Gramsci, *Quaderni*, 1:118, 119, 134, 235, 432; 2:865, 1194, 1197; 3:1619, 1621.

22. ibid., 1:238.

23. P. Vilar, *Une Histoire en Construction*, 355.

24. Gallino, 'Gramsci e le scienze sociali', 84.

25. Gramsci, *Quaderni*, 1:118; 3:1647.

26. ibid., 2:1046, 1402.

27. K. Hempel (1942) 'The function of general laws in history', *Journal of Philosophy* 39 (January), 36.

28. Marx, *Grundrisse*, 605.

29. Gramsci, *Quaderni*, 1:118–9; 3:1647–8.

30. ibid., 2:1194–5, 1197; 3:1619.

31. J. H. Hexter (1961) *Reappraisals in History. New Views on History and Society in Early Modern Europe* (New York: Harper Torchbooks), 11–12.

32. J. H. Randall, Jr., and G. Haines IV (1946) 'Controlling assumptions in the practice of American historians', in *Theory and Practice in Historical Study: A Report of the Committee on Historiography* (New York: Social Science Research Council), 18.

33. Gramsci, *Quaderni*, 2:873. See also 1:310, 319; 2:865, 1169; 3:1980.

34. ibid., 2:1169; 3:1980

35. ibid., 2:865.

36. C. Hill (1969) *Reformation to Industrial Revolution* (Harmondsworth: Penguin), 20.

37. Randall and Haines, 'Controlling assumptions', 18.

38. Gramsci, *Quaderni*, 1:558.

39. L. Rosiello (1982) 'Linguistica e Marxismo nel pensiero di Antonio Gramsci', *Historiographia Linguistica*, 9, 445.

40. Gramsci, *Quaderni*, 2:872.

41. Bhaskar, *The Possibility of Naturalism*, 62.

42. K. Marx, *A Contribution to the Critique of Political Economy*, 21. References to these statements are found in Gramsci, *Quaderni* 1:455; 2:855; 3:1579, 1774.

43. Bhaskar, *The Possibility of Naturalism*, 36.

44. ibid., 12.

45. E. P. Thompson (1978) 'Eighteenth–century English society: class struggle without class?' *Social History* 3 (May), 133.

46. Gramsci, *Quaderni*, 1:451; 2:1446–7.

47. M. Brodbeck (1966) 'Methodological individualisms: definition and reduction', in *Philosophical Analysis and History*, ed. W. H. Dray (New

York: Harper and Row), 321.

48. Gramsci, *Quaderni*, 1:451; 2:1447.

49. M. Mandelbaum (1951) 'A note on emergence', in *Freedom and Reason*, ed. S. W. Baron, Nagel and K. S. Pinson (Glencoe, Illinois: The Free Press), 175–6.

50. Gramsci, *Quaderni*, 1:47; 3:2022.

51. ibid., 1:451; 2:1447.

52. E. Gellner (1959) 'Holism *versus* individualism in history and sociology', in *Theories of History*, ed. P. Gardiner (Glencoe, Illinois: The Free Press), 501.

53. Gramsci, *Quaderni*, 1:451; 2:1447.

54. Gramsci, *Quaderni*, 2:872.

55. ibid.

56. ibid., 3:1992.

57. ibid., 1:456; 3:1581–2.

58. N. Kondratieff (1984) *The Long Wave Cycle*, trans. G. Daniels (New York: Richardson Snyder), 93.

59. F. Braudel (1969) *Écrits sur l'Historie* (Paris: Flammarion), 11–13.

60. ibid., 50.

61. ibid., 51–2.

62. ibid., 58–9.

63. P. Burke (1980) *Sociology and History* (London: George Allen & Unwin), 25.

64. T. Stoianovich (1976) *French Historical Method. The Annales Paradigm* (Ithaca: Cornell University Press).

65. Gramsci, *Quaderni*, 2:1100–1; 3:2176.

66. ibid., 3:2141. See also 1:70–1.

67. ibid., 1:455.

68. ibid., 3:1579.

69. ibid., 1:444; see also 2:1443.

70. ibid., 1:455; 3:1579–80.

71. ibid., 3:1959–60.

72. ibid., 1:38; 3:2042.

73. ibid., 3:1774.

74. ibid., 2:797.

75. ibid.

76. ibid., 3:1579–80.

77. J. C. Portantiero (1979) 'Gramsci y el análisis de coyuntura (algunas notas)', *Revista Mexicana de Sociología* 41 (Jan.–Mar.), 59.

78. ibid., 60–1.

79. Gramsci, *Quaderni*, 3:1580; 1:456.

80. J. Fontana i Lázaro (1967) 'Gramsci i la ciencia històrica', *Nous Horitzons* 12, 40.

81. Gramsci, *Quaderni*, 3:1583; 1:457.

82. Fontana 'Gramsci i la Ciencia Històrica', 40.

83. E. P. Thompson (1978) *The Poverty of Theory and Other Essays* (New York and London: Monthly Review Press), 124.

84. M. Aymard (1978) 'Impact of the *Annales* school in Mediterranean

countries', *Review* 1 (Winter–Spring), 62–3.
85. Salamini, *The Sociology of Political Praxis*, 79.
86. Gramsci, *Quaderni*, 2:856–7, 1429–30.
87. ibid., 2:1430.
88. ibid., 2:862; 3:1565–6.
89. ibid., 2:862.
90. ibid., 2:1253.
91. ibid., 2:1430.
92. ibid., 2:1429–30.
93. ibid., 1:442; 2:1433.
94. ibid., 2:1433.
95. ibid., 2:1236.
96. ibid., 2:1284.
97. ibid., 3:1926.
98. ibid., 2:1334.
99. ibid., 3:1755.
100. ibid., 1:440.
101. ibid., 1:503.
102. ibid.
103. ibid., 2:1.
104. ibid., 1:503; 2:1316.
105. ibid., 1:503.
106. ibid., 2:1316.
107. ibid., 1:445; 2:1445.
108. Bloch, *French Rural History* 54–5.
109. Gramsci, *Quaderni*, 1:452, 2:1505.
110. ibid., 3:2139.
111. ibid., 1:384–85.
112. P. Anderson 'The Antinomies of Antonio Gramsci', *New Left Review* 100, 20.
113. Gramsci, *Quaderni*, 2:1508–9.
114. ibid., 2:1053.
115. ibid., 3:1767.
116. Bhaskar, *The Possibility of Naturalism*, 12.
117. Gramsci, *Quaderni*, 2:1430.
118. ibid., 2:1246.
119. C. B. Macpherson(1962) *The Political Theory of Possessive Individualism. Hobbes to Locke* (Oxford: Oxford University Press), 3.
120. Gramsci, *Lettere del Carcere*, 313–14.
121. Gramsci, *Quaderni*, 2:1018, 1478.
122. ibid., 2:1248.
123. ibid., 2:1018, 1479.
124. ibid., 2:1477.
125. ibid., 1:444.
126. ibid., 2:1019, 1479.
127. Marx, *Grundrisse*, 101.
128. Gramsci, *Quaderni*, 2:1433. See also 1:435.
129. Marx, *Grundrisse*, 101.

130. Gramsci, *Quaderni*, 2:1235.

131. R. Kosellek (1982) 'Concepts of historical time and social history', in *Philosophy of History and Contemporary Historiography*, D. Carr *et al.* eds (Ottawa: University of Ottawa Press), 121.

132. ibid., 122.

133. Gramsci, *Quaderni*, 2:1279.

134. ibid., 2:1061.

135. Gallino, 'Gramsci e le scienze sociali', 86–7.

136. Razeto and Misuraca, *Sociologia e Marxismo*, 60.

137. ibid., 68.

138. Gramsci, *Quaderni*, 2:1245.

139. ibid., 3:1765–6.

140. ibid., 3:1650.

141. ibid., 2:755.

142. ibid., 2:1246.

143. ibid., 2:1479; see also 2:1089.

144. ibid., 3:1557.

145. ibid., 2:1059, 1403.

146. Bhaskar, *The Possibility of Naturalism*, 27.

147. Gramsci, *Quaderni*, 3:1810.

148. ibid., 2:1403.

149. ibid., 2:1403–4; see also 2:1059.

150. Texier, 'Gramsci, nécessité et créativité historique', 65.

151. Gramsci, *Quaderni*, 2:826.

152. ibid., 3:2010.

153. ibid., 3:2012.

154. ibid., 3:2287–8.

155. ibid., 3:1687.

156. ibid., 1:444; see also 2:1443.

157. Marx, *Capital*, 1:19.

158. Gramsci, *Quaderni*, 2:826.

159. ibid., 2:1404.

160. ibid., 2:826.

161. ibid.

162. W. J. Runciman (1973) 'What is Structuralism?' in *The Philosophy of Social Explanation*, ed. A. Ryan (Oxford: Oxford University Press), 199–200.

163. Gramsci, *Quaderni*, 1:234, 235.

164. Marx, *Grundrisse*, 101.

165. S. James (1984) *The Content of Social Explanation*, (Cambridge: Cambridge University Press), 3.

166. Gramsci, *Quaderni*, 2:1375.

167. Bhaskar, *The Possibility of Naturalism*, 73–4.

168. V. Melchiore (1966) 'Sullo storicismo di Gramsci', *Humanitas* 21 (June), 586.

169. ibid., 590.

170. Gramsci, *Quaderni*, 2:1035; 3:1877.

171. ibid., 2:1484.

172. ibid., 2:750.
173. ibid., 2:855.
174. ibid., 2:1273.
175. ibid., 3:1875–6.
176. ibid., 3:1875.
177. ibid., 2:887.
178. ibid., 3:1878.
179. ibid., 2:1280–1.
180. ibid., 1:443–4; 2:1442–3.
181. T. Benton (1977) *The Philosophical Foundations of the Three Sociologies* (London: Routledge & Kegan Paul), 171.
182. Gramsci, *Quaderni*, 2:1035; 3:1878.
183. ibid., 2:1437.
184. ibid., 2:1018, 1478.
185. Badaloni, *Il Marxismo di Gramsci*, 133.
186. A. Sánchez Vázquez *et al.* (1975) *Estructuralismo y Marxismo* (Barcelona: Ediciones Grijalbo, S.A.), 43–4.
187. Gramsci, *Quaderni*, 2:869.
188. C. Rodríguez-Aguilera guezAguilerade Prat (1983) 'Gramsci i la història d'Italia', *L'Avenç*, 56, 58.

CHAPTER THREE

1. N. Bobbio (1979) 'Gramsci and the conception of civil society', in *Gramsci and Marxist Theory*, ed. C. Mouffe (London: Routledge & Kegan Paul), 31.
2. ibid., 33.
3. ibid., 35.
4. J. Texier (1979) 'Gramsci, theoretician of the superstructures. On the Concept of Civil Society', in *Gramsci and Marxist Theory*, ed. C. Mouffe, 49.
5. ibid., 67.
6. ibid., 52.
7. ibid., 71.
8. H. Portelli (1972) *Gramsci et le Bloc Historique* (Paris: Presses Universitaires de France), 10.
9. ibid., 97.
10. ibid., 11.
11. G. Nardone (1971) *Il Pensiero di Gramsci* (Bari: De Donato Editore), 41.
12. ibid., 42.
13. ibid., 39.
14. ibid., 42.
15. ibid., 41.
16. ibid., 332.
17. Salamini, *The Sociology of Political Praxis*, 146.
18. ibid., 12. See also 119, 146.

19. ibid., 119.

20. ibid., 146.

21. P. Misuraca (1977) "Sulla ricostruzione Gramsciana dei concetti di struttura e superstruttura", *Ressegne Italiana di Sociologia* 18 (July–Sept.), 440.

22. ibid., 444.

23. A. S. Sassoon (1980) *Gramsci's Politics* (London: Croom Helm), 184.

24. ibid., 241, n.6.

25. ibid., 139.

26. Gramsci, *Quaderni*, 1:437.

27. ibid., 2:869.

28. ibid., 2:1051.

29. ibid., 2:1052.

30. ibid., 2:1091.

31. ibid., 2:1316.

32. ibid., 3:1569; see also 2:977.

33. ibid.

34. Sassoon, *Gramsci's Politics*, 216.

35. C. Buci–Glucksmann (1980) *Gramsci and the State*, trans. D. Fernbach (London: Lawrence and Wishart), 77.

36. Gramsci, *Quaderni*, 3:2139.

37. ibid.

38. ibid., 3:2139–40.

39. ibid., 3:2143.

40. ibid., 3:2145.

41. ibid., 2:1281–2.

42. ibid., 3:2145–6.

43. ibid., 3:2165.

44. ibid., 3:2171.

45. ibid., 3:2172.

46. ibid., 1:73.

47. ibid., 3:2148.

48. ibid., 3:2149.

49. ibid. See also 1:73.

50. ibid., 3:2149–50. See also 1:73.

51. ibid., 2:903.

52. For a comprehensive and useful treatment of this issue see: F. Cunningham (1987) *Democratic Theory and Socialism* (Cambridge: Cambridge University Press).

53. A. Pizzorno (1970) 'Sul metodo di Gramsci: della storiografia alla scienza politica', in *Gramsci e la Cultura Contemporanea*, ed. P. Rossi, 114.

54. Gramsci, *Quaderni*, 2:1019, 1479; see also 2:1247.

55. ibid., 1:444.

56. ibid., 1:40.

57. ibid., 3:2010.

58. ibid.

59. ibid., 1:40.

60. ibid., 3:2037; see also 1:35.

61. Buci-Glucksmann, *Gramsci and the State*, 26.
62. Gramsci, *Quaderni*, 3:2042, 1:38.
63. ibid., 3:2011.
64. ibid., 1:457; 3:1582–3.
65. ibid., 1:457; 3:1583.
66. ibid., 1:458; 3:1585.
67. ibid., 1:457; 3:1583.
68. ibid.
69. ibid., 1:458; 3:1584.
70. ibid., 1:458; 3:1584–5.
71. Femia, *Gramsci's Political Thought*, 117.
72. Gramsci, *Quaderni*, 2:872.
73. ibid., 2:1120, 3:1612.
74. ibid., 2:1058.
75. ibid., 2:1246.
76. E. P. Thompson, 'Eighteenth-century English society: class struggle without classes?, 147.
77. Gramsci, *Quaderni*, 3:1561.
78. ibid., 3:1561–2.
79. ibid., 3:1563–4.
80. ibid., 3:1564.
81. ibid., 1:433–4.
82. ibid., 1:433.
83. Femia, *Gramsci's Political Thought*, 116.
84. Gramsci, *Quaderni*, 2:869.
85. ibid., 2:869, 1422.
86. Fontana, 'Gramsci i la ciencia històrica', 41.
87. ibid., 42.
88. Gramsci, *Quaderni*, 1:332. Cited by Fontana, 'Gramsci i la ciencia històrica', 42.
89. R. Simon (1982) *Gramsci's Political Thought. An Introduction* (London: Lawrence and Wishart), 15.
90. ibid., 18.
91. ibid., 91.
92. Laclau and Mouffe, *Hegemony and Socialist Strategy*, 69.
93. Gramsci, *Quaderni*, 1:41.
94. ibid., 3:2010.
95. ibid., 2:914.
96. ibid., 2:1084.
97. ibid., 2:1236.
98. A. S. Sassoon (1982) 'Hegemony, war of position and political intervention', in *Approaches to Gramsci*, ed. A. S. Sassoon (London: Writers and Readers Publishing Cooperative Society), 95.
99. Sassoon, *Gramsci's Politics*, 113.
100. Gramsci, *Quaderni*, 2:866.
101. ibid., 1:117; 3:2057.
102. ibid., 3:1254.
103. ibid., 3:2057; see also 1:117–8.

104. ibid., 1:41.

105. ibid., 3:2010.

106. ibid., 3:1588.

107. J. A. Davis (1979) 'Introduction: Antonio Gramsci and Italy's passive revolution', in *Gramsci and Italy's Passive Revolution*, ed. J. A. Davis (London: Croom Helm), 14.

108. Gramsci, *Quaderni*, 2:1084.

109. ibid., 1:58; 3:1636.

110. ibid., 3:2010.

111. Gramsci, *Lettere del Carcere*, 616.

112. N. Machiavelli (1976) *Il Principe e Altre Opere Politiche* (Milano: Garzanti Editore), 65.

113. R. A. Dahl (1963) *Modern Political Analysis* (Engelwood Cliffs, NJ: Prentice Hall Inc.), 73.

114. C. Buci-Glucksmann (1982), 'Hegemony and consent: a political strategy', in *Approaches to Gramsci*, ed. A. S. Sassoon, 118.

115. Femia, *Gramsci's Political Thought*, 37.

116. Buci-Glucksmann, 'Hegemony and consent: a political strategy', 120.

117. Gramsci, *Quaderni*, 1:461; 3:1591.

118. ibid., 3:2145, 2171–2.

119. ibid., 1:42; 3:2012.

120. ibid., 2:1236.

121. ibid., 1:42; 3:2012.

122. ibid., 2:1519.

123. ibid., 2:1273.

124. ibid., 3:1591; also 1:123.

125. C. Mouffe (1981) 'Hegemony and the integral state in Gramsci: towards a new concept of politics', in *Silver Linings. Some Strategies for the Eighties*, ed. G. Bridges and R. Brunt (London: Lawrence and Wishart), 175.

126. ibid., 173.

127. Gramsci, *Quaderni*, 2:1058, cited in Mouffe, 'Hegemony and the integral state in Gramsci', 174.

128. ibid., 2:1236, cited in Mouffe, 'Hegemony and the integral state in Gramsci', 173.

129. ibid., 3:1875, cited in Mouffe, 'Hegemony and the integral state in Gramsci', 175.

130. Mouffe, 'Hegemony and the integral state in Gramsci', 175.

131. C. Mouffe (1979) 'Hegemony and ideology in Gramsci', in *Gramsci and Marxist Theory*, ed. C. Mouffe, 193.

132. Laclau and Mouffe, *Hegemony and Socialist Strategy*, 68.

133. ibid., 69.

134. E. Laclau (1984), 'Transformations of advanced industrial societies and the theory of the subject', in *Rethinking Ideology: a Marxist Debate*, ed. S. Hanninen and L. Paldan (Berlin: Argument Verlag), 42.

135. Althusser and Balibar, *Reading Capital*, 17.

136. Laclau and Mouffe, *Hegemony and Socialist Strategy*, 113.

137. ibid., 105.

138. Gramsci, *Quaderni*, 2:1236.

139. ibid., 2:1254.

140. Marx, *Capital*, 1:293.

141. Gramsci, *Quaderni*, 3:1591; see also 1:461.

142. Buci-Glucksmann, *Gramsci and the State*, 70.

143. Gramsci, *Quaderni*, 2:810–11.

144. ibid., 2:763–4.

145. ibid., 2:1566.

146. B. de Giovanni (1979) 'Lenin and Gramsci: state, politics, and party', in *Gramsci and Marxist Theory*, ed. C. Mouffe, 273–4.

147. Gramsci, *Quaderni*, 3:2175.

148. ibid., 1:372; 3:2287.

149. ibid., 3:1590.

150. G. Bonomi (1975) 'La Théorie Gramscienne de l'état', *Les Temps Modernes* 30 (Feb.), 977. He cites Gramsci, *Quaderni*, 2:2020, in which Gramsci notes that in 'common speech the name of state is given to state life and that it is vulgarly understood as the whole of the state'.

151. Simon, *Gramsci's Political Thoughts*, 73.

152. ibid., 72.

153. Gramsci, *Quaderni*, 3:2287. See also 1:303.

154. ibid., 1:56; 3:1565, 2314.

155. ibid., 3:1254.

156. Bonomi, 'La Théorie Gramscienne de l'état', 989.

157. C. Luporini (1979) 'La Politique et l'étatique: une our deux critiques?' in *Marx et sa Critique de la Politique*, E. Balibar *et al.* (Paris: Francois Maspero), 9.

158. Gramsci, *Quaderni*, 2:937.

CONCLUSION

1. Gramsci, *Quaderni* 2:1426.

2. ibid., 2:1271.

3. ibid., 2:1272.

4. ibid., 2:1255.

5. ibid., 2:1236.

6. ibid., 2:1255.

7. ibid., 2:1241.

8. Y. Cloutier (1983) 'Gramsci et la question de l'idéologie', *Philosophiques* 10 (Oct.), 253.

9. Gramsci, *Quaderni*, 2:1327.

10. ibid., 2:1303.

BIBLIOGRAPHY

WORKS BY GRAMSCI

In Italian

Gramsci, A. (1954) *L'Ordine Nuovo (1919–1920)*, Turin: Einaudi Editore.
(1958) *Scritti Giovanili (1914–1918)*, Turin: Einaudi Editore.
(1960) *Soto la Mole (1916-1920)*, Turin: Einaudi Editore.
(1965) *Lettere dal Carcere*, ed. S. Caprioglio and E. Fubini, Turin:
Einaudi Editore.
(1966) *Socialismo e Fascismo. L'Ordine Nuovo (1921-1922)*, Turin:
Einaudi Editore.
(1971) *La Costruzione del Partito Comunista (1923-1926)*, Turin: Einaudi
Editore.
(1975) *Quaderni del Carcere*, 4 vols, ed. V. Gerratana, Turin: Einaudi
Editore.

English Translations

Gramsci, A. (1957) *The Modern Prince and Other Writings*, trans. L. Marks,
New York: International Publishers.
(1971) *Selections from the Prison Notebooks*, ed. and trans. G. Hoare and
G. Nowell-Smith, New York: International Publishers.
(1973) *Letters from Prison*, trans. L. Lawner, New York: Harber & Row.
(1975) *History, Philosophy and Culture in the Young Gramsci*, ed. P.
Cavalcanti and P. Piccone, St. Louis: Telos Press.
(1977) 'Notes on Journalism', *Telos* 32, 139-51.
(1977) *Selections from Political Writings, 1910-1920*, ed. J. Mathews and
Q. Hoare, New York: International Publishers.
(1978) *Selections from Political Writings, 1921-1926*, trans. and ed. Q.
Hoare, New York: International Publishers.
(1979) 'Science and scientific ideologies', *Telos* 41, 151-5.
(1984) 'Notes on language', *Telos* 59, 127-50.
(1985) *Selections from Cultural Writings*, ed. D. Forgus and G.
Nowell-Smith, London: Lawrence and Wishart.

210

Marzani, C. (1957) *The Open Marxism of Antonio Gramsci*, New York: Cameron Associations.

BIBLIOGRAPHIES

Biondi, M. (1977) *Guida Bibliografica a Gramsci*, Cesena: Libreria Adamo Bettini.

Cozens, P. (1977) *Twenty Years of Antonio Gramsci: A Bibliography of Gramsci and Gramsci Studies Published in English, 1957-1977*, London: Lawrence and Wishart.

Fubini, E. (1970) 'Bibliografia Gramsciana', in *Gramsci e la Cultura Contemporanea. Atti del Convegno Internazionale tenuto a Cagliari il 23-27 Aprile* 1967, ed. P. Rossi, 477-544, Rome: Editori Riuniti-Istituto Gramsci.

(1977) 'Bibliografia Gramsciana, 1968-1977', in *Politica e Storia in Gramsci. Atti del Convegno Internazionale di Studi Gramsciani. Firenze, 9-11 Dicembre, 1977* ed. F. Ferri, 649-733, Rome: Editori Riuniti-Instituto Gramsci.

Kaye, H. J. (1981) 'Antonio Gramsci: an annotated bibilography of studies in English', *Politics and Society* 10, 335-53.

WORKS ON GRAMSCI

Adamson, W. (1978) 'Beyond "Reform or Revolution": notes on political education in Gramsci, Habermas, and Arendt', *Theory and Society* 4 (November), 429-60.

(1979) 'Towards the Prison Notebooks: the evolution of Gramsci's thinking on political organization', *Polity* 7 (Fall), 38-64.

(1980) 'Gramsci's interpretation of Fascism', *Journal of the History of Ideas* 41 (October-December), 615-33.

(1980) *Hegemony and Revolution. A Study of Antonio Gramsci's Political and Cultural Theory*, Berkeley: University of California Press.

(1987) 'Gramsci and the politics of civil society', *Praxis International* 7 (October 1987-January 1988), 320-39.

Adler, F. (1977) 'Factory councils, Gramsci and the industrialists', *Telos*, 31, 67-90.

Agazzi, E. *et al.*(1979) *Gramsci un Eredità Contrastata. La Nuova Sinistra Rilegge Gramsci*, Milan: Edizioni Ottaviano.

Albers, D. (1980) 'Gramsci ja-Bauer nein?' *Das Argument* 22 (March-April), 221-4.

(1983) *Versuch Über Otto Bauer und Antonio Gramsci: Zur Politischen Theorie des Marxismus*, Berlin: Argument-Verlang.

Amendola, G. (1978) *Antonio Gramsci nella Vita Culturale e Politica Italiana*, Naples: Guida Editori.

Amodio, L.(1986) 'Rosa Luxemburg e Gramsci. Continuita e differnze', *Il Politico* 51 (March), 183-94.

Anderson, P. (1968) 'Introduction to Antonio Gramsci, 1919-1921', *New*

Left Review, 51, 22-7.

(1976) 'The Antinomies of Antonio Gramsci', *New Left Review*, 100, 5-78.

Arnold, D. (1984) 'Gramsci and peasant subalternity in India', *Journal of Peasant Studies* 11 (July), 155-77.

Asaro Mazzola, G. (1980) *Gramsci fuori dal Mito*, Rome: A. Armando.

Asor Rosa, A. (1978) 'Gramsci and Italian cultural history', *Praxis*, 41, 107-13.

Auciello, N. (1974) *Socialismo ed Egemonia in Gramsci e Togliatti*, Bari: De Donato.

Badaloni, N. (1970) 'Il fondamento teorico dello storicismo Gramsciano', in *Gramsci e la Cultura Contemporanea. Atti del Convegno Internazionale tenuto a Cagliari il 23-27 Aprile 1967*, ed. P. Rossi, Rome: Editori Riuniti-Istituto Gramsci, vol. 2, 73-80.

(1974) 'Gramsci et le problème de la revolution', *Dialectiques* 4-5, 103-25.

(1975) 'L'Historicisme de Gramsci face au Marxisme contemporain', *Les Temps Modernes* 30 (February), 1019-47.

(1975) *Il Marxismo di Gramsci*, Turin: Einaudi Editori.

(1979) 'Gramsci and the problem of the revolution', in *Gramsci and Marxist Theory*, ed. C. Mouffe, London: Routledge & Kegan Paul, 80-109.

Badaloni, N. *et al.* (1977) *Attualita di Gramsci. L'Egemonia, lo Stato, la Cultura, il Metodo, il Partito*, Milan, Il Saggiatore.

Badia, G. (1970) 'Gramsci et Rosa Luxemburg', *La Nouvelle Critique* 30, 71-3.

Baldan, A. (1977) 'Gramsci as an historian of the 1930s', *Telos* 31, 100-11.

(1978) *Gramsci come Storico. Studio sulle Fonti dei 'Quaderni del Carcere'*, Bari: Dedalo Libri.

Bates, T. R. (1974) 'Antonio Gramsci and the Soviet experiment in Italy', *Societas* 4 (Winter), 39-54.

(1975) 'Gramsci and the theory of hegemony', *Journal of the History of Ideas*, 36 (April-June), 351-66.

(1976) 'Antonio Gramsci and the Bolshevization of the PCI', *Journal of Contemporary History* 11, 115-31.

Bausola, A. (1967), 'Gramsci e Croce', in *Filosofia e Storia del Pensiero Crociano*, Milan: Edizioni Vita e Pensiero.

Bellingeri, E. (1975) *Dall'Intellettuale al Politico. Le 'Cronache Teatrali' di Gramsci*, Bari: Dedalo Libri.

Benney. M.(1983) 'Gramsci on law, morality, and power', *International Journal of the Sociology of Law* 11 (May), 191-208.

Benot, Y. (1975) 'Gramsci en France', *La Pensee* 184, 3-24.

Bergami, G. (1977) *Il Giovane Gramsci e il Marxismo. 1911-1918*, Milan: Feltrinelli Editore.

(1978) 'Gramsci e il Fascismo nel primo tempo del Partito Comunista d'Italia', *Belfagor*, 33 (March), 159-72.

(1979) 'Antonio Gramsci', *Belfagor* 34 (July), 411-34.

(1981) *Gramsci Communista Critico. Il Politico e il Pensatore*, Milan: Franco Angeli Editore.

Bermudo Avail, J. M. (1979) *De Gramsci a Althusser*, Barcelona: Horsori.

Bischoff, J. (1981) *Einfuhrüng Gramsci*, Hamburg: USA-Verlag.

Bobbio, N.(1976) *Gramsci e la Concezione della Società Civile*, Milan: Feltrinelli.

(1979) 'Gramsci and the conception of civil society', in *Gramsci and Marxist Theory*, ed. C. Mouffe, London: Routledge & Kegan Paul, 21-47.

Boekelman, M. A. (1973) 'On the political theory of Antonio Gramsci', *Alive Magazine* 3, 37-42.

Boelhower, W.(1980) 'Antonio Gramsci and the myth of America in Italy during the 1930s', *Minnesota Review* 15 (Fall), 34-52.

(1981) 'Antonio Gramsci's sociology of literature', *Contemporary Literature* 22 (Fall), 574–99.

Boggs, G. (1972) 'Gramsci's "Prison Notebooks"', *Socialist Revolution* 2 (September-October), 79-118.

(1972) 'Gramsci's "Prison Notebooks": part 2', *Socialist Revolution* 2 (November-December), 29-56.

(1974) 'Gramsci's theory of the Factory Councils: nucleus of the socialist state', *Berkeley Journal of Sociology* 19, 171-87.

(1976) *Gramci's Marxism*, London: Pluto Press.

(1979) 'Marxism and the role of intellectuals', *New Political Science* 2-3, 7-23.

(1980) 'Gramsci and Eurocommunism', *Radical America* 14 (May-June) 7-23.

(1982) 'Gramsci and Eurocommunism', in *Continuity and Change in Marxism*, ed. N. Fischer, Atlantic Highlands: Humanities Press, 189-200.

(1984) *The Two Revolutions: Gramsci and the Dilemmas of Western Marxism*. Boston: South End, 1984.

Bolognini, R. (1973) 'Cultura e classe operaia in Gramsci', *Istituto Giangiacomo Feltrinelli. Annali* 15, 1295-317.

Bonetti, P. (1980) *Gramsci el la Società Liberaldemocratica*, Bari: Laterza & Figli.

Bonino, G. (1972) *Gramsci e il Teatro*, Turin: Einaudi Editore.

Bonomi, G. (1973) *Partito e Revoluzione in Gramsci*, Milan: Feltrinelli Editore.

(1973) 'La teoria della rivoluzione in Gramsci', *Istituto Giangiacomo Feltrinelli Annali* 15, 1276-94.

(1975) 'La théorie Gramscienne de l'état', *Les Temps Modernes* 30 (February), 878-98.

Borghese, L. (1981) 'Tia Alena in bicicletta. Gramsci traduttore dal Tedesco e teorico della traduzione', *Belfagor* 36 (November), 632-65.

Bosi, A. (1975) 'O trabalho dos intelectuais segundo Gramsci', *Debate & Critica* 6, 105-13.

Bozal, V. (1976) *El Intelectual Colectivo y el Pueblo*, Madrid: Comunicación.

Broccoli, A. (1972) *Antonio Gramsci e l'Educazione come Egemonia*,

Florence: La Nuova Italia.

Buci-Glucksmann, C. (1974) 'Gramsci et l'état', *Dialectiques* 4-5, 5-27.

(1975) *Gramsci et l'État: Pour une Théorie Matérialiste de la Philosophie,* Paris: Fayard.

(1979) 'State, transition and passive revolution', in *Gramsci and Marxist Theory,* ed. C. Mouffe, London: Routledge & Kegan Paul, 207-36.

(1980) *Gramsci and the State,* trans. D. Fernbach, London: Lawrence and Wishart.

(1982) 'Hegemony and consent: a political strategy', in *Approaches to Gramsci,* ed. A. S. Sassoon, London: Writers and Readers Publishing Cooperative Society, 116-26.

Buzzi, A. R. (1967) *La Theorie Politique d'Antonio Gramsci,* Paris: Béatrice Nauwelaertes; Louvain: Editions Nauwelaertes.

Cain, M. (1983), 'Gramsci, the state and the place of law, in *Legality, Ideology, and the State,* ed. D. Sugarman, London: Academic Press, 95-117.

Calabro, G. P. (1982) *Antonio Gramsci. La 'Transizione' Politica,* Naples: Edizione Scientifiche Italiane.

Calzolari, A. (1969) 'Structure and superstructure in Gramsci', *Telos* 2, 33-42.

Cammet, J. M. (1967) *Antonio Gramsci and the Origins of Italian Communism,* Stanford: Stanford University Press, 1967.

(1971) 'Socialism and participatory democracy', in *The Revival of American Socialism,* ed. G. Fischer, New York: Oxford University Press, 41-60.

Capucci, F. (1978) *Antonio Gramsci. Materialismo Storico e la Filosofia di Benedetto Croce,* L'Aquila: L. U. Japadre Editore.

Caracciolo, A., and Scalia, G. (eds) (1959) *La Citta Futura. Saggi sulla Figura e il Pensiero di Antonio Gramsci,* Milan: Feltrinelli Editore.

Carducci, N. (1973) *Gli Intellettuali e l'Ideologia Americana nell'Italia Letteraria degli Anni Trenta,* Manduria: Lucaita Editore.

Carocci, G. (1948) 'Un intellettuale fra Lenin e Croce', *Belfagor* 3 (July), 435-45.

Carrannante, A. (1973) 'Antonio Gramsci e i problemi della lingua Italiana', *Belfagor* 28 (September), 544-56.

Cereja, F. (1973) *Intellettuale e Politica. Dall'Epoca Giolittiana all'Affermazione del Fascismo,* Turin: G. Giappichelli Editore.

Cerroni, U. (1978) *Lèssico Gramsciano,* Rome: Editori Riuniti.

Cheal, D. J. (1979) 'Hegemony, ideology and contradictory consciousness', *Sociological Quarterly* 20 (Winter), 109-18.

Chemotti, S. (1975) *Umanesimo, Rinascimento, Machiavelli nella Critica Gramsciana,* Rome: Bulzoni Editore.

Cirese, A. M. (1973) *Cultura Egemonica e Culture Subalterne,* Palermo: Palumbe.

(1974) 'Conception du monde, philosophie spontanée, folklore', *Dialectiques* 4-5, 73-100.

(1976) *Intellettuali, Folklore, Istinto di Classe. Note su Verga, Deledda,*

Scotellaro, Gramsci, Turin: Einaudi Editore.

Clarke, M. N. (1977) *Antonio Gramsci and the Revolution that Failed,* New Haven: Yale University Press.

Cloutier, Y. (1983) 'Gramsci et la question de l'idéologie', *Philosophiques* 10 (October), 243-53.

Coassin-Spiegel, H. (1983) *Gramsci und Althusser. Eine Kritik der Althusserschen Rezeption von Gramscis Philosopie,* Berlin: Argument-Verlag.

Colletti, L. (1971) 'Antonio Gramsci and the Italian revolution', *New Left Review* 65, 87-94.

Cortesi, L. (1975) 'Palmiro Togliatti, la "Svolta di Salermo" e l'eredità Gramsciana', *Belfagor* 30 (January), 1-44.

Cox. R. W. (1983) 'Gramsci, hegemony and international relations: an essay in method', *Millennium* 12 (Summer), 163-75.

Cristofolini, P. (1976) 'Sulla dialettica di Gramsci e la storia filosofica delle "facoltà"', *Aut Aut,* 151, 68-72.

Davidson, A. (1972) 'The varying seasons of Gramscian studies', *Political Studies* 20 (December) 448-61.

—— (1973) 'Gramsci and reading Machiavelli', *Science and Society* 37 (Spring), 56-80.

—— (1974) 'Gramsci and Lenin, 1917-1922', *Socialist Register,* 125-50.

—— (1977) *Antonio Gramsci: Towards an Intellectual Biography,* London: Merlin Press.

—— (1984) 'Gramsci, the peasantry, and popular culture', *Journal of Peasant Studies* 11 (July), 139-53.

Davis, J. A. (ed.) (1979) *Gramsci and Italy's Passive Revolution,* London: Croom Helm.

Dawson, D. (1982) 'Educational hegemony and the phenomenology of community participation', *Journal of Educational Thought* 16 (December), 150-60.

De Felice, F. (1966) 'Questione meriodinale e problema dello stato in Gramsci', *Rivista Storica del Socialismo* 9 (January-April), 118-220.

—— (1971) *Serrati, Bordiga, Gramsci e il Problema della Rivoluzione in Italia, 1919-1920,* Bari: De Donato Libri.

de Giovanni, B. (1979) 'Lenin and Gramsci: State politics and party', in *Gramsci and Marxist Theory,* ed. C. Mouffe, London: Routledge & Kegan Paul, 259-88.

de Giovanni, B., Gerratana, V., and Paggi, L. (1977) *Egemonia Stato Partito in Gramsci,* Rome: Editori Riuniti.

Debray, R. (1970) 'Schema for a study of Gramsci', *New Left Reivew,* 59, 48-52.

Di Giorgi, P. L. (1979) 'Gramsci e l'economia politica classica', *La Critica Sociologica* 49, 76-81.

Eley, G. (1984) 'Reading Gramsci in English: observations on the reception of Antonio Gramsci in the English-speaking world 1957-82', *European History Quarterly* 14 (October), 441-78.

Entwistle, H., (1978) 'Antonio Gramsci and the school as hegemonic', *Educational Theory* 28 (Winter), 23-33.

(1979) *Antonio Gramsci: Conservative Schooling for Radical Politics*, London: Routledge & Kegan Paul.

Femia, J. V. (1975) 'Hegemony and consciousness in the thought of Antonio Gramsci', *Political Studies* 23 (March), 29-48.

(1979) 'Gramsci, the *Via Italiana* and the classical Marxist-Leninist approach to revolution', *Government and Opposition* 14 (Winter), 66-95.

(1981) *Gramsci's Political Thought, Hegemony, Consciousness, and the Revolutionary Process*, Oxford: Oxford University Press.

(1981) 'An historicist critique of revisionist methods for studying the history of ideas', *History and Theory* 20, 113-34.

Fergnani, F. (1959) 'Il contributo filosofico di Gramsci', *Il Pensiero Critico* 3 (July-September), 61-95.

Fernandez Buey, F. (1978) *Ensayos sobre Gramsci*, Barcelona: Materiales.

Ferrari, A. T. (1983) 'Ideologia e sociologia II', *Revista Brasileira de Sociologia* 8 (January) 5-20.

Ferrarotti, F. (1978) 'Legittimità, egemonia e dominio: Gramsci–con e contro Lenin', *La Critica Sociologica* 47, 64-79.

(1984) 'Civil society and state structures in creative tension: Ferguson, Hegel, Gramsci', *State, Culture and Society* 1 (Fall), 3-25.

Ferri, F. (ed.) (1977) *Politica e Storia in Gramsci. Atti del Convegno Internazionale di Studi Gramsciani, Firenze 9-11 Dicembre 1977*, Rome: Editori Riuniti-Istituto Gramsci.

Festa, S. (1976) *Gramsci*, Assisi: Cittadella Editrice.

Finocchiaro, M. (1979) 'Gramsci's Crocean Marxism', *Telos* 41, 17-32.

(1979) 'Science and praxis in Grasmci's critique of Bukharin', *Philosophy and Social Criticism* 6 (January), 25-56.

(1984) 'Croce as seen in a recent work on Gramsci', *Rivista di Studi Crociani* 21 (April-December), 139-54.

(1985) 'Marxism, religion, and science in Gramsci: recent trends in Italian scholarship', *Philosophical Forum* 17 (Winter), 127-55.

Fiori, G. (1966) *Vita di Gramsci*, Bari: Laterza & Figli.

(1970) *Antonio Gramsci: Life of a Revolutionary*, trans. T. Nairn, London: New Left Books.

Fontana i Lázaro, J. (1967) 'Gramsci i la ciencia històrica', *Nous Horizons* 12, 39-44.

Franchini, M. (1978) 'Croce e il Marxismo Italiano', *Rivista di Studi Crociani* 15 (July-December), 237-48.

Franchini, R. (1977) 'Gramsci Marxista Atipico', *Rivista di Studi Crociani* 14 (January-March), 58-61.

Francioni, G. (1984) *L'Officina Gramsciana. Ipotesi sulla Struttura dei Quaderni dal Carcere'*, Naples: Bibliopolis.

Galasso, G. (1969) *Croce, Gramsci e altri Storici*, Milan: Mondadori Editore.

Galli, G. (1976) *Storia del Partito Comunista Italiano*, Milan: Edizioni Il Formichiere.

Gallino, L. (1970) 'Gramsci e le scienze sociali', in *Gramsci e la Cultura Contemporanea, Atti del Convegno Internazionale tenuto a Cagliari il 23-27 Aprile 1967*, ed. P. Rossi, Rome: Editori Riuniti-Istituto Gramsci, vol.

2, 81-108.

García Canelini, N. (1984) 'Gramsci con Bourdieu. Hegemonía, consumo y nuevas formas de organización popular', *Nueva Sociedad* 71, 76-78.

Garaudy, R. (1971) 'Révolution et bloc historique', *L'Homme et la Société* 21, 169-77.

Genovese, E. D. (1967) 'On Antonio Gramsci', *Studies on the Left* 7, 83-107.

Germino, D. (1972) 'The radical as humanist: Gramsci, Croce and the 'Philosophy of Paxis', *Bucknell Review* 20 (Spring) 93-116.

Gerratana, V. (1974) 'Labriola et Gramsci', *Dialectiques* 4-5, 126-32.

Giachetti, R. (1972) 'Antonio Gramsci: the subjective revolution', in *The Unknown Dimension: European Marxism since Lenin*, ed. D. Howard and K. E. Klare, New York: Basic Books, 147-68.

Gibbon, P. (1983) 'Gramsci, Eurocommunism and the Comintern', *Economy and Society* 12 (August), 328-66.

Gitlin, T. (1979) 'News as ideology and contested area: toward a theory of hegemony, crisis, and opposition', *Socialist Review* 48, 11-54.

Giordano, A. (1971) *Gramsci. La Vita il Pensiero i Testi Esemplari*, Milan: Edizioni Accademica.

Girling, J. (1984) 'Thailand in Gramscian perspective', *Pacific Affairs* 57 (Fall), 385-403.

Gómez Pérez, R. (1977) *Gramsci. El Comunismo Latino,* Pamplona: EUNSA.

Grassi, F. (1978) *Gramsci e la 'Critica' della Diplomazia 'Tradizionale',* Lecce: Edizioni Milella.

Grasso, C. (1982) 'Alcuni contributi recenti sui rapporti tra il pensiero di Gramsci e la sociologia', *Quaderni di Sociologia* 29, 349-59.

Greenberg, E. S. (1975) 'The consequences of worker participation: a clarification of the theoretical literature', *Social Science Quarterly* 56 (September), 191-209.

Grisoni, D. and Maggiori, R. (1973) *Lire Gramsci*, Paris: Éditions Universitaires.

(1975) 'L'Actualisation de l'Utopie', *Les Temps Modernes* 30 (February), 879-928

Gruppi, L. (1974) 'Le concept d'egemonie chez A. Gramsci', *Dialectiques,* 4-5, 4-54.

(1977) *Il Concetto di Egemonia in Gramsci*, Rome: Editori Riuniti.

(1979) *Socialismo e Democracia. La Teoria Marxista dello Stato*, Milan: Edizioni del Calendario.

Guglielmi, G. (1976) *Da De Sanctis a Gramsci: Il Linguagio della Critica,* Bologna: Il Mulino.

Guibal, F. (1976) 'Antonio Gramsci', *Études* 39 (November), 459-85 (December), 617-39.

Guiducci, A. (1967) *Dallo Zdanovismo allo Strutturalismo* Milan: Feltrinelli Editori.

Hall, S. , Lumley, B., and McLennan, G. (1977) 'Politics and ideology: Gramsci', *Working Papers in Cultural Studies* 10, 45-76.

Hampel, A. (1977) 'Die KPI zwischen Pluralismus und Totalitarismus: Zur Diskussion um Antonio Gramsci', *Osteuropa* 27 (December) 1069-80.

Harman, C. (1983) *Gramsci versus Reformism*, London: Socialist Workers Party.

Harvey, J. (1967) 'Antonio Gramsci', *Marxism Today* 11 (April), 114-20.

Hawley, J. (1980) 'Antonio Gramsci's Marxism: class, state and work', *Social Problems* 27 (June) 584-600.

Hay, D. (1975) 'Property, authority and the criminal law', in *Albion's Fatal Tree: Crime and Society in Eighteenth-Century England*, ed. D. Hay *et al.*, New York: Pantheon Books, 17-64.

Heeger, R. (1975) *Ideologie und Macht. Eine Analyse von Antonio Gramscis 'Quaderni'*, Stockholm: Upsala.

Hobsbawm, E. J. (1977) 'Gramsci and political theory', *Marxism Today* 21 (July), 205-13.

Hofmann, J.(1984) *The Gramscian Challenge. Coercion and Consent in Marxist Political Theory*, New York: Basil Blackwell.

Holz, H. H., and Sandkuhler, H. J. (1980) *Betr: Gramsci Philosophie und Revolutionare Politik in Italien*, Köln: Pahl-Rugenstein.

Hunt, G. (1986) 'Gramsci, civil society and bureaucracy', *Praxis International* 6, (July), 206-19.

Istituto Gramsci (ed.) *Studi Gramsciani*, Rome: Editori Riuniti.

Jacobitti, E. E. (1975) 'Labriola, Croce, and Italian Marxism', *Journal of the History of Ideas* 36 (April-June), 297-318.
    (1980) 'Hegemony before Gramsci: the case of Benedetto Croce', *Journal of Modern History*, 52 (March), 66-84.

Jessop, B. (1980) 'On recent Marxist theories of law, the state, and juridico-political ideology', *International Journal of the Sociology of Law*, 8 (November), 339-68.

Jocteau, G. C. (1975) *Leggere Gramsci. Una Guida alle Interpretazioni*, Milan: Feltrinelli Editore.

Joll, J. (1977) *Antonio Gramsci*, Glasgow: Fontana.

Kahn, B. L. (1983) 'Antonio Grasmci on reading Marx', *Quarterly Journal of Ideology* 7 (Spring), 43-8.
    (1985) 'Antonio Gramsci's reformulation of Benedetto Croce's speculative idealism', *Idealistic Studies* 15 (January), 18-40.

Kallscheuer, O. (1981) 'Wie von Gramsci Lernen?' *Das Argument* 23 (November-December), 843-9.

Kaminski, F., Karuscheit, H., and Winter, K. (1982) *Antonio Gramsci Philosophie und Praxis*, Frankfurt: Sendler Verlag.

Kann, M. E (1980) 'Antonio Gramsci and modern Marxism', *Studies in Comparative Communism*, 13 (Summer-Autumn), 250-66.

Karabel, J. (1976) 'Revolutionary contradictions: Antonio Grasmsci and the problem of intellectuals', *Politics and Society* 6, 123-72.

Kebir, S. (1980) *Die Kulturkonzeption Antonio Gramscis*, Munich: Damnitz Verlag.

Kellner, D. (1978) 'Ideology, Marxism, and advanced capitalism', *Socialist Review* 42, 37-65.

Kiernan, V. G. (1972) 'The socialism of Antonio Gramsci', in *Essays in Socialist Humanism*, ed. K. Coates, Nottingham: Spokesman Books, 63-89.

(1972) 'Gramsci's Marxism', *Socialist Register*, 1-33.

Kilminster, R. (1979) *Praxis and Method: A Socio-Dialogue with Lukács, Gramsci, and the Early Frankfurt School*, Boston: Routledge and Kegan Paul.

King, M. L. (1978) 'The social role of the intellectuals: Antonio Gramsci and the Italian Renaissance', *Soundings* 61 (Spring), 23-46.

Kiros, T. (1985) *Toward the Construction of a Theory of Political Action; Antonio Gramsci. Consciousness, Participation and Hegemony*, Lanham: University Press of America.

Kolakowski, L. (1981) *Main Currents of Marxism*, vol. 3: *The Breakdown*, 220-52, London: Oxford University Press.

Kosik, K. (1967) 'Gramsci et la philosophie de la praxis', *Praxis* 3, 328-32.

Kramer, A. (1984) 'Antonio Gramsci über das Bundnis zwischen Arbeiterklasse und Intelligenz', *Beitrage zur Geschichte der Arbeiterbewegung* 26, 313-24.

Krancberg, S. (1986) 'Common sense and philosophy in Gramsci's "Prison Notebooks"', *Studies in Soviet Thought* 32 (August), 163-81.

La Rocca, T. (1981) *Gramsci e la Religione*, Brescia: Editirice Queriniana.

Lacasta, J. I. (1981) *Revolución Socialista e Idealismo en Gramsci*, Madrid: Editorial Revolución.

Laclau, E., and Mouffe, C. (1985) *Hegemony and Socialist Strategy: Towards a Radical Democratic Politics*, trans. W. Moore and P. Cammack, London: Verso.

Lajacono, G. (1977) *Gramsci, Nuove Linee del PCI ed Eurocomunismo*, Rovigo: Istituto Padano di Arti Grafiche.

Lajolo, L. (1980) *Gramsci un Uomo Sconfitto*, Milan: Rizzoloi Editore.

Laso Prieto, J. M. (1973) *Introducción al Pensamiento de Gramsci*, Madrid: Editorial Ayuso.

(1978) 'Perspectiva actual de Labriola, Gramsci y Togliatti', *Sistema* 27, 111-27.

Lears, T. J. J. (1985) 'The concept of cultural hegemony: problems and possibilities', *American Historical Review* 90 (June), 567-93.

Lentini, G. (1967) *Gramsci e Croce*, Palermo: Mori.

Leonetti, A. (1970) *Note su Gramsci*, Urbino: Argalia Editore.

Lepre, A. (1978) *Gramsci secondo Gramsci*, Naples: Liguori Editore.

Lisa, A. (1973) *Memorie. In Carcere con Gramsci*, Milan: Feltrinelli Editore.

Lombardi, F. (1971) *La Pédagogie d'Antonio Gramsci*, Toulouse: Editions Edouard Privat.

Lombardi Satriani, L. M. (1974) *Antropologia Culturale e Analisi della Cultura Subalterna*, Chapter 1: 'Le osservazioni Gramsciane sul folklore: dal "pittoresco" alla "contrapposizione"', 16-36, Florence: Guaraldi Editore.

(1977) 'La quistione criminale tra "Scuola Antropologica Moderna" e "Regole di Condotta"', in *Politica e Storia in Gramsci. Atti del Convegno*

Internazionale di Studi Gramsciani Firenze, 9-11 Dicembre 1977, 2 vol., ed.
F. Ferri, Rome: Editori Riuniti, Istituto Gramsci, 2:236–49.

Lombardi Satriani, L. M., and Meligrana, M. (1975) *Diritto Egemone e Diritto Popolare. La Calabria negli Studi di Demologia Giuridica,* Florence: Guaraldi Editore.

Longo, L. (1967) *Gramsci Oggi,* Rome: Editori Riuniti.

López Calera, N. M. (1979) 'Gramsci y el derecho', *Sistema* 32, 77-89.

Lowly, M. (1975) 'Notes sur Lukács et Gramsci', *L'Homme et la Société* 35-36, 79-88.

Luperini, R. (1977) 'Gramsci, la critica "neogiolittiana" e gli intellecttuali del primo novecento', *Belfagor* 32 (July), 365-94.

Luporini, C. (1974) *Dialettica e Materialisimo,* Rome: Editori Riuniti.

Macciocchi, M-A. (1974) *Pour Gramsci,* Paris: Editions du Seuil.
   (1976) 'Gramsci et la question du fascisme' in *Elements pour une Analyse du Fascisme,* vol. 1, ed. M-A. Macciocchi, Paris: Union Général d'Etition, 21-61.

Maduro, O. (1977) 'New Marxist approaches to the relative autonomy of religion', *Sociological Analysis* 38 (Winter), 359-67.

Maiello, R. (1980) *Vita di Antonio Gramsci,* Turin: ERI.

Maier, B., and Semana, P. (1978) *Antonio Gramsci. Introduzione e Guida allo Studio dell'Opera Gramsciana,* Florence: Le Monnier.

Mammucari, M., and Miserocchi, A. (1979) *Gramsci a Roma 1924-26,* Milan: La Pietra.

Manacorda, M. A. (1970) *Il Principio Educativo in Gramsci. Americanismo e Conformismo,* Rome: A. Armando.

Mancina, C. (1977) *A Proposito di Alcuni Temi Gramsciani. Riflessioni sul Seminario 'Egemonia, Stato, Partito in Gramsci',* Rome: Tipolitotografia Salemi.

Mancini, F. (1973) *Worker Democracy and Political party in Gramsci's Thinking,* SAIS-Bologna: Johns Hopkins University Press.

Mancini, F., and Galli, G. (1968) 'Gramsci's Presence', *Government and Opposition* 3 (Summer) 325-38.

Mandolfo, S. (1983) *Contributi alla Lettura di Antonio Gramsci,* Catania: Bonanno Editore.

Mansfield, S. R. (1984) 'Introduction to Gramsci's "Notes on Language", *Telos* 59, 119-26;.

Marković, M. (1967) 'Gramsci on the unity of philosophy and politics', *Praxis* 3, 333-9.

Marks, L. (1956) 'Antonio Gramsci', *Marxist Quarterly* 3 (October), 225-38.

Marramao, G. (1972) 'Per una critica dell'ideologia de Gramsci', *Quaderni Piacentini* 46, 74-92.

Martinelli, A. (1968) 'In defense of the dialectic: Antonio Gramsci's theory of revolution', *Berkeley Journal of Sociology* 13, 1-27.

Martinez Lorca, A. (1981) *El Problema de los Intelectuales y el Concepto de Cultura en Gramsci,* Malaga: Universidad de Malaga.

Mastroianni, G. (1972) *Da Croce a Gramsci,* Urbino: A. Armando.
   (1984) 'Quattro punti da rivedere nel Gramsci del "Quaderni"',

Giornale Critico della Filosofia Italiana 63 (May-August), 260-7.

Matteuci, N. (1951) *Antonio Gramsci e la Filosofia della Prassi*, Milan: A Giuffre.

Maturi, W. (1962) *Interpretazioni del Risorgimento*, Turin: Einaudi Editore. (1981) *Invito alla Lettura di Gramsci*, Milan: U. Mursia.

Maya, C. (1982) 'El concepto del estado en los "Cuadernos de la Cárcel"', *Cuadernos Políticos* 33, 7-19.

McLellan, D. (1979) *Marxism after Marx. An Introduction*, Chapter 14: 'Gramsci', 175-95, London: Macmillan.

Melchiorre, V. (1966) 'Sullo storicismo de A. Gramsci', *Humanitas* 11 (June), 585-995.

Melchiorre, V., Vigna, C., and DeRosa, G. (1979) *Antonio Grasmci*, 2 vols, Roma: Citta Nuova Editrica.

Mercer, C. (1978) 'Culture and ideology in Gramsci' *Red Letters* 8, 19-40. (1980) 'After Gramsci', *Screen Education* 36, 5-15.

Merolle, V. (1974) *Gramsci e la Filosofia della Prassi*, Rome: Bulzoni Editore.

Merrington, J. (1968) 'Theory and practice in Gramsci's Marxism', *Socialist Register*, 145-76.

Misuraca, P. (1977) 'Sulla ricostruzione Gramsciana dei concetti di struttura e superstrutta', *Rassegna Italiana di Sociologia* 18 (July-September), 439-51.

Molyneux, J. (1978) *Marxism and the Party*, Chapter 7: 'Gramsci's Modern Prince'. London: Pluto Press.

Mondolfo, R. (1962) *Da Ardigò a Gramsci*, Milan: Nuova Accademia. (1968) *Umanismo di Marx. Studi Filosofici 1908-66*, Turin: Einaudi Editore.

Mottu, H., and Castiglione, M. (1977) *Religione Popolare in un' Ottica Protestante. Gramsci, Cultura Subalterna e Lotte Contadine*, Turin: Claudiana.

Mouffe, C. (1979) ed. *Gramsci and Marxist Theory*, London: Routledge & Kegan Paul.

Mouffe, C. (1979) 'Hegemony and ideology in Gramsci', in *Gramsci and Marxist Theory*, ed. C. Mouffe, London: Routledge & Kegan Paul, 168-204.

(1981) 'Hegemony and the integral state: towards a new concept of politics', in *Silver Linings. Some Strategies for the Eighties*, ed. G. Bridges and R. Brunt, London: Lawrence and Wishard, 167-87.

Mouffe, C., and Sassoon, A. S. (1977) 'Gramsci in France and Italy: a review of the literature', *Economy and Society* 61 (February), 31-68.

Mura, G. (1966) 'Antonio Gramsci tra storicismo e intellettualismo', *Civitas* 17 (November-December), 87-108.

Nardone, G. (1971) *Il Pensiero di Gramsci*, Bari: De Donato Editore. (1977) *L'Umano in Gramsci. Evento Politico e Comprensione dell'Evento Poliltico*, Bari: Dedalo Libri.

Nemeth, T. (1978) 'Gramsci's concept of constitution', *Philosophy and Social Criticism* 5 (September-October), 295-318.

(1981) *Gramsci's Philosopy*, Brighton: Harvester Press; Atlantic City, NJ:

Humanities Press.

Nesti, A. (1975) 'Gramsci et la religion populaire', *Social Compass* 22, 343-54.

Nowell-Smith, G. (1977) 'Gramsci and the national popular', *Screen Education* 22, 12-15.

O'Connell, G. (1978) 'The church and Eurocommunism: formation of the Communist mind in the thought of Antonio Gramsci', *The Month* 11 (August), 257-61.

(1978) 'Sources of Italian Euro-Communism: revolutionary strategy of Antonio Grasmci', *The Month* 11 (October), 338-40.

(1978) 'Sources of Italian Euro-Communism: Gramsci, Italian culture and Catholicism', *The Month* (November), 383-8.

Orfei, R. (1965) *Antonio Gramsci; Coscienza Critica del Marxismo,* Casciago: Relazioni Sociali.

Oriol, M. (1984) 'De L'intellectual organique au gestionnaire de la "identité"', *Recherches Sociologiques* 15, 181-94.

Ormea, F. (1975) *Gramsci e il Futuro dell'Uomo,* Rome: Coinas.

Paggi, L. (1970) *Gramsci e il Moderno Principe,* Rome: Editori Riuniti.

(1973) 'La teoria generale del Marxismo in Gramsci', *Istituto Giangiacomo Feltrinelli. Annali* 15, 1318-70.

(1979) 'Gramsci's general theory of Marxism', in *Gramsci and Marxist Theory,* ed. C. Mouffe, London: Routledge & Kegan Paul, 113-67.

Palla, M. (1986) 'Il Gramsci abbandonato', *Belfagor* 61 (September) 581-6.

Paris, R. (1967) 'Il Gramsci di Tutti', *Giovane Critica* 15-16, 48-61.

(1979) 'Gramsci en France', *Revue Française de Science Politique* 29, 5-18.

Paternostro, R. (1977) *Critica, Marxismo, Storicismo Dialettico,* Rome: Bulzoni Editore.

Patterson, T. (1975) 'Notes on the historical application of Marxist cultural theory', *Science and Society* 34 (Fall), 257-91.

Pellicani, L. (1976) *Gramsci e la Questione Comunista,* Florence: Vallecchi Editore.

(1981) *Gramsci. An Alternative Communism?* Stanford, Ca.: Hoover Institution Press.

Peregalli, A. (ed.) (1978) *Il Comunismo di Sinistra e Gramsci,* Bari: Dedalo Libri.

Pereyra, C. (1979) 'Gramsci: estado y sociedad civil', *Cuadernos Políticos* 21, 66-74.

(1984) *El Sujeto de la Historia,* Madrid: Alianza Editorial.

Perez G. (1979) *Gramscis Theorie der Ideologie,* Frankfurt: Haag+Herchen Verlag.

Perrotta, A. (1973) 'Il tema della classi dirigente nel pensiero Meridionalista: Da P. Villari a G. Dorso', *Sociologia* 7 (January) 69-108.

Perlini, T. (1974) *Gramsci e il Gramscismo,* Milan: CELUC.

Piccone, P. (1974) 'Gramsci's Hegelian Marxism', *Political Theory* 2 (September), 32-45.

(1976) 'Grasmci's Marxism: beyond Lenin and Togliatti', *Theory and Society* 3 (Winter), 485-512.

(1977) 'From Spaventa to Gramsci', *Telos* 31, 35-65.

(1983) *Italian Marxism*, Berkeley: University of California Press.

Pierini, F. (1978) *Gramsci e la Storiologia della Rivoluzione (1914-1920). Studio Storico-Semantico*, Rome: Edizioni Paoline.

Piotte, J-M. (1970) *La Pensée Politique de Gramsci*, Paris: Anthropos.

Pipa, A. (1983) 'Gramsci as a (non) literary critic', *Telos* 57, 83-92.

Pipparo, L. (1979) *Lingua, Intellettuali, Egemonia in Gramsci*, Bari: Laterza & Figli.

Pizzorno, A. (1969) 'A propos de la Méthode de Grasmci, de l'historiographie a la science politique', *L'Homme et la Société* 8, 161-71.

(1970) 'Sul metodo di Gramsci: dalla storiografia alla scienza politica', in *Gramsci e la Cultura Contemporanea. Atti del Convegno Internazionale tenuto a Cagliari il 23-27 Aprile 1967*, vol. 2, ed. P. Rosi, Rome: Editore Riuniti-Istituto Gramsci, 109-26.

Pontusson, J. (1980) 'Gramsci and Eurocommunism. A comparative analyis of conceptions of class rule and socialist transition', *Berkeley Journal of Sociology* 24-25, 185-248.

Portantiero, J. C. (1979) 'Gramsci y el análisis de coyuntura (Algunas Notas)', Revista Mexicana de Sociología 41 (January-March), 59-73.

(1981) *Los Usos de Gramsci*, Mexico: Folios.

Portelli, H. (1972) *Gramsci et le Bloc Historique*, Paris: Presses Universitaires de France.

(1974) *Gramsci et la Question Religieuse*, Paris: Anthropos.

(1974) 'Jacobinisme et antijacobinisme', *Dialectiques* 4-5, 28-43.

(1973) 'Gramsci et les elections', *Les Temps Modernes* 30 (February), 999-1018.

Pozzolini, A. (1970) *Antonio Gramsci: An Introduction to his Thought*, trans. A. F. Showstack, London: Pluto Press.

(1972) *Che Cosa Ha "Veramente" Detto Gramsci*, Rome: Ubaldini Editore.

Prestipino, G. (1979) *Da Gramsci a Marx. Il Bloco Logico-Storico*, Rome: Editori Riuniti.

Priester, K. (1976) 'Antonio Gramsci und der Italienische Marxismus', *Neue Politische Literatur* 21, 182-207.

(1977) 'Zur Staadstheorie bei Antonio Gramsci', *Das Argument* 19 (July-August), 515-32.

Ragazzini, D. (1976) *Società Industriale e Formazione Umana nel Pensiero di Gramsci*, Rome: Editori Riuniti.

Ramos, V. Jr. (1982) 'The concepts of ideology, hegemony, and organic intellectuals in Gramsci's Marxism', *Theoretical Review* 30 (September-October) 8-34.

Razeto Migliaro, L., and Misuraca, P. (1978) *Sociologia e Marxismo nella Critica di Gramsci. Dalla Critica della Sociologia alla Scienza della Storia e della Politica*, Bari: De Donato Editore.

Ricci, F. (1969) 'A. Gramsci, theoricien politique', *La Nouvelle Critique* 28, 16-20.

Richardson, T. (1978) 'Science, ideology and commonsense: on Antonio Gramsci and Althu...r', in *Politics, Ideology and the State*, ed. S. Hibbin, London: Lawrence and Wishart, 99-122.

Riechers, C. (1970) *Antonio Gramsci, Marxismus in Italien*, Frankfurt: Europische Verlaganstalt.

Risset, J. (1969) 'Lettura di Gramsci', *Critica Marxista* 7, 130-58.

(1970) 'Lecture de Gramsci', *Tel Quel* 42, 46-73.

Rodríguez-Aguilera de Prat, C. (1983) 'Gramsci i la historia d'Italia', *L'Avenç* 56, 58-63.

(1984) *Gramsci y la Via Nacional al Socialismo*, Madrid: Ediciones Akal.

Rodriguez-Lores, J. (1971) *Die Grudstruktur des Marxismus. Gramsci un die Philosophie der Praxis*, Frankfurt: Makol Verlag.

Romano, F. (1973) *Gramsci e il Liberalismo Antiliberale*, Rome: Cremonese.

Romano, S. (1965) *Antonio Gramsci*, Turin: Unione Tipografico Editrice.

Rossi, P. (1970) *Gramsci e la Cultura Contemporanae. Atti del Convegno Internazionale tenuto a Cagliari il 23-27 Aprile 1967*, 2 vols, Rome: Editori Riuniti-Istituto Gramsci.

Rosiello, L. (1982) 'Linguistica e Marxismo nel pensiero de Antonio Gramsci' *Histrriographia Linguistica* 9, 432-52.

Roth, G. (1972) *Gramscis Philosophie der Praxis. Eine Neue Deutung des Marxismus*. Düsseldorf: Patmos-Verlag.

Rutigliano, E. (1977) 'The ideology of labour and capitalist rationality in Gramsci', *Telos* 31, 91-9.

Salamini, L. (1974) 'Gramsci and Marxist sociology of knowledge: an analysis of hegemony-ideology-knowledge', *Sociological Quarterly* 15 (Summer), 359-80.

(1975) 'The specificity of Marxist sociology in Gramsci's theory', *Sociological Quarterly* 16 (Winter), 65-86.

(1976) 'Towards a sociology of intellectuals: a structural analysis of Gramsci's Marxist theory', *Sociological Analysis and Theory* 6 (February), 1-36.

(1981) *The Sociology of Political Praxis. An Introduction to Gramsci's Theory*, London: Routledge & Kegan Paul.

(1981) 'Gramsci and Marxist sociology of language', *International Journal of the Sociology of Language* 32, 27-44.

Sallach, D. L. (1974) 'Class domination and ideological hegemony', *Sociological Quarterly* 15 (Winter), 38-50.

Salvadori, M. (1970) *Gramsci e il Problema Storico della Democrazia*, Turin: Einaudi Editore.

(1979) 'Actualité de Gramsci', *Dialectiques* 4-5, 133-50.

(1976) 'Gramsci e il PCI: due concezioni dell'egemonia', *Mondoperaio* 11, 59-69.

(1979) 'Grasmci and the PCI: two conceptions of hegemony', in *Gramsci and Marxist Theory*, ed. C. Mouffe, London: Routledge & Kegan Paul, 237-58.

Sanguinetti, F. (1982) 'Gramsci e Machiavelli, Bari: Laterza & Figli.

Sassano, F. (1974) '"L'Unita" sotto la guida di Gramsci: il quotidiano del PCI dalla fondazione alle leggi speciali', *Il Mulino* 23 (September-October), 799-821.

Sassoon, A. S. (1978) 'Hegemony and political intervention', in *Politics,*

224

Ideology and the State, ed. S. Hibbin, London: Lawrence and Wishart, 9-39.

(1980) *Gramsci's Politics,* London: Croom Helm.

(1980) 'Gramsci: a new concept of democracy', in *Marxism and Democracy,* ed. A. Hunt, London: Lawrence and Wishart, 80-99.

(1982) 'Hegemony, war of position and political intervention', in *Approaches to Gramsci,* ed. A. S. Sassoon, London: Writers and Readers Publishing Cooperative Society, 94-115.

(1982) 'Passive revolution and the politics of reform', in *Approaches to Gramsci,* London: Writers and Readers Publishing Cooperative Society, 127-48.

Sassoon, A. S. (ed.) (1982) *Approaches to Gramsci,* London: Writers and Readers Publishing Cooperative Society.

Schmidt, A. (1973) *History and Structure. An Essay on Hegelian-Marxist and Structuralist Theories of History,* trans. J. Herf, Cambridge, Mass.: MIT.

Scott, J. (1977) 'Hegemony and the Peasantry', *Politics and Society* 7, 267-96.

Shafir, G. (1985) 'Interpretative sociology and the philosophy of praxis: comparing Max Weber and Antonio Gramsci', *Praxis International* 5 (April) 63-74.

Sillanpoa, W. P. (1981) 'Pasolini's Gramsci', *MLN* 96 (January), 120-37.

Simon, R. (1977) 'Gramsci's concept of hegemony', *Marxism Today* 21 (March) 78-86.

(1982) *Gramsci's Political Thought. An Introduction,* London: Lawrence and Wishart.

Simpson, P. (1978) 'The whalebone in the corset: Gramsci on education, culture and change', *Screen Education* 28, 5-22.

Smith, C. (1977) 'Antonio Gramsci and the New Left', *Labour Review* 1 (September), 217-31.

Spriano, P. (1965) *Gramsci e L'Ordine Nuovo (1919-1920),* Rome: Editori Riuniti.

(1977) *Gramsci e Gobetti,* Turin: Giulio Einaudi.

(1977) *Gramsci in Carcere e il Partito,* Rome: Editori Riuniti.

(1979) *Antonio Gramsci and the Party: the Prison Years,* trans. J. Fraser, London: Lawrence and Wishart.

Stipevic, N. (1968) *Gramsci e i Problemi Letterari,* Milan: Mursia.

Storey, J. (1985) 'Mathew Arnold: the politics of an organic intellectual', *Literature and History* 11 (Autumn), 217-28.

Suppa, S. (1976) *Il Primo Gramsci: Gli Scritti Politici Giovanili (1914-1918),* Naples: Jovene.

Tamburano, G. (1963) *Antonio Gramsci,* Milan: Sugar Edizioni.

Telo, M. (1975) 'Il ruolo dei Ceti Medi nei "Quaderni del Carcere" di Antonio Gramsci', *Il Politico* 40 (March), 127-40.

Texier, J. (1966) *Gramsci,* Paris: Seghers.

(1968) 'Gramsci, théoricien des superstructures. Sur le concept de société civile', *La Pensée* 139, 35-60.

(1973) 'Gramsci: nécessité et créativité historique', *La Nouvelle Critique* 69, 61-8.

(1974) 'Gramsci sort-il du purgatoire ou va-t-il en enfer?' *Nouvelle Critique* n. s. 76, 33-8.

(1979) 'Gramsci, theoretician of the superstructures', in *Gramsci and Marxist Theory*, ed. C. Mouffe, London: Routledge & Kegan Paul, 48-79.

Thibaudeau, J. (1974) 'Premiers notes sur les "Ecrits de Prison" de Gramsci pour placer la litterature dans la théorie Marxiste', *Dialectiques* 4-5, 57-82.

(1976) 'Preliminary notes on the Prison Writings of Gramsci: the place of literature in Marxian theory', *Praxis* 3, 3-29.

Todd, N. (1974) 'Ideology in Gramsci and Mao', *Journal of the History of Ideas* 35 (January-March) 148-56.

Togliatti, P. (1967) *Gramsci*, ed. E. Ragioneri, Rome: Editori Riuniti.

(1979) *On Gramsci and Other Writings*, ed. D. Sassoon, London: Lawrence and Wishart.

Torres Novoa, C. A. (1978) 'Filosofía polítca y sujeto histórico-político del cambio social: notas sobre Lenin y Gramsci', *Estudios Filosóficos* 27 (May-August) 287-98.

Tosel, A. (1983) 'Gramsci, philosophie de la praxis et refórme intellectuelle et moral', *La Pensée* 235, 39-48.

(1984) 'Philosophie de la praxis et dialectique', *La Pensée* 237, 100-20.

Turnatori, G., and Lodi, G. (1974) 'Classes in Southern Italy: Salvemini's, Dorso's and Gramsci's analyses', *Sociology* 4 (Summer-Fall), 84-147.

Vargas-Machuca Ortega, R. (1982) *El Poder de la Razón. La Filosofía de Gramsci*, Madrid: Editorial Tecnos.

(1983) 'Política y cultura en la interpretación Gramsciana de la hegemonía', *Sistema* 54-55, 73-91.

Vasale, C. (1979) *Politica e Religione in A. Gramsci. L'Ateodicea della Secolarizzazione*, Rome: Edizioni di Storia e Letteratura.

(1979) 'Il "Moderno Principe" come Chiesa laica? Religione e politica in Antonio Gramsci', *Sociologia* 13 (May-December), 245-66.

Veauvy, C. (1978) 'Gramsci et la question agraire (Les Reports Ouvriers-Paysans-Intellectuelles)', *Peuples Méditerranéens* 5, 73-106.

Veljak, L. (1983) *Filoxofija Prakse Antonija Gramscija*, Belgrade: Izdaje Radionica SIC.

Vinco, R. (1983) *Una Fede senza Futuro? Religione e Mondo Cattolico in Gramsci*, Verona: Casa Editrice Mazziana.

Vranicki, P. (1967) 'Antonio Gramsci et le sens du socialisme', *Praxis* 3, 323-37.

Waiss, O. (1982) 'Socialismo y hegemonía', *Nueva Sociedad* 62, 97-112.

Welton, M. (1982) 'Gramsci's contribution to the analysis of public education knowledge', *Journal of Educational Thought* 16 (December) 140-9.

White, S. (1972) 'Gramsci and the Italian Communist Party', *Government and Opposition* 7 (Spring), 186-205.

Williams, G. A. (1960) 'Gramsci's concept of "egemonia"', *Journal of the History of Ideas* 21 (December), 586-99.

(1975) *Proletarian Order: Antonio Gramsci and the Origins of Italian Communism*, London: Pluto Press.

(1978) 'Gramsci', *New Society* 43 (February), 245-8.

Wolfe, A. (1974) 'New directions in the Marxist theory of politics', *Politics and Society* 4 (Winter), 131-59.

Woolcock, J. A. (1985) 'Politics, ideology and hegemony in Gramsci's theory', *Social and Economic Studies* 34 (September), 199-210.

Zanardo, A. (1974) *Filosofia e Socialismo*, Rome: Editori Riuniti.

OTHER RELEVANT WORKS

Althusser, L. (1970) 'Les appareils ideologiques d'Etat,' *La Pensée* 151, 3-30.

Althusser, L., and Balibar, E. (1970) *Reading Capital*, trans. B. Brewster, London: New Left Books.

Asor Rosa, A. (1973) *Intellettuali e Classe Operaia*, Florence: La Nuova Italia.

Aymard, M. (1978) 'The impact of the *Annales* school in Mediterranean countries', *Review* 1 (Winter-Spring), 53-64.

Badaloni, N. (1975) *Marxismo come Storicismo*, Milan: Feltrinelli Editore.

Baglieri, J. (1980) 'Italian Fascism and the crisis of liberal hegemony: 1901-1922', in *Who Were the Fascists. Social Roots of European Fascism*, ed. S. U. Larsen, B. Hagtvet, and J. P. Myklebust, Bergen: Universitetsforlaget, 318-36.

Balibar, E. *et al.* (1979) *Marx et sa Critique de la Politique*, Paris: Farancois Maspero.

Benton, T. (1977) *Philosophical Foundations of the Three Sociologies*, London: Routledge & Kegan Paul.

Bhaskar, R. (1979) *The Possibility of Naturalism*, Atlantic Highlands: Humanities Press.

Bloch, M. (1966) *French Rural History. An Essay on its Basic Characteristics*, trans. J. Sondheimer, Berkeley and Los Angeles: University of California Press.

Braudel, F. (1969) *Écrits sur l'Histoire*, Paris: Flammarion.

Brodbeck, M. (1966) 'Methodological individualisms: definition and reduction', in *Philosopohical Analysis and History*, ed. W. H. Dray, New York: Harper and Row, 297-329.

Bukharin, N. (1969) *Historical Materialism. A System of Sociology*, Ann Arbor: University of Michigan Press.

Burke, P.(1980) *Sociology and History*, London: George Allen & Unwin.

Claudín, F. (1970) *La Crisis del Movimiento Comunista*, Paris: Ruedo Ibérico.

Callinicos, A. (1983) *Marxism and Philosophy*, Oxford: Oxford University Press.

Colletti, L. (1976) *Il Marxismo e Hegel*, 2 vols, Bari: Laterza & Figli.

Collingwood, R. G. (1946) *The Idea of History*, Oxford: Oxford University Press.

Coppa, F. J. (1971) *Planning, Protectionism, and Politics in Liberal Italy; Economics and Politics in the Giolittian Age*, Washington, DC.: Catholic University of America Press.

Coward, R., Ellis, J. (1977) *Language and Materialism. Developments in Semiology and the Theory of the Subject*. London: Routledge & Kegan Paul.

Croce, B. (1907) *Ciò che è Vivo e Ciò che è Morto della Filosofia di Hegel*, Bari: Laterza & Figli.

(1909) *Logica come Scienza del Concetto Puro*, Bari: Laterza & Figli.

(1920) *Teoria e Storia della Storiografia*, 2nd edn, Bari: Laterza & Figli.

(1928) *Storia d'Italia dal 1871 al 1915*, 2nd edn, Bari: Laterza & Figli. 'Antistoricismo', *La Critica* 27, 401-9.

(1932) *Storia di Europa nel Secolo Decimonono*, Bari: Laterza & Figli.

(1939) 'Il concetto della filosofia come storicismo assoluto', *La Critica* 37, 253-68.

(1950) *Croce, the King, and the Allies. Extracts from a Diary by Benedetto Croce. July 1944-June 1945*, trans. S. Sprigge, London: George Allen & Unwin.

(1963) 'Eternità e storicità della filosofia', in *Ultimi Saggi*, 333-440, Bari: Laterza & Figli.

(1967) *Etica e Politica*, Bari: Laterza & Figli.

(1978) *Materialismo Storico ed Economia Marxistica*, Bari: Laterza & Figli.

Cruz, M. (1981) *El Historicismo. Ciencia Social y Filosofía*, Barcelona: Montesinos Editor.

Cunningham, F. (1987) *Democratic Theory and Socialism*, Cambridge: Cambridge University Press.

Cuoco, V. (1966) *Saggio Storico sulla Rivoluzione di Napoli*, Milan: Rizzoli Editore.

Dahl, R. A. (1963) *Modern Political Analysis*, Englewood Cliffs: Prentice-Hall.

Day, R. B. (1976) 'The theory of the long cycle: Kondratiev, Trotsksy, Mandel', *New Left Review* 99, 67-82.

Dilthey, W. (1976) *Selected Writings*, ed. and trans. H. P. Rickman, Cambridge: Cambridge University Press.

(1961) *Meaning in History*, ed. H. P. Rickman, London: George Allen & Unwin.

Engels, F. (1946) *Feuerbach and the End of Classical German Philosophy*, Moscow: Progress Publishers.

Fontana, J. (1985) 'Bastardos y Ladrones', *Revista de Occidente* 45, 83-100.

Gardiner, P. (1952) *The Nature of Historical Explanation*, London: Oxford University Press.

Gellner, E. (1959) 'Holism versus Individualism in history and sociology', in *Theories of History*, ed. P. Gardiner, Glencoe: The Free Press, 489-503.

Gentile, G. (1974) *La Filosofia di Marx*, ed. V. A. Bellezza, Florence: Sansoni.

Gilliam, H. (1976) 'The dialectics of realism and idealism in modern historiographic theory', *History and Theory* 15 (October) 231-56.

228

Hegel, G. W. P. (1977) *Pheonomenology of Spirit*, trans. A V. Miller, Oxford: Oxford University Press.

Hempel, C. G. (1942) 'The function of general laws in history', *Journal of Philosophy* 39 (January-December) 36-48.

Hexter, J. H. (1963) *Reappraisals in History. New Views on History and Society in Early Modern Europe*, New York: Harper and Row.

Hill, C. (1969) *Reformation to Industrial Revolution*, Harmondsworth: Penguin.

Hughes, S.(1977) *Consciousness and Society*, rev. ed, New York: Vintage Books.

Iggers, G. G. (1983) *The German Conception of History. The National Tradition of Historical Thought from Herder to the Present*, Middletown: Weslyan University Press.

James, S. (1984) *The Content of Social Explanation*, Cambridge: Cambridge University Press.

Kant, I. (1929) *Critique of Pure Reason*, trans. N. K. Smith, London: Macmillan.

(1963) *On History*, ed. L. W. Beck, Indianapolis: Bobbs-Merril Co.

Kondratieff, N. (1984) *The Long Wave Cycle*, trans. G. Daniels, New York: Richardson & Snyder.

Koselleck, R. (1982) 'Concepts of historical time and social history', in *Philosophy of History and Contemporary Historiography*, ed. D. Carr *et al.*, Ottawa: University of Ottawa Press, 113-26.

Labriola, A. (1973) *Scritti Filosofici e Politici*, 2 vols, ed. F. Sbarbieri, Turin: Einaudi Editore.

Laclau, E. (1977) *Politics and Ideology in Marxist Theory. Capitalism-Fascism-Populism* London: NLB.

(1980) 'Togliatti and politics', *Politics and Power* 2, 251-8.

(1984) 'Transformations of advanced industrial societies and the theory of the subject', in *Rethinking Ideology*, ed. S. Hanninen and L. Paldan, Berlin: Argument Verlag, 39-44.

Laclau, E., and Mouffe, C. (1981) 'Socialist strategy. Where next?' *Marxism Today* 25 (January), 17-22.

Lee, D., E., and Beck, R. N. (1954) 'The meaning of "Historicism"'. *American Historical Review* 59 (April) 568-77.

Lenin, V. I. (1970) *Materialism and Empirio-Criticism*, Moscow: Progress Pubishers.

(1972) *The State and Revolution*, Moscow: Progess Publishers.

Machiavelli, N. (1976) *Il Principe e Altre Opere Politiche*, Milan: Garzanti Editore.

McLennan, G. (1981) *Marxism and the Methodologies of History*, London: Verso and NLB.

(1984) 'History and theory: contemporary debates and directions', *Literature and History* 10 (Autumn), 139-64.

Macpherson, C. B. (1962) *The Political Theory of Possessive Individualism, Hobbes to Locke*, Oxford: Oxford University Press.

Mandelbaum, M. H. (1948) 'A critique of philosophies of history', *Journal of Philosophy* 45 (July), 365-78.

(1951) 'A note on emergence', in *Freedom and Reason. Studies in Philosophy and Jewish Culture in Memory of Morris Raphael Cohen*, ed. S. W. Baron, E. Nagel, and K. S. Pinson, Glencoe: The Free Press, 175-83.

Marx, K. (n.d., 1967, 1971) *Capital. A Critique of Political Economy*, 3 vols., ed. F. Engels, Moscow: Progress Publishers.

(1970) *A Contribution to the Critique of Political Economy*, trans. M. Dobb, Moscow: Progress Publishers.

(1970) *Critique of Hegel's 'Philosophy of Right'* trans. J. O'Malley, Cambridge: Cambridge University Press.

(1973) *Grundrisse. Foundations of the Critique of Political Economy*, trans. M. Nicolaus, New York: Vintage Books.

(1973) *The Poverty of Philosophy*, Moscow: Progress Publishers.

Marx, K., and Engels, F. (1965) *Selected Correspondence*, 2nd edn, ed. S. Ryazanskaya, Moscow: Progress Publishers.

(1973) *The German Ideology*, Moscow: Progress Publishers.

Meikle, S. (1985) *Essentialism in the Thought of Karl Marx*, London: G. Duckworth.

Miliband, R. (1977) *Marxism and Politics*, Oxford: Oxford University Press.

Ortega y Gasset, J. (1965) *Kant. Hegel. Dilthey*, Madrid: Revista de Occidente.

Philip, A. (1927) *Le Problème Ouvrier aux États-Unis*, Paris: Librairie Felix Alcan.

Popper, K. (1961) *The Poverty of Historicism*, London: Routledge & Kegan Paul.

Rand, C.G. (1964) 'Two meanings of historicism in the writings of Dilthey, Troeltsch and Meinecke', *Journal of the History of Ideas* 25 (October-December), 503-18.

Randall Jr. J. H., and Haines IV, G. (1946;) 'Controlling assumptions in the practice of American historians', in *Theory and Practice in Historical Study: A Report of the Committee on Historiography*, ed. Social Science Research Council Committee on Historiography, New York: Social Science Research Council, 15-52.

Ranke, L. von (1973) *The Theory and Practice of History*, ed. G. G. Iggers and K. von Moltke, Indianapolis and New York: Bobbs-Merrill Co.

Rossi, P. (1957) 'Benedetto Croce e lo storicismo assoluto', *Il Mulino* 6 (May), 322–54.

(1957) 'Karl Popper e la critica neopositivista allo storicismo', *Rivista di Filosofia* 48, 46-73.

(1960) *Storia e Storicismo nella Filosofia Contemporanea*, Milan: Lerici Editori.

(1975) 'The ideological valences of twentieth-century historicism', *History and Theory* 14, 15-29.

Runciman, W. G. (1973) 'What is Structuralism?', in *The Philosophy of Social Explanation*, ed. A. Ryan, Oxford: Oxford University Press, 189-202.

Saladino, S. (1970) *Italy from Unification to 1919. Growth and Decay of a*

Liberal Regime, New York: Thomas Y. Crowell.

Salamone, A. W. (1945) *Italian Democracy in the Making. The Political Scene in the Giolittian Era, 1900-1914,* with an introduction by G. Salvemini, Philadelphia: University of Pensylvania Press.

Sánchez Vázquez, A. *et al.* (1975) *Estructuralismo y Marxismo,* Barcelona: Ediciones Grijalbo.

Stoianovich, T. (1976) *French Historical Method: The 'Annales' Paradigm* Ithaca: Cornell University Press.

Thompson, E. P. (1978) 'Eighteenth-century English society: class struggle without class?' *Social History* 3 (May) 133-65.

(1978) *The Poverty of Theory and Other Essays,* New York and London: Monthly Review Press.

Tilgher, A. (1935) *Critica dello Storicismo,* Modena: Guanda Editore.

Togiatti, P. (1970) *Lezioni sul Fascismo,* Rome: Editori Riuniti.

Tuchanska, B. (1980) 'The methodological problem of the development of science *versus* the historical problem of how science performs its social functions', *Polish Sociological Review* 3, 5-24.

Vacca, G. (ed.) (1972) *Politica e Teoria nel Marxismo Italiano 1959-1969,* Bari: De Donato Libri.

Vico, G. (1972) *Opere,* vol. 1: *Della Antichissima Sapienza degli Italiani Rivelata delle Origine della Lingua Lantina,* ed. R. Parenti, Naples: Casa Editrice Fulvio Rossi.

(1976) *Principj di Scienza Nuova,* 3 vols, ed. F. Nicolini, Turin: Einaudi Editori.

Vilar, P. (1962) *La Catalogne dans l'Espagne Moderne,* 3 vols, Paris: SEVPEN.

(1982) *Une Histoire en Construction. Approche Marxiste et Problématiques Conjuncturelles,* Paris: Editions du Seuil.

(1981) 'Suggèrencies sobre alguns problemes historiogràfics actuals: Nacionalisme, conjuntura, crítica de la informaciò i politica i història', *Quaderns del Centre de Treball i Documentació* 1, 55-65.

NAME INDEX

SUBJECT INDEX